THE BRITISH POETS,

PUBLISHED BY

LITTLE, BROWN AND COMPANY.

A COMPLETE COLLECTION,

FROM CHAUCER TO WORDSWORTH,

Handsomely Printed in neat 16mo. Volumes.

Price 75 Cents per Volume, in Cloth.

(For sale also in full calf and half calf binding.)

The following volumes are already issued:—

Akenside	1 vol.	Marvell	1 vol.
Ballads	8 vols.	Milton	3 vols.
Beattie	1 vol.	Montgomery	5 "
Burns	3 vols.	Moore	6 "
Butler	2 "	Parnell & Tickell	1 vol.
Byron	10 "	Pope	3 vols.
Campbell	1 vol.	Prior	2 "
Chatterton	2 vols.	Scott	9 "
Churchill	3 "	Shakespeare	1 vol.
Coleridge	3 "	Shelley	3 vols.
Collins	1 vol	Skelton	3 "
Cowper	3 vols.	Southey	10 "
Donne	1 vol.	Spenser	5 "
Dryden	5 vols.	Surrey	1 vol.
Falconer	1 vol.	Swift	3 vols.
Gay	2 vols.	Thomson	2 "
Goldsmith	1 vol.	Vaughan	1 vol.
Gray	1 "	Watts	1 "
Herbert	1 "	White	1 "
Herrick	2 vols.	Wordsworth	7 vols
Hood	4 "	Wyatt	1 vol.
Keats	1 vol.	Young	2 vols.

Each work sold separately.

This Collection, of which one hundred and twenty-eight volumes are already issued, is intended to embrace the works of the most distinguished authors, from Chaucer to Wordsworth, with selections from the minor poets; accompanied with biographical, historical, and critical notices

and portraits, — the whole forming a far more complete, elegant, and cheap edition of the British Poets than has ever appeared before.

The numerous testimonials to the excellence of this series, which the publishers have received, both from the press and the public, in all parts of the country, would seem to indicate that a popular want has been met by this edition, which is universally acknowledged to be the best ever issued, both in point of editorship and mechanical execution.

Notices of the Press.

"We cannot speak too highly in praise of this edition — the only one that deserves the name of 'complete' — of the British Poets." — *Boston Daily Advertiser.*

"We really know nothing more worthy of the cordial support of the American public than the Boston edition of the English Poets." — *New York Times.*

"A fairer printed, a more tasteful, or more valuable set of books, cannot be placed in any library." — *New York Courier and Inquirer.*

"The best, the most permanently valuable, the most convenient, and the cheapest edition of the standard poetical literature of Great Britain ever published." — *Home Journal.*

"We regard it as the most beautiful and convenient library edition of the British Poets yet published." — *Philadelphia Evening Bulletin.*

"We do not know any other edition of the English Poets which combines so much excellence." — *Bibliotheca Sacra.*

"Of the typographical beauty and literary accuracy of this edition, the most flattering things have been said by the most competent authorities, and we have rarely witnessed such complete unanimity among critics as this Boston enterprise has elicited." — *Ballou's Pictorial.*

borne a large office in the culture of mind and style for past generations, and for our elders now upon the stage; and we can wish for those entering active or literary life, access to no purer, or more copious, or more stimulating fountains of thought, sentiment, and motive, than are here." — *North American Review.*

"The judgment of the most competent and respected authority has been passed upon these works, and has decided that they are eminently worthy of being kept in constant use." — *Christian Examiner.*

"The value and popularity of the works included in this series will increase as those who read the English language become cultivated, and wish for compositions of the highest rank. For school and family libraries, these books are just what is needed; they are of convenient size, and attractive outward appearance, — their contents are models of composition, their spirit is liberal and manly, — their tone and influence moral and religious, without cant, or a weakness of any kind." — *Boston Transcript.*

"It is superfluous to praise the Essays, — they are by general consent esteemed models of pure English style, and are full of entertainment, knowledge of the world, and moral instruction, — they will be read with pleasure as long as the English language lives." — *New York Commercial Advertiser.*

"No greater service can be done in the cause of good letters than the extensive dissemination of these standard compositions. They embrace the best models of style in the English language." — *Boston Daily Advertiser.*

"As models of English prose they stand unrivalled, and deserve a place in every library, public or private, but especially in every school and town library in the country." — *Boston Atlas.*

"A series of standard works, the value and popularity of which have only increased with time." — *New York Times.*

"No more desirable edition has ever been published." — *New York Evening Post.*

Oliver Goldsmith.

THE

POETICAL WORKS

OF

OLIVER GOLDSMITH.

WITH A LIFE,

BY

THOMAS BABINGTON MACAULAY.

BOSTON:
LITTLE, BROWN AND COMPANY.
NEW YORK: BLAKEMAN AND MASON.
CINCINNATI: RICKEY AND CARROLL.
M.DCCC.LXII.

ADVERTISEMENT.

THE Memoir of Goldsmith which accompanies this edition is taken from the tenth volume of the new edition of the Encyclopædia Brittanica.

The Anecdotes of Goldsmith which follow the Memoir, were collected by the Rev. John Mitford, and appended to his Life of Goldsmith. He says: "I should with reluctance have deprived my readers of what information might be collected from them; but I am not sufficiently satisfied of the veracity of all to authorize their reception in the narrative of the Poet's Life. I have, therefore, collected them into an Appendix, where they appear under the sanction of the narrators' names, who are alone responsible for their truth."

CONTENTS.

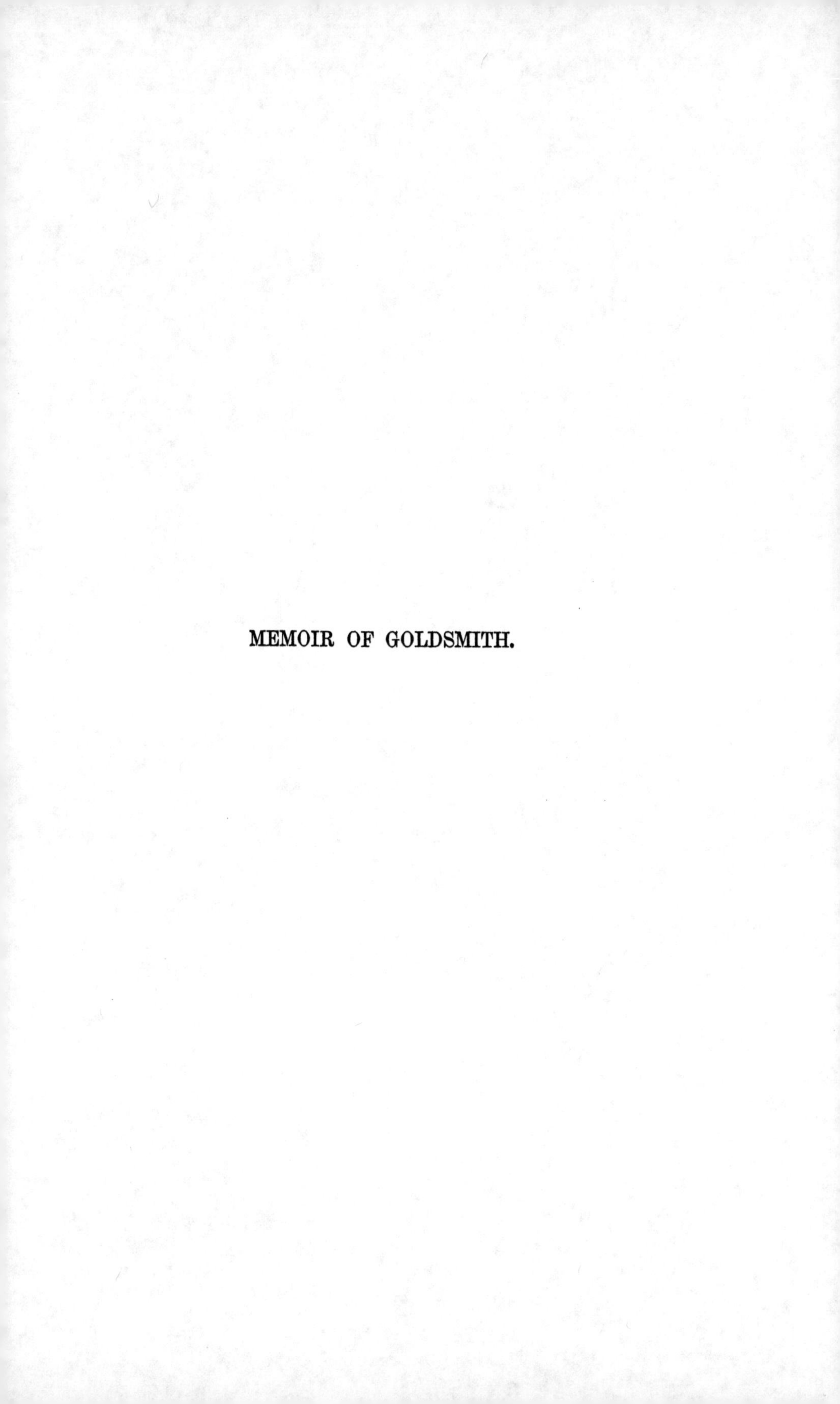

MEMOIR OF GOLDSMITH.

MEMOIR OF GOLDSMITH.

BY THOMAS BABINGTON MACAULAY.

Oliver Goldsmith was one of the most pleasing English writers of the eighteenth century. He was of a Protestant and Saxon family which had been long settled in Ireland, and which had, like most other Protestant and Saxon families, been, in troubled times, harassed and put in fear by the native population. His father, Charles Goldsmith, studied in the reign of Queen Anne, at the diocesan school of Elphin, became attached to the daughter of the schoolmaster, married her, took orders, and settled at a place called Pallas, in the county of Longford. There he with difficulty supported his wife and children on what he could earn, partly as a curate, and partly as a farmer.

At Pallas, Oliver Goldsmith was born in November, 1728. That spot was then, for all practical purposes, almost as remote from the busy and splendid capital in which his later years were passed, as any clearing in Upper Canada, or any sheep-walk in Australasia, now is. Even at this day, those enthusiasts who venture to make a pilgrimage to the birthplace of the poet, are forced to perform the latter part of their journey on foot. The hamlet lies far from any high road, on a dreary plain which, in wet weather, is often a lake. The lanes would break any jaunting car to pieces; and there are ruts and sloughs through which the most strongly built wheels cannot be dragged.

While Oliver was still a child, his father was presented to a living worth about £200 à year, in the county of Westmeath. The family accordingly quitted their cottage in the wilderness for a spacious house on a frequented road, near the village of Lissoy. Here the boy was taught his letters by a maid-servant, and was sent in his seventh year to a village school kept by an old quartermaster on half-pay, who professed to teach nothing but reading, writing, and arithmetic, but who had an inexhaustible fund of stories about ghosts, banshees, and fairies, about the great Rapparee chiefs, Baldearg O'Donnell and galloping Hogan, and about the exploits of Peterborough and Stanhope, the surprise of Monjuich, and the glorious disaster of Brihuega. This man must have been of the Protestant religion; but he was of the aboriginal race, and not only spoke the Irish language, but could pour forth unpremeditated Irish verses. Oliver early became, and through life continued to be, a passionate admirer of the Irish music, and especially of the compositions of Carolan, some of the last notes of whose harp he heard. It ought to be added that Oliver, though by birth one of the Englishry, and though connected by numerous ties with the Established Church, never showed the least sign of that contemptuous antipathy with which, in his days, the ruling minority in Ireland too generally regarded the subject majority. So far indeed was he from sharing in the opinions and feelings of the caste to which he belonged, that he conceived an aversion to the Glorious and Immortal Memory, and, even when George the Third was on the throne, maintained that nothing but the restoration of the banished dynasty could save the country.

From the humble academy kept by the old soldier, Goldsmith was removed in his ninth year. He went to several grammar-schools, and acquired some knowledge of the ancient languages. His life at this time seems to have been far from happy. He had, as appears from the admirable portrait of him at Knowle, features harsh even to ugliness. The smallpox had set its mark on him with more than usual severity. His stature was small, and his limbs ill put together. Among boys, little tenderness is shown to personal defects; and the ridicule excited by poor Oliver's appearance, was heightened by a peculiar simplicity and a disposition to blunder which he retained to the last. He became the common butt of boys and masters, was pointed at as a fright in the play-ground, and flogged as a dunce in the school-room. When he had risen to eminence, those who had once derided him, ransacked their memory for the events of his early years, and recited repartees and couplets which had dropped from him, and which, though little noticed at the time, were supposed, a quarter of a century later, to indicate the powers which produced the Vicar of Wakefield and the Deserted Village.

In his seventeenth year, Oliver went up to Trinity College, Dublin, as a sizar. The sizars paid nothing for food and tuition, and very little for lodging; but they had to perform some menial services, from which they have long been relieved. They swept the court; they carried up the dinner to the fellows' table, and changed the plates and poured out the ale of the rulers of the society Goldsmith was quartered, not alone, in a garret, on the window of which his name, scrawled by himself, is still read with interest. From such garrets, many men of less parts than his have made their way to the woolsack or to the episcopal bench. But Goldsmith, while he suffered all the humiliations, threw away all the advantages of his situation. He neglected the studies of the place, stood low at the examinations, was turned down to the bottom of his class for playing the buffoon in the lecture-room, was severely reprimanded for pumping on a constable, and was caned by a brutal tutor for giving a ball in the attic story of the college to some gay youths and damsels from the city.

While Oliver was leading at Dublin a life divided between squalid distress and squalid dissipation, his father died, leaving a mere pittance. The youth obtained his bachelor's degree, and left the university. During some time, the humble dwelling to which his widowed mother had retired, was his home. He was now in his twenty-first year; it was necessary that he should do something; and his education seemed to have fitted him to do nothing but to dress himself in gaudy colours, of which he was as fond as a magpie, to take a hand at cards, to sing Irish airs, to play the flute, to angle in summer, and to tell ghost stories by the fire in winter. He tried five or six professions in turn without success. He applied for ordination; but, as he applied in scarlet clothes, he was speedily turned out of the episcopal palace. He then became tutor in an opulent family, but soon quitted his situation in consequence of a dispute about play. Then he determined to emigrate to America. His relations, with much satisfaction, saw him set out for Cork on a good horse, with thirty pounds in his pocket.

But in six weeks he came back on a miserable hack, without a penny, and informed his mother that the ship in which he had taken his passage, having got a fair wind while he was at a party of pleasure, had sailed without him. Then he resolved to study the law. A generous kinsman advanced fifty pounds. With this sum, Goldsmith went to Dublin, was enticed into a gaming house, and lost every shilling. He then thought of medicine. A small purse was made up; and in his twenty-fourth year, he was sent to Edinburgh. At Edinburgh, he passed eighteen months in nominal attendance on lectures, and picked up some superficial information about chemistry and natural history. Thence he went to Leyden, still pretending to study physic. He left that celebrated university, the third university at which he had resided, in his twenty-seventh year, without a degree, with the merest smattering of medical knowledge, and with no property but his clothes and his flute. His flute, however, proved a useful friend. He rambled on foot through Flanders, France, and Switzerland, playing tunes which everywhere set the peasantry dancing, and which often procured for him a supper and a bed. He wandered as far as Italy. His musical performances, indeed, were not to the taste of the Italians; but he contrived to live on the alms which he obtained at the gates of convents. It should, however, be observed, that the stories which he told about this part of his life, ought to be received with great caution; for strict veracity was never one of his virtues; and a man who is ordinarily inaccurate in narration, is likely to be more than ordinarily inaccurate when he talks about his own travels. Goldsmith, indeed, was so regardless of truth as to assert in print that he was present at a most interesting conversation between Voltaire and Fontenelle, and that this conversation took place at Paris. Now, it is certain that Voltaire never was within a hundred leagues of Paris during the whole time which Goldsmith passed on the continent.

In 1756, the wanderer landed at Dover, without a shilling, without a friend, and without a calling. He had, indeed, if his own unsupported evidence may be trusted, obtained from the University of Padua a doctor's degree; but this dignity proved utterly useless to him. In England, his flute was not in request: there were no convents; and he was forced to have recourse to a series of desperate expedients. He turned strolling player; but his face and figure were ill suited to the boards even of the humblest theatre. He pounded drugs, and ran about London with phials for charitable chemists. He joined a swarm of beggars, which made its nest in Axe Yard. He was for a time usher of a school, and felt the miseries and humiliations of this situation so keenly, that he thought it a promotion to be permitted to earn his bread as a bookseller's hack; but he soon found the new yoke more galling than the old one, and was glad to become an usher again. He obtained a medical appointment in the service of the East India Company; but the appointment was speedily revoked. Why it was revoked, we are not told. The subject was one on which he never liked to talk. It is probable that he was incompetent to perform the duties of the place. Then he presented himself at Surgeon's Hall for examination, as mate to a naval hospital. Even to so humble a post he was found unequal. By this time the schoolmaster, whom he had served for a morsel of food and the third part of a bed, was no more. Nothing remained but to return to the lowest drudgery of literature. Goldsmith took a garret in a miserable court, to which he had to climb from the brink of Fleet Ditch by a dizzy ladder of flagstones called Breakneck Steps. The court and the ascent have long disappeared; but old Londoners well remember both. Here, at thirty, the unlucky adventurer sat down to toil like a galley slave.

In the succeeding six years, he sent to the press some things which have survived, and many which have perished. He produced articles for reviews, magazines, and newspapers; children's books, which, bound in gilt paper and adorned with hideous woodcuts, appeared in the window of the once far-famed shop at the corner of Saint Paul's

Churchyard; An Inquiry into the State of Polite Learning in Europe, which, though of little or no value, is still reprinted among his works; a Life of Beau Nash, which is not reprinted,[1] though it well deserves to be so; a superficial and incorrect, but very readable, History of England, in a series of letters purporting to be addressed by a nobleman to his son; and some very lively and amusing Sketches of London Society, in a series of letters purporting to be addressed by a Chinese traveller to his friends. All these works were anonymous; but some of them were well known to be Goldsmith's; and he gradually rose in the estimation of the booksellers for whom he drudged. He was, indeed, emphatically a popular writer. For accurate research or grave disquisition, he was not well qualified by nature or by education. He knew nothing accurately; his reading had been desultory; nor had he meditated deeply on what he had read. He had seen much of the world; but he had noticed and retained little more of what he had seen than some grotesque incidents and characters which had happened to strike his fancy. But, though his mind was very scantily stored with materials, he used what materials he had in such a way as to produce a wonderful effect. There have been many greater writers; but perhaps no writer was ever more

1 [See Cunningham's edition of the Works of Goldsmith, vol. iv.]

uniformly agreeable. His style was always pure and easy, and, on proper occasions, pointed and energetic. His narratives were always amusing, his descriptions always picturesque, his humour rich and joyous, yet not without an occasional tinge of amiable sadness. About every thing that he wrote, serious or sportive, there was a certain natural grace and decorum, hardly to be expected from a man a great part of whose life had been passed among thieves and beggars, street-walkers and merry-andrews, in those squalid dens which are the reproach of great capitals.

As his name gradually became known, the circle of his acquaintance widened. He was introduced to Johnson, who was then considered as the first of living English writers; to Reynolds, the first of English painters; and to Burke, who had not yet entered parliament, but had distinguished himself greatly by his writings and by the eloquence of his conversation. With these eminent men, Goldsmith became intimate. In 1763, he was one of the nine original members of that celebrated fraternity which has sometimes been called the Literary Club, but which has always disclaimed that epithet, and still glories in the simple name of The Club.

By this time, Goldsmith had quitted his miserable dwelling at the top of Breakneck Steps, and had taken chambers in the more civilized region of the Inns of Court. But he was still often reduced to pitiable shifts. Towards the close of 1764, his rent was so long in arrear that his landlady one morning called in the help of a sheriff's officer. The debtor, in great perplexity, despatched a messenger to Johnson; and Johnson, always friendly, though often surly, sent back the messenger with a guinea, and promised to follow speedily. He came, and found that Goldsmith had changed the guinea, and was railing at the landlady over a bottle of Madeira. Johnson put the cork into the bottle, and entreated his friend to consider calmly how money was to be procured. Goldsmith said that he had a novel ready for the press. Johnson glanced at the manuscript, saw that there were good things in it, took it to a bookseller, sold it for £60, and soon returned with the money. The rent was paid; and the sheriff's officer withdrew. According to one story, Goldsmith gave his landlady a sharp reprimand for her treatment of him; according to another, he insisted on her joining him in a bowl of punch. Both stories are probably true. The novel which was thus ushered into the world, was the Vicar of Wakefield.

But before the Vicar of Wakefield appeared in print, came the great crisis of Goldsmith's literary life. In Christmas week, 1764, he published a poem, entitled the Traveller. It was the first work to which he had put his name; and it at once raised him to the rank of a legitimate English classic. The opinion of the most skilful critics was, that nothing finer had appeared in verse since the fourth book of the Dunciad. In one respect, the Traveller differs from all Goldsmith's other writings. In general, his designs were bad, and his execution good. In the Traveller, the execution, though deserving of much praise, is far inferior to the design. No philosophical poem, ancient or modern, has a plan so noble, and at the same time so simple. An English wanderer, seated on a crag among the Alps, near the point where three great countries meet, looks down on the boundless prospect, reviews his long pilgrimage, recalls the varieties of scenery, of climate, of government, of religion, of national character, which he has observed, and comes to the conclusion, just or unjust, that our happiness depends little on political institutions, and much on the temper and regulation of our own minds.

While the fourth edition of the Traveller was on the counters of the booksellers, the Vicar of Wakefield appeared, and rapidly obtained a popularity which has lasted down to our own time, and which is likely to last as long as our language. The fable is indeed one of the worst that ever was constructed. It wants not merely that probability which ought to be found in a tale of common English life, but that consistency which ought to be found even in the wildest fiction about witches, giants, and fairies. But the earlier chapters have all the sweetness of pastoral poetry, together with all the vivacity of comedy. Moses and his spectacles, the vicar and his monogamy, the sharper and his cosmogony, the squire proving from Aristotle that relatives are related, Olivia preparing herself for the arduous task of converting a rakish lover by studying the controversy between Robinson Crusoe and Friday, the great ladies with their scandal about Sir Tomkyn's amours and Dr. Burdock's verses, and Mr. Burchell with his "Fudge," have caused as much harmless mirth as has ever been caused by matter packed into so small a number of pages. The latter part of the tale is unworthy of the beginning. As we approach the catastrophe, the absurdities lie thicker and thicker; and the gleams of pleasantry become rarer and rarer.

The success which had attended Goldsmith as a novelist, emboldened him to try his fortune as a dramatist. He wrote the Good-natured Man, a piece which had a worse fate than it deserved. Garrick refused to produce it at Drury Lane. It was acted at Covent Garden in 1768, but was coldly received. The author, however, cleared by his benefit nights, and by the sale of the copyright, no less than £500, five times as much as he had made by the Traveller and the Vicar of Wakefield together. The plot of the Good-natured Man is, like almost all Goldsmith's plots, very ill constructed. But some passages are exquisitely ludicrous; much more ludicrous, indeed, than suited the taste of the town at that time. A canting, mawkish play, entitled False Delicacy, had just had an immense run. Sentimentality was all the mode. During some years, more tears were shed at comedies than at tragedies; and a pleasantry which moved the audience to any thing more than a grave smile, was reprobated as low. It is not strange, therefore, that the very best scene in the Good-natured Man, that in which Miss Richland finds her lover attended by the bailiff and the bailiff's follower in full court dresses, should have been mercilessly hissed, and should have been omitted after the first night.

In 1770 appeared the Deserted Village. In mere diction and versification, this celebrated poem is fully equal, perhaps superior to the Traveller; and it is generally preferred to the Traveller by that large class of readers who think, with Bayes in the Rehearsal, that the only use of a plan is to bring in fine things. More discerning judges, however, while they admire the beauty of the details, are shocked by one unpardonable fault which pervades the whole. The fault which we mean, is not that theory about wealth and luxury which has so often been censured by political economists. The theory is indeed false; but the poem, considered merely as a poem, is not necessarily the worse on that account. The finest poem in the Latin language, indeed the finest didactic poem in any language, was written in defence of the silliest and meanest of all systems of natural and moral philosophy. A poet may easily be pardoned for reasoning ill; but he cannot be pardoned for describing ill, for observing the world in which he lives so carelessly, that his portraits bear no resemblance to the originals, for exhibiting as copies from real life monstrous combinations of things which never were and never could be found together. What would be thought of a painter who should mix August and January in one landscape, who should introduce a frozen river into a harvest scene? Would it be a sufficient defence of such a picture to say that every part was exquisitely coloured, that the green hedges, the apple-trees loaded with fruit, the wagons reeling under the yellow sheaves, and the sun-burned reapers wiping their foreheads, were very fine, and that the ice and the boys sliding were also very fine? To such a picture the Deserted Village bears a great resemblance. It is made up of incongruous parts. The village in its happy days, is a true English village. The village in its decay, is an Irish village. The felicity and the misery which Goldsmith has brought close together, belong to two different countries, and to two different stages in the progress of society. He had assuredly never seen in his native island such a rural paradise, such a seat of plenty, content, and tranquillity, as his Auburn.

He had assuredly never seen in England all the inhabitants of such a paradise turned out of their homes in one day, and forced to emigrate in a body to America. The hamlet he had probably seen in Kent; the ejectment he had probably seen in Munster; but by joining the two, he has produced something which never was and never will be seen in any part of the world.

In 1773, Goldsmith tried his chance at Covent Garden with a second play, She Stoops to Conquer. The manager was not without great difficulty induced to bring this piece out. The sentimental comedy still reigned, and Goldsmith's comedies were not sentimental. The Good-natured Man had been too funny to succeed; yet the mirth of the Good-natured Man was sober when compared with the rich drollery of She Stoops to Conquer, which is, in truth, an incomparable farce in five acts. On this occasion, however, genius triumphed. Pit, boxes, and galleries were in a constant roar of laughter. If any bigoted admirer of Kelly and Cumberland ventured to hiss or groan, he was speedily silenced by a general cry of "turn him out," or "throw him over." Two generations have since confirmed the verdict which was pronounced on that night.

While Goldsmith was writing the Deserted Village and She Stoops to Conquer, he was employed on works of a very different kind, works from which he derived little reputation, but much profit. He compiled for the use of schools a History of Rome, by which he made £300, a History of England, by which he made £600, a History of Greece, for which he received £250, a Natural History, for which the booksellers covenanted to pay him 800 guineas. These works he produced without any elaborate research, by merely selecting, abridging, and translating into his own clear, pure, and flowing language, what he found in books well known to the world, but too bulky or too dry for boys and girls. He committed some strange blunders; for he knew nothing with accuracy. Thus, in his History of England, he tells us that Naseby is in Yorkshire; nor did he correct this mistake when the book was reprinted. He was very nearly hoaxed into putting into the History of Greece an account of a battle between Alexander the Great and Montezuma. In his Animated Nature, he relates, with faith and with perfect gravity, all the most absurd lies which he could find in books of travels about gigantic Patagonians, monkeys that preach sermons, nightingales that repeat long conversations. "If he can tell a horse from a cow," said Johnson, that is the extent of his knowledge of zoology." How little Goldsmith was qualified to write about the physical sciences, is sufficiently proved by two anecdotes. He on one occasion denied that the sun is longer in the northern than in the southern signs. It was vain to cite the authority of Maupertuis. "Maupertuis!" he cried, "I understand those matters better than Maupertuis." On another occasion, he, in defiance of the evidence of his own senses, maintained obstinately, and even angrily, that he chewed his dinner by moving his upper jaw.

Yet, ignorant as Goldsmith was, few writers have done more to make the first steps in the laborious road to knowledge easy and pleasant. His compilations are widely distinguished from the compilations of ordinary bookmakers. He was a great, perhaps an unequalled, master of the arts of selection and condensation. In these respects, his histories of Rome and of England, and still more his own abridgments of these histories, well deserved to be studied. In general, nothing is less attractive than an epitome; but the epitomes of Goldsmith, even when most concise, are always amusing; and to read them is considered by intelligent children, not as a task, but as a pleasure.

Goldsmith might now be considered as a prosperous man. He had the means of living in comfort, and even in what to one who had so often slept in barns and on bulks, must have been luxury. His fame was great, and was constantly rising. He lived in what was intellectually far the best society of the kingdom, in a society in which no talent or accomplishment was wanting, and in which the art of conversation was cultivated with splendid success. There probably were never four talkers more admirable in four different ways than Johnson, Burke, Beauclerk, and Garrick; and Goldsmith was on terms of intimacy with all the four. He aspired to share in their colloquial renown; but never was ambition more unfortunate. It may seem strange that a man who wrote with so much perspicuity, vivacity, and grace, should have been, whenever he took a part in conversation, an empty, noisy, blundering rattler. But on this point the evidence is overwhelming. So extraordinary was the contrast between Goldsmith's published works and the silly things which he said, that Horace Walpole described him as an inspired idiot. "Noll," said Garrick, "wrote like an angel, and talked like poor Pol." Chamier declared that it was a hard exercise of faith to believe that so foolish a chatterer could have really written the Traveller. Even Boswell could say, with contemptuous compassion, that he liked very well to hear honest Goldsmith run on. "Yes, sir," said Johnson, "but he should not like to hear himself." Minds differ as rivers differ. There are transparent and sparkling rivers from which it is delightful to drink as they flow; to such rivers, the minds of such men as Burke and Johnson may be compared. But there are rivers of which the water, when first drawn, is turbid and noisome, but becomes pellucid as crystal and delicious to the taste if it be suffered to stand till it has deposited a sediment; and such a river is a type of the mind of Goldsmith. His first thoughts on every subject were confused even to absurdity, but they required only a little time to work themselves clear. When he wrote, they had that time; and therefore his readers pronounced him a man of genius; but when he talked, he talked nonsense, and made himself the laughing-stock of his hearers. He was painfully sensible of his inferiority in conversation; he felt every failure keenly; yet he had not sufficient judgment and self-command to hold his tongue. His animal spirits and vanity were always impelling him to try to do the one thing which he could not do. After every attempt he felt that he had exposed himself, and writhed with shame and vexation; yet the next moment he began again.

His associates seem to have regarded him with kindness, which, in spite of their admiration of his writings, was not unmixed with contempt. In truth, there was in his character much to love, but very little to respect. His heart was soft even to weakness; he was so generous that he quite forgot to be just; he forgave injuries so readily, that he might be said to invite them, and was so liberal to beggars, that he had nothing left for his tailor and his butcher. He was vain, sensual, frivolous, profuse, improvident. One vice of a darker shade was imputed to him, envy. But there is not the least reason to believe that this bad passion, though it sometimes made him wince and utter fretful exclamations, ever impelled him to injure by wicked arts the reputation of any of his rivals. The truth probably is, that he was not more envious, but merely less prudent than his neighbours. His heart was on his lips. All those small jealousies, which are but too common among men of letters, but which a man of letters, who is also a man of the world, does his best to conceal, Goldsmith avowed with the simplicity of a child. When he was envious, instead of affecting indifference, instead of damning with faint praise, instead of doing injuries slyly and in the dark, he told everybody that he was envious. "Do not, pray, do not talk of Johnson in such terms," he said to Boswell, "you harrow up my very soul." George Steevens and Cumberland were men far too cunning to say such a thing. They would have echoed the praises of the man whom they envied, and then have sent to the newspapers anonymous libels upon him. Both what was good and what was bad in Goldsmith's character, was to his associates a perfect security that he would never commit such villany. He was neither ill-natured enough, nor long-headed enough, to be guilty of any malicious act which required contrivance and disguise.

Goldsmith has sometimes been represented as a man of genius, cruelly treated by the world, and doomed to struggle with difficulties, which at last broke his heart. But no representation can be more remote from the truth. He did, indeed, go through much sharp misery before he had done any thing considerable in literature. But after his name had appeared on the title-page of the Traveller, he had none but himself to blame for his distresses. His average income, during the last seven years of his life, certainly exceeded £400 a year, and £400 a year ranked, among the incomes of that day, at least as high as £800 a year would rank at present. A single man living in the Temple, with £400 a year, might then be called opulent. Not one in ten of the young gentlemen of good families, who were studying the law there, had so much. But all the wealth which Lord Clive had brought from Bengal, and Sir Lawrence Dundas from Germany, joined together, would not have sufficed for Goldsmith. He spent twice as much as he had. He wore fine clothes, gave dinners of several courses, paid court to venal beauties. He had also, it should be remembered, to the honour of his heart, though not of his head, a guinea, or five, or ten, according to the state of his purse, ready for any tale of distress, true or false. But it was not in dress or feasting, in promiscuous amours or promiscuous charities, that his chief expense lay. He had been from boyhood a gambler, and at once the most sanguine and the most unskilful of gamblers. For a time he put off the day of inevitable ruin by temporary expedients. He obtained advances from booksellers, by promising to execute works which he never began. But at length this source of supply failed. He owed more than £2000; and he saw no hope of extrication from his embarrassments. His spirits and health gave way. He was attacked by a nervous fever, which he thought himself competent to treat. It would have been happy for him if his medical skill had been appreciated as justly by himself as by others. Notwithstanding the degree which he pretended to have received at Padua, he could procure no patients. "I do not practise," he once said; "I make it a rule to prescribe only for my friends." "Pray, dear Doctor," said Beauclerk, "alter your rule; and prescribe only for your enemies." Goldsmith now, in spite of this excellent advice, prescribed for himself. The remedy aggravated the malady. The sick man was induced to call in real physicians; and they at one time imagined that they had cured the disease. Still, his weakness and restlessness continued. He could get no sleep. He could take no food. "You are worse," said one of his medical attendants, "than you should be from the degree of fever which you have. Is your mind at ease?" "No, it is not," were the last recorded words of Oliver Goldsmith. He died on the 3d of April, 1774, in his forty-sixth year. He was laid in the churchyard of the Temple; but the spot was not marked by any inscription, and is now forgotten. The coffin was followed by Burke and Reynolds. Both these great men were sincere mourners. Burke, when he heard of Goldsmith's death, had burst into a flood of tears. Reynolds had been so much moved by the news, that he had flung aside his brush and palette for the day.

A short time after Goldsmith's death, a little poem appeared, which will, as long as our language lasts, associate the names of his two illustrious friends with his own. It has already been mentioned that he sometimes felt keenly the sarcasm which his wild blundering talk brought upon him. He was, not long before his last illness, provoked into retaliating. He wisely betook himself to his pen; and at that weapon he proved himself a match for all his assailants together. Within a small compass he drew with a singularly easy and vigorous pencil the characters of nine or ten of his intimate associates. Though this little work did not receive his last touches, it must always be regarded as a masterpiece. It is impossible, however, not to wish that four or five likenesses which have no interest for posterity, were wanting to that noble gallery, and that their places were supplied by sketches of Johnson and Gibbon, as happy and vivid as the sketches of Burke and Garrick.

Some of Goldsmith's friends and admirers honoured him with a cenotaph in Westminster Abbey. Nollekens was the sculptor; and Johnson wrote the inscription. It is much to be lamented that Johnson did not leave to posterity a more durable and a more valuable memorial of his friend. A life of Goldsmith would have been an inestimable addition to the Lives of the Poets. No man appreciated Goldsmith's writings more justly than Johnson; no man was better acquainted with Goldsmith's character and habits; and no man was more competent to delineate with truth and spirit the peculiarities of a mind in which great powers were found in company with great weaknesses. But the list of poets to whose works Johnson was requested by the booksellers to furnish prefaces, ended with Lyttelton, who died in 1773. The line seems to have been drawn expressly for the purpose of excluding the person whose portrait would have most fitly closed the series. Goldsmith, however, has been fortunate in his biographers. Within a few years, his life has been written by Mr. Prior, by Mr. Washington Irving, and by Mr. Forster. The diligence of Mr. Prior deserves great praise; the style of Mr. Washington Irving is always pleasing; but the highest place must, in justice, be assigned to the eminently interesting work of Mr. Forster.

ANECDOTES OF GOLDSMITH,

FROM

I. NORTHCOTE'S LIFE OF REYNOLDS.
II. CRADOCK'S MEMOIRS.
III. DAVIES'S LIFE OF GARRICK.
IV. BOSWELL'S LIFE OF JOHNSON.
V. MISS HAWKINS'S ANECDOTES.
VI. COLMAN'S RANDOM RECORDS.
VII. CUMBERLAND'S MEMOIRS.
VIII. NORTHCOTE'S CONVERSATIONS.
IX. HAWKINS'S LIFE OF JOHNSON.

ANECDOTES OF GOLDSMITH.

NORTHCOTE'S LIFE OF REYNOLDS.

In the course of this year, Sir Joshua took another trip to Paris, from which he had scarcely returned when Mr. Bennet Langton renewed, in a very pressing manner, an invitation which he had given to him and Goldsmith to spend some part of the autumn with him and his lady, the Countess of Rothes, at their seat in Lincolnshire. With this obliging request, however, he was unable to comply; and Goldsmith, in a letter to Mr. Langton, declining the invitation on the part of both, says, 'Reynolds is just returned from Paris, and finds himself now in the case of a truant, that must make up for his idle time by diligence: we have therefore agreed to postpone our journey till next summer.'

In fact, at this period Sir Joshua may be said to have been at the zenith of his eminence, as we see him now employed in portraying the most illustrious personages in every different department, whilst his intimacy was sedulously sought after by all degrees of persons.

Much of the attention which even Goldsmith personally met with was undoubtedly owing to the patronage of his admired friend; yet Sir Joshua used to say that Goldsmith looked at or considered public notoriety or fame as one great parcel, to the whole of which he laid claim, and whoever partook of any part of it, whether dancer, singer, sleight-of-hand man, or tumbler, deprived him of his right, and drew off the attention of the world from himself, and which he was striving to gain.

Notwithstanding this, he lamented that whenever he entered into a mixed company, he struck a kind of awe on them, which deprived him of the enjoyment and freedom of society, and which he then made it his endeavour to dispel by playing wanton and childish pranks in order to bring himself to the wished-for level.

It was very soon after my first arrival in London, where every thing appeared new and wonderful to me, that I expressed to Sir Joshua my impatient curiosity to see Dr. Goldsmith, and he promised I should do so on the first opportunity. Soon afterwards Goldsmith came to dine with him, and immediately on my entering the room, Sir Joshua, with a designed abruptness, said to me, 'This is Dr. Goldsmith: pray, why did you wish to see him?' I was much confused by the suddenness of the question, and answered, in my hurry, 'Because he is a notable man.' This, in one sense of the word, was so very contrary to the character and conduct of Goldsmith, that Sir Joshua burst into a hearty laugh, and said that Goldsmith should in future always be called the notable man.

What I meant, however, to say was, that he was a man of note or eminence.

He appeared to me to be very unaffected and good-natured; but he was totally ignorant of the art of painting, and this he often confessed with much gaiety.

It has been often said of Goldsmith, that he was ever desirous of being the object of attention in all companies where he was present, which the following anecdote may serve to prove: —

On a summer's excursion to the continent, he accompanied a lady and her two beautiful daughters into France and Flanders, and often expressed a little displeasure at perceiving that more attention was paid to them than to himself. On their entering a town, I think Antwerp, the populace surrounded the door of the hotel at which they alighted, and testified a desire to see those beautiful young women; and the ladies, willing to gratify them, came into a balcony at the front of the house, and Goldsmith with them; but perceiving that it was not himself who was the object of admiration, he presently withdrew, with evident signs of mortification, saying, as he went out, 'There are places where I am the object of admiration also.'

One day when Drs. Goldsmith and Johnson were at dinner with Sir Joshua, a poem, by a poet already alluded to, was presented to Sir Joshua, by his servant, from the author. Goldsmith immediately laid hold of it and began to read it, and at every line cut almost through the paper with his finger-nail, crying out, 'What d—d nonsense is this!' when Sir Joshua caught it out of his hands, saying, 'No, no, don't do so; you shall not spoil my book, neither;' for the Doctor could not bear to hear of another's fame.

Sir Joshua was always cautious to preserve an unblemished character, and careful not to make any man his enemy. I remember, when he was told of some very indiscreet speech or action of Goldsmith, he quickly said, 'What a fool he is thus to commit himself, when he has so much more cause to be careful of his reputation than I have of mine!' well recollecting that even the most trivial circumstance which tells against an eminent person will be remembered as well as those in his favour, and that the world watches those who are distinguished for their abilities with a jealous eye.

To Goldsmith, in particular, he was always attentive; a man of whom it has been not unaptly said, that his carelessness of conduct and frivolity of manners obscured the goodness of his heart. Mr. Cumberland, in his own Memoirs, has a passage peculiarly illustrative of this, where he says that 'Sir Joshua Reynolds was very good to him, and would have drilled him into better trim and order for society, if he would have been amenable; for Reynolds was a perfect gentleman, had good sense, great propriety, with all the social attributes, and all the graces of hospitality, equal to any man. He well knew how to appreciate men of talents, and how near akin the Muse of Poetry was to that art of which he was so eminent a master. From Goldsmith he caught the subject of his famous Ugolino: what aids he got from others, if he got any, were worthily bestowed and happily applied.'

Mr. Cumberland, however, is perhaps rather inaccurate in his assertion respecting the painting of 'Ugolino,' which was finished in this year (1773), and begun, not long before, as an historical subject.

The fact is, that this painting may be said to have been produced as an historical picture by an accident; for the head of the Count had been painted previous to the year 1771, and finished on what we painters call 'a half-length canvas,' and was, in point of expression, exactly as it now stands, but without any intention, on the part of Sir Joshua, of making it the subject of an historical composition, or having the story of Count Ugolino in his thoughts. Being exposed in the picture-gallery, along with his other works, it was seen either by Mr. Edmund Burke or Dr. Goldsmith, I am not certain which, who immediately exclaimed, that it struck him as being the precise person, countenance, and expression of the Count Ugolino, as described by Dante in his 'Inferno.'

When Goldsmith's comedy of 'She Stoops to Conquer' was to be brought out on the stage, on the 15th of March, in this year, he was at a loss what name to give it, till the very last moment, and then, in great haste, called it, 'She Stoops to Conquer, or the Mistakes of a Night.' Sir Joshua, who disliked this name for a play, offered a much better to him, saying, 'You ought to call it the Belle's Stratagem; and if you do not, I will damn it.' However, Goldsmith chose to name it himself, as above; and Mrs. Cowley has since given that name to one of her comedies.

Goldsmith was in great anxiety about its success; he was much distressed in his finances at the time, and all his hopes hung on the event; and at the dinner preceding the representation of his play, his mouth became so parched and dry, from the agitation of his mind, that he was unable to swallow a single mouthful. The actors themselves had great doubts of its success; but, contrary to their expectations, the play was received with great applause; Sir Joshua and a large party of friends going for the purpose of supporting it if necessary. The dinner-party, which took place at the Shakespeare, is humorously described by Cumberland. Dr. Johnson took the head of the table, and there were present the Burkes, Caleb Whiteford, Major Mills, &c. &c.

I remember Dr. Goldsmith gave me an order soon after this,

with which I went to see this comedy; and the next time I saw him, he inquired of me what my opinion was of it. I told him that I would not presume to be a judge of its merits; he then said, 'Did it make you laugh?' I answered, 'Exceedingly.' 'Then,' said the Doctor, 'that is all I require.'

One day Dr. Johnson and Dr. Goldsmith meeting at Sir Joshua Reynolds's table, the conversation turned on the merits of that well-known tragedy, Otway's Venice Preserved, which Goldsmith highly extolled, asserting that of all tragedies it was the one nearest in excellence to Shakespeare; when Johnson, in his peremptory manner, contradicted him, and pronounced that there were not forty good lines to be found in the whole play; adding, 'Pooh! what stuff are these lines:—

'What feminine tales hast thou been listening to, of unaired shirts, catarrhs, and toothache, got by thin-soled shoes?'

'True,' replied Goldsmith, 'to be sure that is very like Shakespeare.'

Of this subject, however, I presume my readers will think I have given them enough: I shall, therefore, revert to another friend of Sir Joshua's, poor Goldsmith, who left this world on the 4th of April, 1774; the first, too, of those on whom the epitaphs had been so playfully written, as I have before alluded to in another place.

Just before his death, he had nearly completed a design for the execution of a 'Universal Dictionary of the Arts and Sciences.' Of this he had published the Prospectus, or, at least, had distributed copies of it amongst his friends and acquaintances. It did not meet with any warm encouragement, however, from the booksellers, although Sir Joshua Reynolds, Johnson, Garrick, and several others of his literary connexions, had promised him their assistance on various subjects; and the design was, I believe, entirely given up even previous to his demise.

In the Dedication of his 'Deserted Village' to Sir Joshua Reynolds, already noticed, Goldsmith alludes to the death of his eldest brother, Henry, the clergyman; and his various biographers record another, Maurice, who was a younger brother, and of whom it is stated by Bishop Percy, that, having been bred to no business, he, upon some occasion, complained to Oliver that he found it difficult to live like a gentleman. To this Oliver wrote him an answer, begging that he would, without delay, quit so unprofitable a trade, and betake himself to some handicraft employment. Maurice wisely, as the Bishop adds, took the hint, and bound himself apprentice to a cabinet-maker, and when out of his indentures set up in business for himself, in which he was engaged during the viceroyalty of the late Duke of Rutland; and his shop being in Dublin, he was noticed by Mr. Orde, since Lord Bolton, the Lord Lieutenant's Secretary, who recommended him to the patronage of the duke, out of regard to the memory of his brother.

In consequence of this, he received the appointment of inspector of licences in that metropolis, and was also employed as macebearer by the Royal Irish Academy, then just established. Both of these places were compatible with his business; and in the former he gave proof of great integrity by detecting a fraud committed on the revenue in his department, and one by which he himself might have profited, if he had not been a man of principle. He has now been dead not more than fifteen years. I enter more particularly into his history, from having seen the following passage in one of Oliver's letters to him: 'You talked of being my only brother, — I don't understand you. Where is Charles?'

This, indeed, was a question which Maurice could not answer then, nor for many years afterwards; but as the anecdote is curious, and I have it from a friend on whose authority I can rely, I shall give it a place here nearly in his own words.

My friend informed me, that whilst travelling in the stage-coach towards Ireland, in the autumn of 1791, he was joined at Oswestry by a venerable-looking gentleman, who, in the course of the morning, mentioned that his name was Goldsmith, when one of the party observed, that if he was going to Ireland, that name would be a passport for him. The stranger smiled, and asked the reason why; to which the other replied, that the memory of Oliver was embalmed amongst his countrymen. A tear glistened in the stranger's eye, who immediately answered, 'I am his brother.' The gentleman who had first made the observation on the name looked doubtingly, and said, 'He has but one brother living: I know him well.' 'True,' replied the stranger, 'for it may be said that I am risen from the dead, having been for many years supposed to be no longer in the land of the living. I am Charles, the youngest of the family. Oliver, I know, is dead; but of Henry and Maurice I know nothing.'

On being informed of various particulars of his family, the stranger then told his simple tale; which was, that, having heard of his brother Noll mixing in the first society in London, he took it for granted that his fortune was made, and that he could soon make a brother's also; he therefore left home without notice, but soon found, on his arrival in London, that the picture he had formed of his brother's situation was too highly coloured; that Noll would not introduce him to his great friends, and, in fact, that although out of a jail, he was also often out of a lodging.

Disgusted with this entrance into high life, and ashamed to return home, the young man left London without acquainting his brother with his intentions, or even writing to his friends in Ireland; and proceeded, a poor adventurer, to Jamaica, where he lived for many years without ever renewing an intercourse with his friends, and by whom he was, of course, supposed to be dead; though Oliver may at first have imagined that he had returned to Ireland. Years now passed on, and young Charles, by industry and perseverance, began to save some property; soon after which, he married a widow lady of some fortune; when, his young family requiring the advantages of further education, he determined to return to England, to examine into the state of society, and into the propriety of bringing over his wife and family: on this project he was then engaged, and was proceeding to Ireland to visit his native home, and with the intention of making himself known to such of his relatives as might still be living. His plan, however was to conceal his good fortune until he should ascertain their affection and esteem for him.

On arriving at Dublin, the party separated; and my friend,

a few weeks afterwards, returning from the north, called at the Hotel where he knew Mr. Goldsmith intended to reside. There he met him; when the amiable old man, for such he really was, told him that he had put his plan in execution; had given himself as much of the appearance of poverty as he could with propriety, and thus proceeded to the shop of his brother Maurice, where he inquired for several articles, and then noticed the name over the door, asking if it had any connexion with the famous Dr. Goldsmith.

'I am his brother, his sole surviving brother,' said Maurice.

'What, then,' replied the stranger, 'is become of the others?'

'Henry has long been dead; and poor Charles has not been heard of for many years.'

'But suppose Charles were alive,' said the stranger, 'would his friends acknowledge him?' 'Oh, yes!' replied Maurice, 'gladly indeed!' 'He lives, then; but as poor as when he left you.'

Maurice instantly leaped over his counter, hugged him in his arms, and, weeping with pleasure, cried, 'Welcome, welcome! here you shall find a home and a brother.'

It is needless to add, that this denouement was perfectly agreeable to the stranger, who was then preparing to return to Jamaica to make his proposed family arrangement; but my friend having been engaged for the next twenty years in traversing the four quarters of the globe, — being himself a wanderer, — has never, since that period, had an opportunity of making inquiries into the welfare of the stranger, for whom he had, indeed, formed a great esteem, even on a few days' acquaintance.

Sir Joshua was much affected by the death of Goldsmith, to whom he had been a very sincere friend. He did not touch the pencil for that day; a circumstance most extraordinary for him, who passed no day without a line. He acted as executor, and managed in the best manner the confused state of the Doctor's affairs. At first he intended, as I have already stated, to have made a grand funeral for him, assisted by several subscriptions to that intent, and to have buried him in the Abbey, his pallbearers to have been Lord Shelburne, Lord Louth, Sir Joshua himself, Burke, Garrick, &c.; but, on second thoughts, he resolved to have him buried in the plainest and most private manner possible, observing that the most pompous funerals are soon past and forgotten, and that it would be much more prudent to apply what money could be procured to the purpose of a more substantial and more lasting memorial of his departed friend, by a monument; and he was accordingly privately interred in the Temple burying-ground.

Sir Joshua went himself to Westminster Abbey, and fixed upon a place where Goldsmith's monument now stands, over a door in the Poet's Corner. He thought himself lucky in being able to find so conspicuous a situation for it, as there scarcely remained another so good.

Nollekens, the sculptor, was employed to make the monument, and Dr. Johnson composed the epitaph.

There is a very fine portrait, which is the only original one of Dr. Goldsmith, now at Knowle, the seat of the Duke of Dorset, painted by Sir Joshua.

A lady, who was a great friend of Dr. Goldsmith, earnestly desired to have a lock of his hair to keep as a memorial of him; and his coffin was opened again, after it had been closed up, to procure this lock of hair from his head. This relic is still in the possession of the family, and is the only one of the kind which has been preserved of the Doctor.

An observation of Dr. Beattie, respecting the deceased Poet, in a letter to Mr. Montagu, must not be passed over:—'I am sorry for poor Goldsmith. There were some things in his temper which I did not like, but I liked many things in his genius; and I was sorry to find, last summer, that he looked upon me as a person who seemed to stand between him and his interest. However, when next we meet, all this will be forgotten; and the jealousy of authors, which, Dr. Gregory used to say, was next to that of physicians, will be no more.'

Soon after Goldsmith's death, some people dining with Sir Joshua were commenting rather freely on some part of his works, which, in their opinion, neither discovered talent nor originality. To this Dr. Johnson listened in his usual growling manner for some time; when, at length, his patience being exhausted, he rose with great dignity, looked them full in the face, and exclaimed, 'If nobody was suffered to abuse poor Goldy but those who could write as well, he would have few censors.'

Yet, on another occasion, soon after the death of Goldsmith, a lady of his acquaintance was condoling with Dr. Johnson on their loss, saying, 'Poor Goldsmith! I am exceedingly sorry for him; he was every man's friend!'

'No, madam,' answered Johnson, 'he was no man's friend.'

In this seemingly harsh sentence, however, he merely alluded to the careless and imprudent conduct of Goldsmith, as being no friend even to himself; and, when that is the case, a man is rendered incapable of being of any essential service to any one else.

It has been generally circulated, and believed by many, that Goldsmith was a mere fool in conversation; but, in truth, this has been greatly exaggerated by such as were really fools. In allusion to this notion, Mr. Horace Walpole, who admired his writings, said he was an 'inspired idiot;' and Garrick described him as one,

> ——'for shortness call'd Noll,
> Who wrote like an angel, but talk'd like poor poll.'

Sir Joshua Reynolds mentioned to Boswell that he frequently had heard Goldsmith talk warmly of the pleasure of being liked, and observe how hard it would be if literary excellence should preclude a man from that satisfaction, which he perceived it often did, from the envy which attended it; and therefore Sir Joshua was convinced that he was intentionally more absurd, in order to lessen himself in social intercourse, trusting that his character would be sufficiently supported by his works. If it was his intention to appear absurd in company, he was often very successful. This, in my own opinion, was really the case; and I also think Sir Joshua was so sensible of the advantage of it, that he, yet in a much less degree, followed the same idea, as he never had a wish to impress his company with any awe of the great abilities with which he was endowed, especially when in the society of those high in rank.

I have heard Sir Joshua say that he has frequently seen the whole company struck with an awful silence at the entrance of Goldsmith, but that Goldsmith has quickly dispelled the charm by his boyish and social manners, and he then has soon become the plaything and favourite of the company.

Mr. Boswell in this year records an opinion of Sir Joshua's on the subject of conversation, which may be noticed in this place. When it had been proposed to add some members to the Literary Club (during Goldsmith's life), that writer had said in favour of it, that it would give the club an agreeable variety, that there could then be nothing new among the members, and that they had travelled over each other's minds; to which Johnson answered, 'Sir, you have not travelled over my mind, I promise you.' When Sir Joshua was afterwards told of this, he agreed with Goldsmith, saying, that, 'when people have lived a great deal together, they know what each of them will say on the subject. A new understanding, therefore, is desirable; because, though it may only furnish the same sense upon a question which would have been furnished by those with whom we are accustomed to live, yet this sense will have a different colouring, and colouring is of much effect in every thing else as well as in painting.'

The mention of Goldsmith calls to my recollection a circumstance related to me by Miss Reynolds.

About the year 1770, Dr. Goldsmith lost his mother, who died in Ireland. On this occasion he immediately dressed himself in a suit of clothes of gray cloth, trimmed with black, such as commonly is worn for second mourning. When he appeared the first time after this at Sir Joshua Reynolds's house, Miss F. Reynolds, the sister of Sir Joshua, asked him whom he had lost, as she saw he wore mourning; when he answered, a distant relation only; being shy, as I conjecture, to own that he wore such slight mourning for so near a relative. This appears in him an unaccountable blunder, in wearing such a dress; as all those who did not know his mother, or of her death, would not expect or require him to wear mourning at all, and to all those who knew of his mother's death, it would appear to be not the proper dress of mourning for so near a relative: so that he satisfied nobody, and displeased some; for Miss Reynolds, who afterwards heard of her death, thought it unfeeling in him to call his mother a distant relation.

CRADOCK'S MISCELLANEOUS MEMOIRS.

I THINK my acquaintance with Dr. Goldsmith must have commenced at Mr. Yates's house. My introduction to Mr. Murphy certainly took place there. The Doctor afterwards favoured me with a Prologue for my tragedy of Zobeide, probably in consequence of some application made by the Yates family, and he sent it to me with the following note: —

'Mr. Goldsmith presents his best respects to Mr. Cradock; has sent him the Prologue, such as it is. He cannot take time to make it better. He begs he will give Mr. Yates the proper instructions; and so, even so, he commits him to fortune and the public.'

'For the Right Hon. Lord Clare,
(Mr. Cradock,) Gosfield, Essex.'

This Prologue was evidently intended to be spoken by Mr. Yates, but it was forwarded to Mr. Quick; a comic Prologue, by the husband, in the character of a sailor, would have ill suited with the lofty dignity of the first tragic actress; indeed their names rarely appeared in the same play-bill, they were not calculated for the same meridian.

The following note seems to refer to one of his earlier productions; but I retain neither letter nor written document of any kind from him with a date.

'Mr. Goldsmith's best respects to Mr. Cradock: when he asked him to-day, he quite forgot an engagement of above a week's standing, which has been made purposely for him; he feels himself quite uneasy at not being permitted to have his instructions upon those parts where he must necessarily be defective. He will have a rehearsal on Monday; when, if Mr. Cradock would come, and afterwards take a bit of mutton chop, it would add to his other obligations.

'Sunday morning,

'To J. Cradock, Esq., at the Hotel in Pall Mall.

The first letter I ever received from Dr. Goldsmith was sent to me in Leicestershire, where I had previously altered his Comedy of 'She Stoops to Conquer.'

'MY DEAR SIR, — The Play has met with a success much beyond your expectations or mine. I thank you sincerely for your Epilogue, which, however, could not be used, but with your permission shall be printed. The story, in short, is this: Murphy sent me rather the outline of an Epilogue than an Epilogue, which was to be sung by Mrs. Catley, and which she approved. Mrs. Bulkley, hearing this, insisted on throwing up her part, unless, according to the custom of the theatre, she were permitted to speak the Epilogue. In this embarrassment, I thought of making a quarrelling Epilogue between Catley and her, debating who should speak the Epilogue; but then Mrs. Catley refused, after I had taken the trouble of drawing it out. I was then at a loss indeed: an Epilogue was to be made, and for none but Mrs. Bulkley. I made one, and Colman thought it too bad to be spoken: I was obliged, therefore, to try a fourth time, and I made a very mawkish thing, as you'll shortly see. Such is the history of my stage adventures, and which I have at last done with.

'I cannot help saying that I am very sick of the stage; and though I believe I shall get three tolerable benefits, yet I shall, upon the whole, be a loser, even in a pecuniary light: my ease and comfort I certainly lost while it was in agitation.

'I am, my dear Cradock,

'Your obliged and obedient Servant,

'OLIVER GOLDSMITH.'

'P.S. Present my most humble respects to Mrs. Cradock.'

ADDRESS, IN THE CHARACTER OF TONY LUMPKIN

WELL, the Play ended, and my comrades gone,
Pray what becomes of mother's n'only son?
A hopeful blade! in town I'll fix my station,
And cut a dashing figure through the nation;
Turn Author, Actor, Statesman, Wit, or Beau,
And stalk the Hero of the 'Puppetshow.'
Could I but gain some present firm support,
I'd quickly barter Country Ale for Port.
No 'Piety in Pattens,' I renounce her,
Off in a crack, and carry big Bet Bouncer.
Bill Bullet now can drive a roaring trade,
And picks up Countesses in Masquerade;
Walks round the new Great room * with Dukes and Peers,
And swears he'll never balk his country jeers;
Nay, more, they much admires his lounging gait,
And talks to him as to the Lords of State.
And there's my Comrade, too, that lived o' th' hill,
Odzooks! he quite forgets his father's mill,
Says he was born to figure high in life,
And gets in keeping by a Nabob's wife.
Why should not I, then, in the world appear?
I soon shall have a thousand pounds a year;
What signifies below what men inherit?
In London, there they've some regard for merit.
Mother still talks 'of larning, modes refin'd;'
They're all for making mince-meat of my mind.
I'll no such stuff; for, after all their strife,
'Tis best, what haps in lottery and in life.
I'm off, — the horses scamper through the streets,
And big Bet Bouncer bobs to all she meets;
To every Race, to Pastimes every night,
Not to the Plays (they say), it been't polite;
To Sadler's Wells, perhaps, or Operas go;
And once, perchance, to th' Roratorio.
Then Bet herself shall sit at top o' th' table;
She manages the house, and I the stable;
The rest o' th' time we'll scamper up and down,
And set the fashions, too, to half the town;
Frequent all auctions, money ne'er regard;
Buy pictures, like the great, ten pounds a yard.
Odzooks! we'll make these London gentry say,
We know what's high genteel as well as they.

---

* Pantheon.

Though I was inattentive to my own productions of every sort, I hope I was always careful as to those of others. Dr. Goldsmith presented to me his Threnodia Augustalis, written on the Princess Dowager's death; I gave it up to Mr. Nichols, and have since seen the following extract from Mr. Chalmers's Life of Goldsmith, in the collection of English Poets, published in 1810:—

'The present edition of his poems is copied from the octavo principally, with the addition of the Threnodia Augustalis, a piece which has hitherto escaped the researches of his editors. It is now printed from a copy given by the author to his friend Joseph Cradock, Esq. of Grumley, author of Zobeide, and obligingly lent to me by Mr. Nichols. If it add little to his fame, it exhibits a curious instance of the facility with which he gratified his employers on a very short notice.'

Dr. Percy very kindly introduced me to dine at the Literary Club, at the bottom of St. James's-street, where we met Dr. Goldsmith. The table that day was crowded, and I sat next Mr. Burke; but as Mr. Richard Burke talked much, and the great orator said very little, I was not aware at first who was my neighbour. One of the party near us remarked that there was an offensive smell in the room, and thought it must proceed from some dog that was under the table; but Mr. Burke, with a smile, turned to me, and said, 'I rather fear it is from the beef-steak pie that is opposite to us, the crust of which is made with some very bad butter, that comes from my country.' Just at that moment Dr. Johnson sent his plate for some of it, and Burke helped him to very little, which he soon dispatched, and returned his plate for more. Burke, without thought, exclaimed, 'I am glad that you are able so well to relish this beef-steak pie.' Johnson, not at all pleased that what he eat should ever be noticed, immediately retorted, 'There is a time of life, sir, when a man requires the repairs of a table.'

Before dinner was finished, Mr. Garrick came in, full dressed, made many apologies for being so much later than he intended, but he had been unexpectedly detained at the House of Lords, and Lord Camden had absolutely insisted upon setting him down at the door of the hotel in his own carriage. Johnson said nothing, but he looked a volume.

During the afternoon, some literary dispute arose; but Johnson sat silent, till the Dean of Derry very respectfully said, 'We all wish, sir, for your opinion on the subject.' Johnson inclined his head, and never shone more in his life than at that period: he replied without any pomp; he was perfectly clear and explicit, full of the subject, and left nothing undetermined. There was a pause, and he was then hailed with astonishment by all the company. The evening in general passed off very pleasantly: some talked perhaps for amusement, and others for victory. We sat very late; and the conversation that at last ensued was the direct cause of my friend Goldsmith's poem, called 'Retaliation.'

Dr. Goldsmith and I never quarrelled, for he was convinced that I had a real regard for him; but a kind of civil sparring continually took place between us. 'You are so attached,' says he, 'to Hurd, Gray, and Mason, that you think nothing good can proceed but out of that formal school. Now I'll mend Gray's Elegy, by leaving out an idle word in every line,'—'And for me, Doctor, completely spoil it.'

'The curfew tolls the knell of day,
The lowing herd winds o'er the lea;
The ploughman homeward plods his way,
And ——'

'Enough, enough! I have no ear for more.'

'Cradock (after a pause), I am determined to come down into the country, and make some stay with you, and I will build you an ice-house.'—'Indeed, my dear Doctor,' I replied, 'you will not; you have got the strangest notion in the world of making amends to your friends, wherever you go; I hope, if you favour me with a visit, that you will consider your own company is the best recompense.'—'Well,' says Goldsmith, 'that is civilly enough expressed; but I should like to build you an ice-house: I have built two already, they are perfect, and this should be a pattern to all your country.'

'I dined yesterday,' says he, laying down his papers, 'in

company with three of your friends, and I talked at every thing.'—'And they would spare you in nothing.'—'I cared not for that, I persisted; but I declare solemnly to you, that, though I angled the whole evening, I never once obtained a bite.'

'You are all of you,' continued he, 'absolutely afraid of Johnson: now I attack him boldly, and without the least reserve.'—'You do, Doctor, and sometimes catch a Tartar.'—'If it were not for me, he would be insufferable: if you remember the last time we ever supped together, he sat sulky and growling, but I resolved to fetch him out.'—'You did, and at last he told you that he would have no more of your fooleries.'

It was always thought fair by some persons to make what stories they pleased of Dr. Goldsmith, and the following was freely circulated in ridicule of him: 'That he attended the Fantoccini in Penton-street, and that from envy he wished to excel the dexterity of one of the puppets.' I was of the party, and remember no more than that the Doctor, the Rev. Mr. Ludlam of St. John's College, and some others, went together to see the puppetshow: there we were all greatly entertained, and many idle remarks might possibly be made by all of us during the evening. Mr. Ludlam afterwards laughingly declared, that he believed he must shut up all his experiments at Cambridge and Leicester in future, and take lectures only during the winter from Fantoccinis, and the expert mechanists of both the royal theatres.

The greatest real fault of Dr. Goldsmith was, that, if he had thirty pounds in his pocket, he would go into certain companies in the country, and, in hopes of doubling the sum, would generally return to town without any part of it.

One of the worst affrays that Dr. Goldsmith ever engaged in was with Evans the bookseller, of Paternoster Row. Evans was the editor of the Universal Magazine, and had suffered a most offensive article to be inserted therein, which turned to ridicule not only the Doctor, but some ladies of the highest respectability. The Doctor unfortunately went to dine with the family, in Westminster, just after they had read this insulting article, and they were all most highly indignant at it. The Doctor, agonized all dinner-time, but, as soon as possible afterwards, he stole away, set off in great haste for Paternoster Row, and caned Evans in his own shop. This was every way a terrible affair, and I privately consulted with Dr. Johnson concerning it. He said, 'that this at any time would have been highly prejudicial to Goldsmith, but particularly now;' and he advised me, as I was intimate with both, that I should call upon Evans, and endeavour to get the matter adjusted. I followed his advice, and Evans really behaved very kindly to me on the occasion. I truly urged, 'that this publication had cut off Dr. Goldsmith from the society of one of the most friendly houses that he had ever frequented, and that he could not have tortured him in a more tender point.' Evans calmly attended to me; and, after much negotiation, and the interference of several discreet friends, this vexatious affair was at last finally got rid of. The name of Johnson on such an affray will perhaps remind the reader, that he himself once knocked down a very worthy bookseller in his own shop, at Gray's Inn (as related by Boswell). The story was currently reported, and caused the following extempore, which has never extended before beyond a private circulation:—

'When Johnson, with tremendous step and slow,
Fully determin'd, deigns to fell the foe,
E'en the earth trembles, thunders roll around,
And mighty Osborne's self lies levell'd with the ground.'

'Lie still, sir,' said Johnson, 'that you may not give me a second trouble.' Mr. Nichols once asked Dr. Johnson, 'if the story was true.'—'No, sir, it was not in his shop, it was in my own house.'

I had not seen or heard from Dr. Goldsmith for a very considerable time, till I came to town with my wife, who was to place herself under the care of Mr. Parkinson, dentist, in Fleet-street, for rather a dangerous operation; and we took lodgings in Norfolk-street, that we might be in his neighbourhood. Goldsmith I found much altered, and at times very low; and I devoted almost all my mornings to his immediate service. He wished me to look over and revise some of his works; but, with a select friend or two, I was most pressing that he should publish, by subscription, his two celebrated poems of 'The Traveller' and 'The Deserted Village,' with notes; for he was well aware that I was no stranger to Johnson's having made some little addition to the one, and possibly had suggested some corrections at least for the other; but the real meaning was to give some great persons an opportunity of delicately conveying pecuniary relief, of which the Doctor at that time was particularly in need. Goldsmith readily gave up to me his private copies, and said, 'Pray, do what you please with them.' But, whilst he sat near me, he rather submitted to than encouraged my zealous proceedings.

I one morning called upon him, however, and found him infinitely better than I expected, and in a kind of exulting style he exclaimed, 'Here are some of the best of my prose writings: I have been hard at work ever since midnight, and I desire you to examine them.' 'These,' said I, 'are excellent indeed.' 'They are,' replied he, 'intended as an introduction to a body of arts and sciences.' 'If so, Dr. Goldsmith, let me most seriously entreat, that, as your name is to be prefixed, more care may be taken by those who are to compile the work than has formerly been the case, when Knaresborough was printed for Naseby, and Yorkshire for Northamptonshire; and you know what was the consequence with Mr. Cadell.'

We entered on various topics, and I left him that morning seemingly much relieved.

The day before I was to set out from town for Leicestershire, I insisted upon his dining with us. He replied, 'I will; but on one condition, that you will not ask me to eat any thing.' 'Nay,' said I, 'this answer, Goldsmith, is absolutely unkind; for I had hoped, as we are entirely served from the Crown and Anchor, that you would have named something that you might have relished.' 'Well,' says he, 'if you will but explain it to Mrs. Cradock, I will certainly wait upon you.'

The Doctor found, as usual, at my apartments, newspapers and pamphlets, and with a pen and ink he amused himself as well as he could. I had ordered from the tavern some fish, a roasted joint of lamb, and a tart; and the Doctor either sat down or walked about, just as he liked. After dinner he took some wine with biscuits; but I was soon obliged to leave him for a while, as I had matters to settle for our next day's journey. On my return, coffee was ready; and the Doctor appeared more cheerful (for Mrs. Cradock was always rather a favourite with him), and in the course of the evening he endeavoured to talk and remark as usual, but all was force. He stayed till midnight, and I insisted on seeing him safe home; and we most cordially shook hands at the Temple gate.

Dr. Goldsmith did not live long after our return into Leicestershire, and I have often since regretted that I did not remain longer in town at every inconvenience. Yet, alas! what could I have done? With one or two select friends, I might have stood by his bedside, deeply lamenting his most unfortunate fate, till he, in a last agony, would have exclaimed, —

——— 'Dear friends, adieu!
For, see, the hounds are full in view.'

DR. GOLDSMITH.

I AM aware that what I am about to relate will somewhat subject myself to ridicule. It was the fashion of some authors frequently to retail poor Goldsmith's absurdities; but they, at times, misrepresented or exaggerated. I recollect one evening he had launched out unboundedly, and next morning I ventured to say to him, that 'I was surprised that in that company he would lay himself so open.' His answer was, I believe I did; I fired at them all; I angled all the night, but I caught nothing.' When he was scheming some essay perhaps, he would force the subject on every body, till Johnson has been quite provoked, and at last did say, 'My dear Doctor, let us have no more of your fooleries to-night.' Mr. Boswell and others have given some account of these particular absurdities of Goldsmith relative to the Fantoccini, then exhibiting in London; and as I was present at the greater part of what then passed, I will beg to trespass with all the truth I know. Dr. Goldsmith spoke most highly of the performance in Panton-street, and talked about bringing out a comedy of his own there in ridicule. When the Rev. Wm. Ludlam, the great mechanic, of Leicester, came to town, I often talked about Goldsmith to him, and persuaded him to go and see the puppetshow. He was quite surprised and entertained, and declared that, at the conclusion of the little comedy, the puppets acted so naturally, that, though he placed himself close to the stage, he could scarce detect either string or wire. I was with Goldsmith there; but whether that night or not I cannot specify. Goldsmith merely was made known to Ludlam by me, and his low humour was not ill adapted to Ludlam's own style of conversation; however, I will add Mr. Ludlam's own remark: 'I have caught many a cold by examining the dock-yards; however, in future, I believe, I must come to London, and instead of attending our mechanical societies, and rummaging for improvements afterwards, I must only visit Fantoccinis, and frequent the harlequin farces. I cannot guess where the managers collect all these able mechanists.' Ludlam was likewise excessively fond of music, and I introduced Mrs. Barthelemon to him at Leicester. She was a great favourite; and many of my musical friends very kindly entertained him in town with particular performances, and he was offered to take an interior view of both the great theatres. Ludlam occasionally entertained his friends at Leicester with some Chinese tumblers, which he had made. They were dressed puppets, with quicksilver in the veins, and surprised even at Cambridge. However, on leaving London this time, he turned to me, and slily said, 'The first thing I shall do at my return will be to burn my Chinese tumblers.'

Polly Pattens, in the Puppetshow,* meant Mrs. Yates; but, when Foote mentioned the names of Kelly, Cumberland, and Cradock on the stage, the audience would not permit him to proceed. The scene was printed in the Bon Ton Magazine, and illustrated by a good print, representing Foote, a strong likeness, the Devil, Polly Pattens, Harlequin, Punch, and Stevens.

Goldsmith at that time greatly wished to bring out a comedy;

* This made its first appearance at the Haymarket Theatre, Feb. 15, 1773, under the title of the 'Handsome Housemaid, or Piety in Pattens.' — Ed.

but he had powerful rivals to contend with, who were in full possession of the town. Goldsmith's turn was for very low humour, always dangerous; but when some authors hinted to him, that, for a man to write genteel comedy, it was necessary that he should be well acquainted with high life himself, 'True,' says Goldsmith; 'and if any of you have a character of a truly elegant lady in high life, who is neither a coquette nor a prude, I hope you will favour me with it.' Some one observed that Millament * was the most refined character he recollected in any comedy, neither a prude nor a coquette; and I then ventured to say, that, 'however refined Millament might be, I thought no very delicate lady would now venture upon her raillery of Mirabel, who declares, 'When I'm married to you, I'll positively get up in a morning as early as I please;' and the refined and delicate lady replies, 'Oh, to be sure; get up, idle creature!' The cry was, 'Goldsmith is envious; but surely it was a little irritating to hear the town ring with applause of Garrick, and see him courted everywhere, and in the height of splendour, whilst he perhaps had only to retire impransus to the Temple.'

About the time that I think Boswell wrote a prologue in compliment to Johnson at Lichfield, a proposal was made for the play of the Beaux Stratagem to be acted there, by a party of friends, in honour of Johnson and Garrick. Mr. Yates offered all assistance from Birmingham, where he was then manager, and, if required, to play Scrub. 'No,' says Goldsmith, 'I should of all things like to try my hand at that character.' Several smiled, thinking perhaps of his assuming such a part, who frequently, with his gold-headed cane, assumed the real character of doctor of physic. However, the thought amused Goldsmith at the time. It was the fashion to say, that Goldsmith's turn was merely for low humour; and that his Vicar, his Moses, and his Tony Lumpkin, were characters now obsolete. However, Goldsmith often retaliated with good effect. Dick Yates at that time was much admired in old Fondlewife, and Goldsmith said he 'was surprised, in this refined age, to see Lord

* In the comedy of 'The Constant Couple, or a Trip to the Jubilee,' by George Farquhar, acted at Drury Lane, 1700. — Ed.

North and all his family in the stage-box: to be sure, Mr. Yates being admonished not to sing "The Soldier and the Sailor," in another refined comedy, was a good sign of delicacy.' I was, however, with Mr. Yates at his house just after he had received this order; and he expressed himself in violent terms against it, insomuch that I doubted whether he would play the part of Ben, unless permitted as for forty years past. At last he complied.

I wrote an epilogue in the character of Tony Lumpkin, for 'She Stoops to Conquer,' and likewise the following song:-

TALLY-HO!

A SONG, INTENDED TO HAVE BEEN SUNG BY MR. QUICK, IN THE CHARACTER OF TONY LUMPKIN, IN GOLDSMITH'S COMEDY OF 'SHE STOOPS TO CONQUER.'

MINE alone is the age
When all pleasures engage
    That horses and hounds can bestow;
Among the great folks,
What their whims and their jokes,
    Compar'd with a good Tally-ho!

To learn the soft airs
Of your opera-players,
    For ever the fine ladies go;
Ah! what are such joys
But low trifles and toys,
    Compar'd with a good Tally-ho!

They say that in time
I should marry — refine,
    If to courts and their balls I would go;
But when tied up for life
To a termagant wife,
    In vain I might cry Tally-ho'

The epilogue and song were intended for Mr. Quick. He would, if any one, have carried them both through. The epilogue was thought too personal, and occasioned some dissension, though not with my friend Goldsmith. That curtailed and printed at the end of the comedy was without either my knowledge or consent. Some of the allusions might be rather *trop libre*, but it had reference to Foote's Puppetshow, which certainly was not expected to be strictly correct; nor was the character of Tony Lumpkin too refined. No comic prologue was ever more admired than Garrick's to 'Barbarossa;' but what is a part of it?

I particularly recollect, that when Goldsmith was near completing his 'Natural History,' he sent to Dr. Percy and me, to state that he wished not to return to town, from Windsor, I think, for a fortnight, if we would only complete a proof that lay upon his table in the Temple. It was concerning birds, and many books lay open that he occasionally consulted for his own materials. We met by appointment; and Dr. Percy, smiling, said, 'Do you know any thing about birds?' 'Not an atom,' was my reply: 'do you?' 'Not I,' says he; 'scarce know a goose from a swan: however, let us try what we can do.' We set to work, and our task was not very difficult. Some time after the work appeared, we compared notes, but could not either of us recognize our own share.

I come now to the last day but one I passed with poor Goldsmith (see vol. i. p. 234), whose loss (with whatever faults he might have) I shall ever lament whilst 'memory of him holds its seat.' At his breakfast in the Temple, as sual, I offered every aid in my power as to his works; some amendments had been agreed upon in his 'Deserted Village.' Some of the bad lines in the latter I have by me marked. 'As to my "Hermit," that poem, Cradock, cannot be amended.' I knew he had been offered ten pounds for the copy, and it was introduced into the 'Vicar of Wakefield,' to which he applied himself entirely for a fortnight, to pay a journey to Wakefield. 'As my business then lay there,' said he, 'that was my reason for fixing on Wakefield as the field of action. I never took more pains than in the first volume of my "Natural History;" surely that was good, and I was handsomely paid for the whole.

'My "Roman History," Johnson says, is well abridged.' Indeed, I could have added, that Johnson (when Goldsmith was absent) would frequently say, 'Why, sir, whatever that man touches he adorns;' for, like Garrick, when not present, he considered him as a kind of sacred character. After a general review of papers lying before him, I took leave; when, turning to his study table, he pointed to an article I had procured for him, and said, 'You are kindest to me.' I only replied, 'You mean more rude and saucy than some others.' However, much of the conversation took a more melancholy tone than usual, and I became very uneasy about him.

When I returned to town after his death (see vol. i. p. 236), I had an interview with his nephew, an apothecary in Newman-street, and the two sisters milliners, the Miss Gunns, who resided at a house at the corner of Temple Lane, who were always most attentive to him, and who once said to me most feelingly, 'Oh! sir, sooner persuade him to let us work for him gratis, than suffer him to apply to any other. We are sure that he will pay us if he can.' Circumstanced as he was, I know not what more could have been done for him. It was said he improperly took laudanum; but all was inwardly disturbed. Had the Doctor freely laid open all the debts he had contracted, I am certain that his zealous friends were so numerous that they would freely have contributed to his relief. I mean here explicitly to assert only, that I believe he died miserably, and that his friends were not entirely aware of his distress.

Where the Doctor thought there was a sincere regard, he was not fastidious, but would listen with attention to the remonstrance of one whom he believed to be his friend; and when he assented to give his name, for a mere trifle, to a new publication, about which he never meant to give himself much trouble, I more than once spoke freely to him.

Goldsmith and I (with great satisfaction I now speak it) never had a serious dispute in our lives; we freely gave and took. He rallied me on my Cambridge pedantry, and I hinted at illegitimate education; for, to speak on my mended judgment, Johnson, he, Garrick, and some others, had convinced me 'that all literature was not confined to our own academical world.' Goldsmith truly said, I was nibbling about elegant phrases, whilst he was obliged to write half a volume.

DAVIES'S LIFE OF GARRICK.

Dr. Goldsmith having tried his genius in several modes of writing, in essays, descriptive poetry, and history, was advised to apply himself to that species of composition which is said to have been long the most fruitful in the courts of Parnassus. The writer of plays has been ever supposed to pursue the quickest road to the temple of Plutus.

The Doctor was a perfect heteroclite, an inexplicable existence in creation; such a compound of absurdity, envy, and malice, contrasted with the opposite virtues of kindness, generosity, and benevolence, that he might be said to consist of two distinct souls, and influenced by the agency of a good and bad spirit.

The first knowledge Mr. Garrick had of his abilities was from an attack upon him by Goldsmith, when he was but a very young author, in a book called 'The Present State of Learning.' Amongst other abuses of the times (for the Doctor loved to dwell upon grievances), he took notice of the behaviour of managers to authors. This must surely have proceeded from the most generous principles of reforming what was amiss for the benefit of others, for the Doctor at that time had not the most distant view of commencing dramatic author.

Little did Goldsmith imagine he should one day be obliged to ask a favour from the director of a playhouse; however, when the office of secretary to the Society of Arts and Sciences became vacant, the Doctor was persuaded to offer himself a candidate. He was told that Mr. Garrick was a leading member of that learned body, and his interest and recommendation would be of consequence to enforce his pretensions.

He waited upon the manager, and, in few words, requested his vote and interest. Mr. Garrick could not avoid observing to him, that it was impossible he could lay claim to any recommendation from him, as he had taken pains to deprive himself of his assistance by an unprovoked attack upon his management of the theatre, in his State of Learning. Goldsmith, instead of making an apology for his conduct, either from misinformation or misconception, bluntly replied, 'In truth he had spoken his mind, and believed what he said was very right.' The manager dismissed him with civility; and Goldsmith lost the office by a very great majority, who voted in favour of Dr. Templeman.

The Doctor's reputation, which was daily increasing from a variety of successful labours, was at length lifted so high that he escaped from indigence and obscurity to competence and fame.

The first man of the age, one who, from the extensiveness of his genius and benevolence of his mind, is superior to the little envy and mean jealousy which adhere so closely to most authors, and especially to those of equivocal merit, took pleasure in introducing Dr. Goldsmith to his intimate friends, persons of eminent rank and distinguished abilities. The Doctor's conversation by no means corresponded with the idea formed of him from his writings.

The Duchess of Rambouillet, who was charmed with the tragedies of Corneille, wished to have so great an author amongst her constant visitors, expecting infinite entertainment from the writer of the Cid, the Horace, and Cinna. But the poet lost himself in society; he held no rank with the beaux esprits who met at the hotel of this celebrated lady; his conversation was dry, unpleasant, and what the French call *distrait*. So Dr. Goldsmith appeared in company to have no spark of that genius which shone forth so brightly in his writings; his address was awkward, his manner uncouth, his language unpolished, his elocution was continually interrupted by disagreeable hesitation, and he was always unhappy if the conversation did not turn upon himself.

To manifest his intrepidity in argument, he would generously espouse the worst side of the question, and almost always left it weaker than he found it. His jealousy fixed a perpetual ridicule on his character, for he was emulous of every thing and everybody. He went with some friends to see the entertainment of the Fantoccini, whose uncommon agility and quick evolutions were much celebrated. The Doctor was asked how he liked these automatons. He replied, he was surprised at the applause bestowed on the little insignificant creatures, for he could have performed their exercises much better himself. When his great literary friend was commended in his hearing, he could not restrain his uneasiness, but exclaimed, in a kind of agony, 'No more, I desire you; you harrow up my soul!' More absurd stories may be recorded of Goldsmith than of any man: his absence of mind would not permit him to attend to time, place, or company. When at the table of a nobleman of high rank and great accomplishments, one to whom England stands indebted in many obligations, and it is hoped that he will more and more increase the debt by his continual and vigorous efforts to secure her happiness,—to this great man Goldsmith observed, that he was called by the name of Malagrida; 'but I protest and vow to your lordship, I can't conceive for what reason; for Malagrida* was an honest man.'

In short, his absurdities were so glaring, and his whole conduct so contradictory to common sense, and so opposite to what was expected from a man of his admirable genius, that a gentleman of strong discernment characterised him by the name of the Inspired Idiot.

When the Doctor had finished his comedy of The Good-natured Man, he was advised to offer it to Mr. Garrick. The manager was fully conscious of his merit, and perhaps more ostentatious of his abilities to serve a dramatic author

* A Portuguese Jesuit, put to the stake by the Inquisition under the charge of heresy, his real offence being his intimacy with certain political offenders. The nobleman alluded to was Lord Shelburne.

than became a man of his prudence. Goldsmith was, on his side, as fully persuaded of his own importance and independent greatness. Mr. Garrick, who had been so long treated with the complimentary language paid to a successful patentee and admired actor, expected that the writer would esteem the patronage of his play as a favour: Goldsmith rejected all ideas of kindness in a bargain that was intended to be of mutual advantage to both parties; and in this he was certainly justifiable. Mr. Garrick could reasonably expect no thanks for the acting a new play, which he would have rejected if he had not been convinced it would have amply rewarded his pains and expense. I believe the manager was willing to accept the play; but he wished to be courted to it, and the Doctor was not disposed to purchase his friendship by the resignation of his sincerity. He then applied to Mr. Colman, who accepted his comedy without any hesitation.

The Good-natured Man bears strong marks of that happy originality which distinguishes the writings of Dr. Goldsmith. Two characters in this comedy were absolutely unknown before to the English stage; a man who boasts an intimacy with persons of high rank whom he never saw, and another who is almost always lamenting misfortunes he never knew. Croaker is as strongly designed and as highly finished a portrait of a discontented man, of one who disturbs every happiness he possesses, from apprehension of distant evil, as any character of Congreve, or any other of our English dramatists. Shuter acted Croaker with that warm glee of fancy, and genuine flow of humour, that always accompanied his best and most animated performance. The great applause and profit which attended the acting of this comedy contributed to render the author more important in his own eyes, and in the opinion of the public. But no good fortune could make Goldsmith discreet, nor any increase of fame diminish his envy, or cure the intractability of his temper. John Home was taught by experience, that his connexions with the great were of no avail with the public, and that courtly approbation was no protection from popular dislike; he therefore veiled himself in obscurity, and prevailed upon a young gentleman, his friend, to adopt his play of The Fatal Discovery; but the foster-father performed his assumed character so awkwardly at the rehearsal of this tragedy, that it was soon discovered that the child was not his own; for he submitted to have the piece altered, lopped, and corrected, with such tranquillity of temper as the real parent could not have assumed. Of the true author Goldsmith by chance found out the knowledge; and when the play was announced to the public, it will hardly be credited, that this man of benevolence, for such he really was, endeavoured to muster a party to condemn it; alleging this cogent reason for the proceeding, that such 'fellows ought not to be encouraged.'

Wits are game-cocks to one another;
No author ever lov'd a brother.

The tragedy of The Countess of Salisbury, a play in which Mr. Barry and Mrs. Dancer displayed great powers of acting, was in a good degree of favour with the town. This was a crime sufficient to rouse the indignation of Goldsmith, who issued forth to see it, and with a determined resolution to consign the play to perdition. He sat out four acts of The Countess of Salisbury with great calmness and seeming temper; but, as the plot thickened, and his apprehension began to be terrified with the ideas of blood and slaughter, he got up in a great hurry, saying, loud enough to be heard, 'Brownrig! Brownrig! by G—.'

Goldsmith never wanted literary employment. The booksellers understood the value of his name, and did all they could to excite his industry; and it cannot be denied, that they rewarded his labours generously. In a few years he wrote three histories of England; the first in two pocket volumes in letters, and another in four volumes octavo: the first an elegant summary of British transactions, and the other an excellent abridgment of Hume, and other copious historians. These books are in everybody's hands. The last is a short contraction of four volumes into one duodecimo. For writing these books he obtained £750 or £800.

His squabbles with booksellers and publishers were innumerable; his appetites and passions were craving and violent; he loved variety of pleasures, but could not devote himself to industry long enough to purchase them by his writings. Upon every emergency, half a dozen projects would present themselves to his mind; these he communicated to the men who were to advance money on the reputation of the author; but the money was generally spent long before the new work was half finished, or perhaps before it was commenced. This circumstance naturally produced expostulation and reproach from one side, which was often returned with anger and vehemence on the other. After much and disagreeable altercation, one bookseller desired to refer the matter in dispute to the Doctor's learned friend, a man of known integrity, and one who would favour no cause but that of justice and truth. Goldsmith consented, and was enraged to find that one author should have so little feeling for another as to determine a dispute to his disadvantage, in favour of a tradesman.

His love of play involved him in many perplexing difficulties, and a thousand anxieties; and yet he had not the resolution to abandon a practice for which his impatience of temper and great unskilfulness rendered him totally unqualified.

Though Mr. Garrick did not act his comedy of She Stoops to Conquer, yet, as he was then upon very friendly terms with the author, he presented him with a very humorous prologue, well accommodated to the author's intention of reviving fancy, wit, gaiety, humour, incident, and character, in the place of sentiment and moral preachment.

Woodward spoke this whimsical address in mourning, and lamented pathetically over poor dying Comedy. To her he says: —

—— A mawkish drab of spurious breed,
Who deals in sentimentals, will succeed.

In the close of the prologue, the Doctor is recommended as a fit person to revive poor drooping Thalia, with a compliment which hinted, I imagine, at some public transactions, of not dealing in poisonous drugs.

She Stoops to Conquer, notwithstanding many improbabilities in the economy of the plot, several farcical situations, and some characters which are rather exaggerated, is a lively and faithful representation of nature; genius presides over every scene of this play; the characters are either new, or varied improvements from other plays.

Marlow has a slight resemblance of Charles in the Fop's Fortune, and something more of Lord Hardy in Steele's Funeral; and yet, with a few shades of these parts, he is discriminated from both. Tony Lumpkin is a vigorous improvement of Humphry Gubbins, and a most diverting portrait of ignorance, rusticity, low cunning, and obstinacy.

Hardcastle, his wife and daughter, I think, are absolutely new; the language is easy and characteristical; the manners of the times are slightly, but faithfully, represented; the satire is not ostentatiously displayed, but incidentally involved in the business of the play; and the suspense of the audience is artfully kept up to the last. This comedy was very well acted. Hardcastle and Tony Lumpkin were supported in a masterly style by Shuter and Quick; so was Miss Hardcastle by Mrs. Bulkley. Mrs. Green, in Mrs. Hardcastle, maintained her just title to one of the best comic actresses of the age.

Though the money gained by this play amounted to a considerable sum, more especially so to a man who had been educated in straits and trained in adversity, yet his necessities soon became as craving as ever: to relieve them, he undertook a new History of Greece, and a book of animals, called The History of Animated Nature. The first was to him an easy task; but, as he was entirely unacquainted with the world of animals, his friends were anxious for the success of his undertaking. Notwithstanding his utter ignorance of the subject, he has compiled one of the pleasantest and most instructive books in our language; I mean, that it is not only useful to young minds, but entertaining to those who understand the animal creation.

Every thing of Goldsmith seems to bear the magical touch of an enchanter; no man took less pains, and yet produced so powerful an effect: the great beauty of his composition consists in a clear, copious, and expressive style

Goldsmith's last work was his poem called Retaliation, which the historian of his life says was written for his own amusement, and that of his friends, who were the subject of it. That he did not live to finish it is to be lamented, for it is supposed he would have introduced more characters. What he has left is so perfect in its kind, that it stands not in need of a revisal.

In no part of his works has this author discovered a more nice and critical discernment, or a more perfect knowledge of human nature, than in this poem; with wonderful art he has traced all the leading features of his several portraits, and given with truth the characteristical peculiarities of each: no man is lampooned, and no man is flattered.

The occasion, we are told, to which we owe this admirable poem, was a circumstance of festivity. The literary society to which he belonged proposed to write epitaphs on the Doctor. Mr. Garrick, one of the members, wrote the following fable of Jupiter and Mercury, to provoke Goldsmith to a retaliation.

JUPITER AND MERCURY.

A FABLE.

Here, Hermes, says Jove, who with nectar was mellow,
Go fetch me some clay, I will make an odd fellow.
Right and wrong shall be jumbled, much gold and some dross;
Without cause be he pleas'd, without cause be he cross:
Be sure as I work to throw in contradictions;
A great lover of truth, yet a mind turn'd to fictions.
Now mix these ingredients, which, warm'd in the baking,
Turn to learning and gaming, religion and raking.
With the love of a wench, let his writings be chaste;
Tip his tongue with strange matter, his pen with fine taste.
That the rake and the poet o'er all may prevail,
Set fire to his head, and set fire to his tail.
For the joy of each sex on the world I'll bestow it,
This scholar, rake, Christian, dupe, gamester, and poet.

Though a mixture so odd, he shall merit great fame,
And among brother mortals be Goldsmith his name.
When on earth this strange meteor no more shall appear,
You, Hermes, shall fetch him to make us sport here.

There never was surely a more finished picture, at full length, given to the world, than this warm character of the incomprehensible and heterogeneous Doctor.

And here Doctor Goldsmith's portrait of Mr. Garrick will be introduced with propriety.

Here lies David Garrick. Describe me, who can,
An abridgment of all that was pleasant in man.
As an actor, confess'd without rival to shine;
As a wit, if not first, in the very first line;
Yet, with talents like these, and an excellent heart,
The man had his failings, a dupe to his art.
Like an ill-judging beauty, his colours he spread,
And beplaster'd with rouge his own natural red.
On the stage he was natural, simple, affecting;
'Twas only that, when he was off, he was acting.
With no reason on earth to go out of his way,
He turn'd and he varied full ten times a day:
Though secure of our hearts, yet confoundedly sick,
If they were not his own by finessing and trick.
He cast off his friends, as a huntsman his pack;
For he knew, when he pleas'd, he could whistle them back.
Of praise a mere glutton, he swallow'd what came,
And the puff of a dunce he mistook it for fame;
Till his relish grown callous, almost to disease,
Who pepper'd the highest was surest to please.
But let us be candid, and speak out our mind;
If dunces applauded, he paid them in kind.
Ye Kenricks, ye Kellys, and Woodfalls so grave,
What a commerce was yours, while you got and you gave!
How did Grub-street re-echo the shouts that you rais'd,
While he was be-Roscius'd and you were beprais'd!
But peace to his spirit, wherever it flies,
To act as an angel, and mix with the skies.
Those poets who owe their best fame to his skill,
Shall still be his flatterers, go where he will;
Old Shakespeare receive him with praise and with love,
And Beaumonts and Bens be his Kellys above.

The sum of all that can be said for and against Mr. Garrick, some people think, may be found in these lines of Goldsmith. That the person upon which they were written was displeased with some strokes of this character may be gathered from the following lines, which Mr. Garrick wrote on the Retaliation, soon after it had been produced to the society.

Are these the choice dishes the Doctor has sent us?
Is this the great poet whose works so content us?
This Goldsmith's fine feast, who has written fine books?
Heaven sends us good meat, but the devil sends cooks.

Candour must own that Mr. Garrick, in his verses on Goldsmith, was gentle in describing the subject, as well as delicate in the choice of his expressions, but that Garrick's features in the Retaliation are somewhat exaggerated.

Not long before his death, he had formed a design of publishing an Encyclopedia, or a Universal Dictionary of Arts and Sciences, a prospectus of which he printed and sent to his friends, many of whom had promised to furnish him with articles on different subjects; and amongst the rest Sir Joshua Reynolds, Dr. Johnson, and Mr. Garrick. His expectations from any new-conceived projects were generally very sanguine; but from so extensive a plan his hopes of gain had lifted up his thoughts to an extraordinary height.

The booksellers, notwithstanding they had a very good opinion of his abilities, yet were startled at the bulk, importance, and expense of so great an undertaking, the fate of which was to depend upon the industry of a man with whose indolence of temper and method of procrastination they had long been acquainted. The coldness with which they met his proposal was lamented by the Doctor to the hour of his death, which seems to have been accelerated by a neglect of his health, occasioned by continual vexation of mind, arising from his involved circumstances. Death, I really believe, was welcome to a man of his great sensibility.

The chief materials which compose Goldsmith's character are before the reader; but, as I have with great freedom exposed his faults, I should not have dwelt so minutely upon them, if I had not been conscious, that, upon a just balance of his good and bad qualities, the former would far outweigh the latter.

Goldsmith was so sincere a man that he could not conceal what was uppermost in his mind. So far from desiring to appear in the eye of the world to the best advantage, he took more pains to be esteemed worse than he was, than others do to appear better than they are.

His envy was so childish, and so absurd, that it was easily pardoned, for everybody laughed at it; and no man was ever very mischievous whose errors excited mirth: he never formed any scheme, or joined in any combination, to hurt any man living.

His inviting persons to condemn Mr. Home's tragedy, at first sight wears an ill face; but this was a transient thought of a giddy man, who, upon the least check, would have immediately renounced it, and as heartily joined with a party to support the piece he had before devoted to destruction. It cannot be controverted that he was but a bad economist, nor in the least acquainted with that punctuality which regular people exact. He was more generous than just; like honest Charles, in the School for Scandal, he could not, for the soul of him, make justice keep pace with generosity. His disposition of mind was tender and compassionate; no unhappy person ever sued to him for relief without obtaining it, if he had any thing to give, and, rather than not relieve the distressed, he would borrow. The poor woman with whom he had lodged during his obscurity several years in Green Arbour Court, by his death lost an excellent friend; for the Doctor often supplied her with food from his table, and visited her frequently with the sole purpose to be kind to her. He had his dislike, as most men have, to particular people, but unmixed with rancour. He, least of all mankind, approved Baretti's conversation; he considered him as an insolent, overbearing foreigner; as Baretti, in his turn, thought him an unpolished man, and an absurd companion: but when this unhappy Italian was charged with murder, and afterwards sent by Sir John Fielding to Newgate, Goldsmith opened his purse, and would have given him every shilling it contained; he, at the same time, insisted upon going in the coach with him to the place of his confinement.

BOSWELL'S LIFE OF JOHNSON.

Dr. Goldsmith is one of the first men we now have as an author, and he is a very worthy man too. He has been loose in his principles, but he is coming right.

As Dr. Oliver Goldsmith will frequently appear in this narrative, I shall endeavour to make my readers in some degree acquainted with his singular character. He was a native of Ireland, and a contemporary with Mr. Burke, at Trinity College, Dublin, but did not then give much promise of future celebrity. He, however, observed to Mr. Malone, that 'though he made no great figure in mathematics, which was a study in much repute there, he could turn an ode of Horace into English better than any of them.' He afterwards studied physic at Edinburgh, and upon the Continent; and, I have been informed, was enabled to pursue his travels on foot, partly by demanding at the university to enter the lists as a disputant, by which, according to the custom of many of them, he was entitled to the premium of a crown, when luckily for him his challenge was not accepted; so that, as I once observed to Dr. Johnson, he disputed his passage through Europe. He then came to England, and was successively in the capacities of an usher to an academy, a corrector of the press, a reviewer, and a writer for a newspaper. He had sagacity enough to cultivate assiduously the acquaintance of Johnson, and his faculties were gradually enlarged by the contemplation of such a model. To me and many others it appeared that he studiously copied the manner of Johnson, only indeed upon a smaller scale.

At this time I think he published nothing with his name, though it was pretty generally known that one Dr. Goldsmith was the author of 'An Inquiry into the Present State of Polite Learning in Europe,' and of 'The Citizen of the World,' a series of letters supposed to be written from London by a Chinese. No man had the art of displaying with more advantage as a writer whatever literary acquisitions he made. 'Nihil quod tetigit non ornavit.' His mind resembled a fertile, but thin soil. There was a quick, but not a strong vegetation, of whatever chanced to be thrown upon it. No deep root could be struck. The oak of the forest did not grow there; but the elegant shrubbery and the fragrant parterre appeared in gay succession. It has been generally circulated and believed that he was a mere fool in conversation; but, in truth, this has been greatly exaggerated. He had, no doubt, a more than common share of that hurry of ideas which we often find in his countrymen, and which sometimes produces a laughable confusion in expressing them. He was very much what the French call *un étourdi*, and, from vanity and an eager desire of being conspicuous wherever he was, he frequently talked carelessly without knowledge of the subject, or even without thought. His person was short, his countenance coarse and vulgar, his deportment that of a scholar awkwardly affecting the easy gentleman. Those who were in any way distinguished, excited envy in him to so ridiculous an excess, that the instances of it are hardly credible. When accompanying two beautiful young ladies with their mother on a tour in France, he was seriously angry that more attention was paid to them than to him; and once at the exhibition of the Fantoccini in London, when those who sat next him observed with what dexterity a puppet was made to toss a pike, he could not bear that it should have such praise, and exclaimed with some warmth, 'Pshaw! I can do it better myself.'

He, I am afraid, had no settled system of any sort, so that his conduct must not be strictly scrutinized; but his affections were social and generous, and when he had money he gave it away very liberally.

His desire of imaginary consequence predominated over his

attention to truth. When he began to rise into notice, he said he had a brother who was Dean of Durham; a fiction so easily detected, that it is wonderful how he should have been so inconsiderate as to hazard it.

He boasted to me at this time of the power of his pen in commanding money, which I believe was true in a certain degree, though, in the instance he gave, he was by no means correct. He told me that he had sold a novel for four hundred pounds. This was his 'Vicar of Wakefield.' But Johnson informed me that he had made the bargain for Goldsmith, and the price was sixty pounds. 'And, sir (said he), a sufficient price, too, when it was sold; for then the fame of Goldsmith had not been elevated, as it afterwards was, by his "Traveller;" and the bookseller had such faint hopes of profit by his bargain, that he kept the manuscript by him a long time, and did not publish it till after the "Traveller" had appeared. Then, to be sure, it was accidentally worth more money.'

During all the time in which Dr. Johnson was employed in relating to the circle at Sir Joshua Reynolds's the particulars of what passed between the king and him, Dr. Goldsmith remained unmoved upon a sofa at some distance, affecting not to join in the least in the eager curiosity of the company. He assigned as a reason for his gloom and seeming inattention, that he apprehended Johnson had relinquished his purpose of furnishing him with a Prologue to his play, with the hopes of which he had been flattered; but it was strongly suspected that he was fretting with chagrin and envy at the singular honour Dr. Johnson had lately enjoyed. At length, the frankness and simplicity of his natural character prevailed. He sprung from the sofa, advanced to Johnson, and, in a kind of flutter from imagining himself in the situation which he had just been hearing described, exclaimed, 'Well, you acquitted yourself in this conversation better than I should have done; for I should have bowed and stammered through the whole of it.'

To obviate all the reflections which have gone round the world to Johnson's prejudice, by applying to him the epithet of a bear, let me impress upon my readers a just and happy saying of my friend Goldsmith, who knew him well: 'Johnson, to be sure, has a roughness in his manner; but no man alive has a more tender heart. He has nothing of the bear but his skin.'

Goldsmith, to divert the tedious minutes, strutted about, bragging of his dress, and I believe was seriously vain of it; for his mind was wonderfully prone to such impressions. 'Come, come (said Garrick), talk no more of that. You are, perhaps, the worst — eh, — eh!' Goldsmith was eagerly attempting to interrupt him, when Garrick went on, laughing ironically, 'Nay, you will always look like a gentleman; but I am talking of being well or ill dressed.' 'Well, let me tell you (said Goldsmith), when my tailor brought home my bloom-coloured coat, he said, "Sir, I have a favour to beg of you. — When anybody asks who made your clothes, be pleased to mention John Filby, at the Harrow, in Water Lane."' Johnson: 'Why, sir, that was because he knew the strange colour would attract crowds to gaze at it, and thus they might hear of him, and see how well he could make a coat, even of so absurd a colour.'

He said, 'Goldsmith's Life of Parnell is poor; not that it is poorly written, but that he had poor materials; for nobody can write the life of a man but those who have eat and drunk and lived in social intercourse with him.'

A question was started, how far people who disagree in a capital point can live in friendship together. Johnson said they might. Goldsmith said they could not, as they had not the *idem velle atque idem nolle*, the same likings and the same aversions. Johnson: 'Why, sir, you must shun the subject as to which you disagree. For instance, I can live very well with Burke: I love his knowledge, his genius, his diffusion, and affluence of conversation; but I would not talk to him ot the Rockingham party.' Goldsmith: 'But, sir, when people live together who have something as to which they disagree, and which they want to shun, they will be in the situation mentioned in the story of Bluebeard: "You may look into all the chambers but one." But we should have the greatest inclination to look into that chamber, to talk of that subject.' Johnson (with a loud voice): 'Sir, I am not saying that *you* could live in friendship with a man from whom you differ as to some point; I am only saying that *I* could do it. You put me in mind of Sappho in Ovid.'

Goldsmith told us that he was now busy in writing a natural history, and, that he might have full leisure for it, he had taken lodgings at a farmer's house, near to the sixth milestone on the Edgeware Road, and had carried down his books in two returned postchaises. He said he believed the farmer's family thought him an odd character, similar to that in which the Spectator appeared to his landlady and her children: he was *the gentleman.* Mr. Mickle, the translator of 'The Lusiad,' and I went to visit him at this place a few days afterwards. He was not at home; but, having a curiosity to see his apartment, we went in, and found curious scraps of descriptions of animals scrawled upon the wall with a blacklead pencil.

The subject of ghosts being introduced, Johnson repeated what he had told me of a friend of his, an honest man, and a man of sense, having asserted to him that he had seen an apparition. Goldsmith told us he was assured by his brother, the Rev. Mr. Goldsmith, that he also had seen one.

Of our friend Goldsmith he said, 'Sir, he is so much afraid of being unnoticed, that he often talks merely lest you should forget that he is in the company.' Boswell: 'Yes, he stands forward.' Johnson: 'True, sir; but if a man is to stand forward, he should wish to do it not in an awkward posture, not in rags, not so as that he shall only be exposed to ridicule.' Boswell: 'For my part, I like very well to hear honest Goldsmith talk away carelessly.' Johnson: 'Why yes, sir, but he should not like to hear himself.'

'The misfortune of Goldsmith in conversation is this: he goes on without knowing how he is to get off. His genius is great, but his knowledge is small. As they say of a generous man, it is a pity he is not rich, we may say of Goldsmith, it is a pity he is not knowing. He would not keep his knowledge to himself.

I told him that Goldsmith had said to me a few days before, 'As I take my shoes from the shoemaker, and my coat from the tailor, so I take my religion from the priest.' I regretted this loose way of talking. Johnson: 'Sir, he knows nothing; he has made up his mind about nothing.'

He owned that he thought Hawkesworth was one of his imitators, but he did not think Goldsmith was. Goldsmith, he said, had great merit. Boswell: 'But, sir, he is much indebted to you for his getting so high in the public estimation.' Johnson: 'Why, sir, he has perhaps got sooner to it by his intimacy with me.'

Goldsmith, though his vanity often excited him to occasional competition, had a very high regard for Johnson, which he at this time expressed in the strongest manner in the dedication of his comedy, entitled, 'She Stoops to Conquer.'

We talked of the king's coming to see Goldsmith's new play. 'I wish he would,' said Goldsmith; adding, however, with an affected indifference, 'Not that it would do me the least good.' Johnson: 'Well then, sir, let us say it would do him good (laughing). No, sir, this affectation will not pass; it is mighty idle. In such a state as ours, who would not wish to please the chief magistrate?' Goldsmith I do wish to please him. I remember a line in Dryden, —

"And every poet is the monarch's friend."

It ought to be reversed.' Johnson: 'Nay, there are finer lines in Dryden on this subject: —

> "For colleges on bounteous kings depend,
> And never rebel was to arts a friend."'

General Paoli observed, that successful rebels might. Martinelli: 'Happy rebellions.' Goldsmith: 'We have no such phrase.' General Paoli: 'But have you not the thing?' Goldsmith: 'Yes: all our happy revolutions. They have hurt our constitution, and will hurt it, till we mend it by another happy revolution.' I never before discovered that my friend Goldsmith had so much of the old prejudice in him.

General Paoli, talking of Goldsmith's new play, said, 'Il a fait un compliment très-gracieux à une certaine grande dame;' meaning a duchess of the first rank.

I expressed a doubt whether Goldsmith intended it, in order that I might hear the truth from himself. It, perhaps, was not quite fair to endeavour to bring him to a confession, as he might not wish to avow positively his taking part against the court. He smiled and hesitated. The General at once relieved him, by this beautiful image: 'Monsieur Goldsmith est comme la mer, qui jette des perles et beaucoup d'autres belles choses, sans s'en appercevoir.' Goldsmith: 'Très bien dit, et très élégamment.'

He said, 'Goldsmith should not be for ever attempting to shine in conversation: he has not temper for it, he is so much mortified when he fails. Sir, a game of jokes is composed partly of skill, partly of chance, as a man may be beat at times by one who has not the tenth part of his wit. Now Goldsmith's putting himself against another, is like a man laying a hundred to one who cannot spare the hundred. It is not worth a man's while. A man should not lay a hundred to one, unless he can easily spare it, though he has a hundred chances for him: he can get but a guinea, and he may lose a hundred Goldsmith is in this state. When he contends, if he gets the better, it is a very little addition to a man of his literary reputation: if he does not get the better, he is miserably vexed.'

Goldsmith, however, was often very fortunate in his witty contests, even when he entered the lists with Johnson himself. Sir Joshua Reynolds was in company with them one day, when Goldsmith said that he thought he could write a good fable, mentioned the simplicity which that kind of composition requires, and observed that in most fables the animals introduced seldom talk in character. 'For instance (said he), the fable of the little fishes, who saw birds fly over their heads, and, envying them, petitioned Jupiter to be changed into birds. The skill (continued he) consists in making them talk like little fishes.' While he indulged himself in this fanciful reverie, he observed Johnson shaking his sides, and laughing. Upon which he smartly proceeded, 'Why, Dr. Johnson, this is not so easy as you seem to think; for if you were to make little fishes talk, they would talk like whales.'

During this argument, Goldsmith sat in restless agitation, from a wish to get in and shine. Finding himself excluded, he had taken his hat to go away, but remained for some time with it in his hand, like a gamester, who, at the close of a long night, lingers for a little while, to see if he can have a favourable opening to finish with success. Once when he was beginning to speak, he found himself overpowered by the loud voice of Johnson, who was at the opposite end of the table, and did not perceive Goldsmith's attempt. Thus disappointed of his wish to obtain the attention of the company, Goldsmith in a passion threw down his hat, looking angrily at Johnson, and exclaiming in a bitter tone, 'Take it.' When Toplady was going to speak, Johnson uttered some sound, which led Goldsmith to think that he was beginning again, and taking the words from Toplady. Upon which he seized this opportunity of venting his own envy and spleen, under the pretext of supporting another person: 'Sir,' said he to Johnson, 'the gentleman has heard you patiently for an hour; pray allow us now to hear him.' Johnson (sternly): 'Sir, I was not interrupting the gentleman; I was only giving him a signal of my attention. Sir, you are impertinent.'

Goldsmith made no reply, but continued in the company for some time.

He and Mr. Langton and I went together to the club, where we found Mr. Burke, Mr. Garrick, and some other members, and amongst them our friend Goldsmith, who sat silently brooding over Johnson's reprimand to him after dinner. Johnson perceived this, and said aside to some of us, 'I'll make Goldsmith forgive me;' and then called to him in a loud voice, 'Dr. Goldsmith, something passed to-day where you and I dined: I ask your pardon.' Goldsmith answered placidly, 'It must be much from you, sir, that I take ill.' And so at once the difference was over, and they were on as easy terms as ever, and Goldsmith rattled away as usual.

In our way to the club to-night, when I regretted that Goldsmith would, upon every occasion, endeavour to shine, by which he often exposed himself, Mr. Langton observed that he was not like Addison, who was content with the fame of his writings, and did not aim also at excellency in conversation, for which he found himself unfit; and that he said to a lady, who complained of his having talked little in company, 'Madam, I have but ninepence in ready money, but I can draw for a thousand pounds.' I observed that Goldsmith had a great deal of gold in his cabinet, but, not content with that, was always taking out his purse. Johnson: 'Yes, sir, and that so often an empty purse.'

Goldsmith's incessant desire of being conspicuous in company was the occasion of his sometimes appearing to such disadvantage as one should hardly have supposed possible in a man of his genius.

When his literary reputation had risen deservedly high, and his society was much courted, he became very jealous of the extraordinary attention which was everywhere paid to Johnson. One evening, in a circle of wits, he found fault with me for talking of Johnson as entitled to the honour of unquestionable superiority. 'Sir,' said he, 'you are for making a monarchy of what should be a republic.'

He was still more mortified, when, talking in a company with fluent vivacity, and, as he flattered himself, to the admiration of all who were present, a German, who sat next him, and perceived Johnson rolling himself as if about to speak, suddenly stopped him, saying, 'Stay, stay, Doctor Johnson is going to say something.' This was, no doubt, very provoking, especially to one so irritable as Goldsmith, who frequently mentioned it with strong expressions of indignation.

It may also be observed, that Goldsmith was sometimes content to be treated with an easy familiarity, but, upon occasions, would be consequential and important. An instance of this occurred in a small particular. Johnson had a way of contracting the names of his friends; as Beauclerc, Beau; Boswell, Bozzy; Langton, Lanky; Murphy, Mur; Sheridan, Sherry. I remember one day, when Tom Davies was telling that Dr. Johnson said, 'We are all in labour for a name to Goldy's play,' Goldsmith seemed displeased that such a liberty should be taken with his name, and said, 'I have often desired him not to call me Goldy.'

Chambers, you find, is gone far, and poor Goldsmith is gone much farther. He died of a fever, exasperated, as I believe, by the fear of distress. He had raised money and squandered it by every artifice of acquisition, and folly of expense. But let not his frailties be remembered; he was a very great man.

'Goldsmith,' he said, 'referred every thing to vanity: his virtues, and his vices too, were from that motive. He was not a social man. He never exchanged mind with you.'

He said 'Goldsmith was a plant that flowered late. There appeared nothing remarkable about him when he was young; though, when he had got high in fame, one of his friends begun to recollect something of his being distinguished at college. Goldsmith, in the same manner, recollected more of that friend's early years, as he grew a greater man.'

Goldsmith being mentioned, Johnson observed that it was long before his merit came to be acknowledged. That he once complained to him, in ludicrous terms of distress, 'Whenever I write any thing, the public make a point to know nothing about it;' but that his 'Traveller' brought him into high reputation. Langton: 'There is not one bad line in that poem; not one of Dryden's careless verses.' Sir Joshua: 'I was glad to hear Charles Fox say it was one of the finest poems in the English language.' Langton: 'Why were you glad? You surely had no doubt of this before.' Johnson: 'No; the merit of "The Traveller" is so well established, that Mr. Fox's praise cannot augment it, nor his censure diminish it.' Sir Joshua: 'But his friends may suspect they had too great a partiality for him.' Johnson: 'Nay, sir, the partiality of his friends was always against him. It was with difficulty we could give him a hearing. Goldsmith had no settled notions upon any subject; so he talked always at random. It seemed to be his intention to blurt out whatever was in his mind, and see what would become of it. He was angry, too, when catched in an absurdity; but it did not prevent him from falling into another the next minute. I remember Chamier, after talking with him for some time, said, "Well, I do believe he wrote this poem himself; and, let me tell you, that is believing a great deal." Chamier once asked him, what he meant by "slow," — the last word in the first line of "The Traveller,"—

"Remote, unfriended, melancholy, slow."

Did he mean tardiness of locomotion? Goldsmith, who would say something without consideration, answered, "Yes." I was sitting by, and said, "No, sir; you do not mean tardiness of locomotion; you mean that sluggishness of mind which comes upon a man in solitude." Chamier believed then that I had written the line, as much as if he had seen me write it. Goldsmith, however, was a man, who, whatever he wrote, did it better than any other man could do. He deserved a place in Westminster Abbey, and every year he lived would have deserved it better. He had, indeed, been at no pains to fill his mind with knowledge. He transplanted it from one place to another, and it did not settle in his mind; so he could not tell what was in his own books.'

Talking of Goldsmith, Johnson said he was very envious. I defended him, by observing that he owned it frankly upon all occasions. Johnson: 'Sir, you are enforcing the charge. He had so much envy that he could not conceal it. He was so full of it that he overflowed. He talked of it, to be sure, often enough.'

Goldsmith, in his diverting simplicity, complained one day, in a mixed company, of Lord Camden. 'I met him,' said he, 'at Lord Clare's house in the country, and he took no more notice of me than if I had been an ordinary man.' The company having laughed heartily, Johnson stood forth in defence of his friend: 'Nay, gentlemen,' said he, 'Dr. Goldsmith is in the right. A nobleman ought to have made up to such a man as Goldsmith; and I think it is much against Lord Camden that he neglected him.'

Of Dr. Goldsmith he said, 'No man was more foolish when he had not a pen in his hand, or more wise when he had.'

He said Goldsmith's blundering speech to Lord Shelburne, which has been so often mentioned, and which he really did make to him, was only a blunder in emphasis:—'I wonder they should call your lordship Malagrida, for Malagrida was a very good man,—meant, I wonder they should use Malagrida as a term of reproach.'

'Returning home one day from dining at the chaplain's table, he told me that Dr. Goldsmith had given a very comical and unnecessarily exact recital there of his own feelings when his play was hissed; telling the company how he went indeed to the Literary Club at night, and chatted gaily among his friends, as if nothing had happened amiss;—that, to impress them still more forcibly with an idea of his magnanimity, he even sung his favourite song about an old woman tossed in a blanket seventeen times as high as the moon; 'but all this while I was suffering horrid tortures,' said he, 'and verily believe that if I had put a bit into my mouth, it would have strangled me on the spot, I was so excessively ill: but I made more noise than usual to cover all that, and so they never perceived my not eating, nor I believe at all imagined to themselves the anguish of my heart. But when all were gone except Johnson here, I burst out a crying, and even swore that I would never write again.' 'All which, Doctor,' said Dr. Johnson, amazed at his odd frankness, 'I thought had been a secret between you and me, and I am sure I would not have said any thing about it for the world. Now see,' repeated he, when he told the story, 'what a figure a man makes who thus unaccountably chooses to be the frigid narrator of his own disgrace. *Il volto sciolto, ed i pensieri stretti*, was a proverb made on purpose for such mortals, to keep people, if possible, from being thus the heralds of their own shame; for what compassion can they gain by such silly narratives? No man should be expected to sympathize with the sorrows of vanity. If then you are mortified by any ill usage, whether real or supposed, keep at least the account of such mortifications to yourself, and forbear to proclaim how meanly you are thought of by others, unless you desire to be meanly thought of by all.'

'Poor Goldsmith was to him indeed like the earthen pot to the iron one in Fontaine's Fables: it had been better for him, perhaps, that they had changed companions oftener, yet no experience of his antagonist's strength hindered him from continuing the contest. He used to remind me always of that verse in Berni, —

> 'Il pover uomo che non sen'era accorto,
> Andava combattendo — ed era morto.'

Dr. Johnson made him a comical answer one day, when seeming to repine at the success of Beattie's Essay on Truth. 'Here's such a stir,' said he, 'about a fellow that has written one book, and I have written many.' 'Ah, Doctor,' said his friend, 'there go two-and-forty sixpences, you know, to one guinea.'

Here was exemplified what Goldsmith said of him, with the aid of a very witty image from one of Cibber's comedies: 'There is no arguing with Johnson; for, if his pistol misses fire, he knocks you down with the butt-end of it.'

Of Goldsmith's Traveller he used to speak in terms of the highest commendation. A lady, I remember, who had the pleasure of hearing Dr. Johnson read it from the beginning to the end on its first coming out, to testify her admiration of it, exclaimed, 'I never more shall think Dr. Goldsmith ugly.' In having thought so, however, she was by no means singular, an instance of which I am rather inclined to mention, because it involves a remarkable one of Dr. Johnson's ready wit; for this lady, one evening being in a large party, was called upon after supper for her toast, and seeming embarrassed, she was desired to give the ugliest man she knew, and she immediately named Dr. Goldsmith, on which a lady on the other side of the table rose up and reached across to shake hands with her, it being the first time they had met; on which Dr. Johnson said, 'Thus the ancients, on the commencement of their friendships, used to sacrifice a beast betwixt them.'

Sir Joshua, I have often thought, never gave a more striking proof of his excellence in portrait-painting, than in giving dignity to Dr. Goldsmith's countenance, and yet preserving a strong likeness. But he drew after his mind, or rather his genius, if I may be allowed to make that distinction, assimilating the one with his conversation, the other with his works. Dr. Goldsmith's cast of countenance, and indeed his whole figure from head to foot, impressed every one at first sight with an idea of his being a low mechanic, particularly, I believe, a journeyman tailor. A little concurring instance of this I well remember. One day at Sir Joshua Reynolds's, in company with some gentlemen and ladies, he was relating with great indignation an insult he had just received from some gentleman he had accidentally met (I think at a coffee-house). 'The fellow,' he said, 'took me for a tailor;' on which all the party either laughed aloud, or showed they suppressed a laugh.

Dr. Johnson seemed to have much more kindness for Goldsmith than Goldsmith had for him. He always appeared to be overawed by Johnson, particularly when in company with people of any consequence, always as if impressed with some fear of disgrace; and, indeed, well he might. I have been witness to many mortifications he has suffered in Dr. Johnson's company: one day in particular, at Sir Joshua's table, a gentleman, to whom he was talking his best, stopped him in the midst of his discourse, with 'Hush! hush! Dr. Johnson is going to say something.'

At another time, a gentleman who was sitting between Dr. Johnson and Dr. Goldsmith, and with whom he had been disputing, remarked to another, loud enough for Goldsmith to hear him, 'That he had a fine time of it, between Ursa major and Ursa minor.'

MISS HAWKINS'S MEMOIRS.

When Goldsmith expressed an inclination to visit Aleppo, for the purpose of importing some of the mechanical inventions in use there, Dr. Johnson said, 'Goldsmith will go, and he will bring back a frame for grinding knives, which he will think a convenience peculiar to Aleppo.' After he had published his 'Animated Nature, Johnson said, 'You are not to infer from this compilation Goldsmith's knowledge on the subject; if he knows that a cow has horns, it is as much as he does know.'

On this it is apposite to remark the exalted ideas which we entertain in early life of the intellectual acquisition of writers. We fancy that what they tell must be written from the dictation of their own memory. When we have more experience, we find that there is often as much work for the feet as for the fingers, in the committing a few pages to paper; and that the claim to admiration is founded rather in knowing where to seek what we want, than in possessing it. Enviable indeed are the few who carry their libraries in their heads.

Of the two following, I had the former from Mr. Langton; and the latter my father had from Mr. Cadell.

Goldsmith happened once to stop at an inn on the road, in a parlour of which was a very good portrait, which he coveted, believing it a Vandyke: he therefore called in the mistress of the house, asked her if she set any value on that old-fashioned picture; and, finding that she was wholly a stranger to its worth, he told her it bore a very great resemblance to his aunt Salisbury, and that, if she would sell it cheap, he would buy it. A bargain was struck, a price infinitely below the value was paid. Goldsmith took the picture away with him, and had the satisfaction to find, that by this scandalous trick he had indeed procured a genuine and very saleable painting of Vandyke's.

Soon after Goldsmith had contracted with the booksellers for his History of England, for which he was to be paid five hundred guineas, he went to Cadell, and told him he was in the utmost distress for money, and in imminent danger of being arrested by his butcher or baker. Cadell immediately called a meeting of the proprietors, and prevailed on them to advance him the whole, or a considerable part of the sum, which, by the original agreement, he was not entitled to till a twelvemonth after the publication of his work. On a day which Mr. Cadell had named for giving this needy author an answer, Goldsmith came and received the money, under pretence of instantly satisfying his creditors. Cadell, to discover the truth of his pretext, watched whither he went, and, after following him to Hyde Park Corner, saw him get into a postchaise, in which a woman of the town was waiting for him, and with whom, it afterwards appeared, he went to Bath to dissipate what he had thus fraudulently obtained.

Have I told of my father's being invited by Goldsmith to

look at a book in which was some information that might be useful to him, and, instead of lending it to him, tearing out the leaves?

COLMAN'S RANDOM RECORDS.

OLIVER GOLDSMITH, several years before my luckless presentation to Johnson, proved how 'Doctors differ.' I was only five years old when Goldsmith took me on his knee, while he was drinking coffee, one evening, with my father, and began to play with me; which amiable act I returned with the ingratitude of a peevish brat, by giving him a very smart slap on the face: it must have been a tingler, for it left the marks of my little spiteful paw upon his cheek. This infantile outrage was followed by summary justice, and I was locked up by my indignant father in an adjoining room, to undergo solitary imprisonment in the dark. Here I began to howl and scream most abominably; which was no bad step towards liberation, since those who were not inclined to pity me might be likely to set me free, for the purpose of abating a nuisance.

At length a generous friend appeared to extricate me from jeopardy, and that generous friend was no other than the man I had so wantonly molested by assault and battery, — it was the tender-hearted Doctor himself, with a lighted candle in his hand, and a smile upon his countenance, which was still partially red from the effects of my petulance. I sulked and sobbed, and he fondled and soothed, till I began to brighten. Goldsmith, who in regard to children was like the Village Preacher he has so beautifully described, — for

> 'Their welfare pleased him, and their cares distress'd,' —

seized the propitious moment of returning good humour; so he put down the candle, and began to conjure. He placed three hats, which happened to be in the room, upon the carpet, and a shilling under each: the shillings, he told me, were England, France, and Spain. 'Hey, presto, cockolorum!' cried the Doctor, and, lo! on uncovering the shillings which had been dispersed, each beneath a separate hat, they were all found congregated under one. I was no politician at five years old, and therefore might not have wondered at the sudden revolution which brought England, France, and Spain all under one crown; but, as I was also no conjurer, it amazed me beyond measure. Astonishment might have amounted to awe for one who appeared to me gifted with the power of performing miracles, if the good-nature of the man had not obviated my dread of the magician; but, from that time, whenever the Doctor came to visit my father,

> 'I pluck'd his gown, to share the good man's smile;'

a game at romps constantly ensued, and we were always cordial friends and merry playfellows. Our unequal companionship varied somewhat in point of sports as I grew older, but it did not last long; my senior playmate died, alas! in his forty-fifth year, some months after I had attained my eleventh. His death, it has been thought, was hastened by 'mental inquietude.' If this supposition be true, never did the turmoils of life subdue a mind more warm with sympathy for the misfortunes of our fellow-creatures. But his character is familiar to every one who reads: in all the numerous accounts of his virtues and his foibles, his genius and absurdities, his knowledge of nature and his ignorance of the world, his 'compassion for another's woe' was always predominant; and my trivial story of his humouring a froward child weighs but as a feather in the recorded scale of his benevolence.

CUMBERLAND'S MEMOIRS.

At this time I did not know Oliver Goldsmith even by person. I think our first meeting chanced to be at the British Coffee-house. When we came together, we very speedily coalesced; and I believe he forgave me for all the little fame I had got by the success of my West Indian, which had put him to some trouble, for it was not in his nature to be unkind; and I had soon an opportunity of convincing him how incapable I was of harbouring resentment, and how zealously I took my share in what concerned his interest and reputation. That he was fantastically and whimsically vain, all the world knows; but there was no settled and inherent malice in his heart. He was tenacious, to a ridiculous extreme, of certain pretensions that did not, and by nature could not, belong to him, and, at the same time, inexcusably careless of the fame which he had powers to command. His table-talk was (Garrick aptly compared it) like a parrot, whilst he wrote like Apollo; he had gleams of eloquence, and at times a majesty of thought; but, in general, his tongue and his pen had two very different styles of talking. What foibles he had he took no pains to conceal; the good qualities of his heart were too frequently obscured by the carelessness of his conduct and the frivolity of his manners. Sir Joshua Reynolds was very good to him, and would have drilled him into better trim and order for society, if he would have been amenable; for Reynolds was a perfect gentleman, had good sense, great propriety, with all the social attributes and all the graces of hospitality, equal to any man. He knew well how to appreciate men of talents, and how near akin the Muse of Poetry was to that art of which he was so eminent a master. From Goldsmith he caught the subject of his famous Ugolino; what aids he got from others, if he got any, were worthily bestowed and happily applied.

There is something in Goldsmith's prose that to my ear is uncommonly sweet and harmonious; it is clear, simple, easy to be understood; we never want to read his period twice over, except for the pleasure it bestows; obscurity never calls us back to a repetition of it. That he was a poet there is no doubt; but the paucity of his verses does not allow us to rank him in that high station where his genius might have carried him. There must be bulk, variety, and grandeur of design, to constitute a first-rate poet. The Deserted Village, Traveller, and Hermit, are all specimens, beautiful as such; but they are only bird's eggs on a string, and eggs of small birds too. One great magnificent *whole* must be accomplished before we can pronounce upon the *maker* to be the ὁ ποιητης. Pope himself never earned this title by a work of any magnitude but his Homer; and that, being a translation, only constituted him an accomplished versifier. Distress drove Goldsmith upon undertakings neither congenial with his studies, nor worthy of his talents. I remember him, when in his chamber in the Temple, he showed me the beginning of his 'Animated Nature;' it was with a sigh, such as genius draws, when hard necessity diverts it from its bent to drudge for bread, and talk of birds and beasts and creeping things, which Pidcock's showmen would have done as well. Poor fellow! he hardly knew an ass from a mule, nor a turkey from a goose, but when he saw it on the table. But publishers hate poetry, and Paternoster Row is not Parnassus. Even the mighty Doctor Hill, who was not a very delicate reader, could not make a dinner out of the press, till, by a happy transformation into Hannah Glass, he turned himself into a cook, and sold receipts for made dishes to all the savoury readers in the kingdom. Then, indeed, the press acknowledged him second in fame only to John Bunyan; his pasty kept pace in sale with Nelson's Feasts, and when his own name was fairly written out of credit, he wrote himself into immortality under an alias. Now, though necessity, I should rather say the desire of finding money for a masquerade, drove Oliver Goldsmith upon abridging history and turning Buffon into English, yet I much doubt if, without that spur, he would ever have put his Pegasus into action; no, if he had been rich, the world would have been poorer than it is by the loss of all the treasures of his genius and the contributions of his pen.

Oliver Goldsmith began at this time to write for the stage; and it is to be lamented that he did not begin at an earlier period of life to turn his genius to dramatic compositions, and much more to be lamented, that, after he had begun, the succeeding period of his life was so soon cut off. There is no doubt but his genius, when more familiarized to the business, would have inspired him to accomplish great things. His first comedy of the 'Good-natured Man' was read and applauded in its manuscript by Edmund Burke, and the circle in which he then lived and moved. Under such patronage it came with those testimonials to the director of Covent Garden Theatre, as could not fail to open all the avenues to the stage, and bespeak all the favour and attention from the performers and the public, that the applauding voice of him, whose applause was fame itself, could give it. This comedy has enough to justify the good opinion of its literary patron, and secure its author against any loss of reputation; for it has the stamp of a man of talents upon it, though its popularity with the audience did not quite keep pace with the expectations that were grounded on the fiat it had antecedently been honoured with. It was a first effort, however, and did not discourage its ingenious author from invoking his muse a second time. It was now, whilst his labours were in perfection, that I first met him at the British Coffee-house, as I have already related, somewhat out of place. He dined with us as a visitor, introduced, as I think, by Sir Joshua Reynolds; and we held a consultation upon the naming of his comedy, which some of the company had read, and which he detailed to the rest after his manner with a great deal of good-humour. Somebody suggested, 'She Stoops to Conquer,' — and that title was agreed upon. When I perceived an embarrassment in his manner towards me, which I could readily account for, I lost no time to put him at his ease, and I flatter myself I was successful. As my heart was ever warm towards my contemporaries, I did not counterfeit, but really felt a cordial interest in his behalf; and I had soon the pleasure to perceive that he credited me for my sincerity. 'You and I,' said he, 'have very different motives for resorting to the stage. I write for money, and care little about fame.' I was touched by this melancholy confession, and from that moment busied myself assiduously amongst all my connexions in his cause. The whole company pledged themselves to the support of the ingenious poet, and faithfully kept their promise to him. In fact, he needed all that could be done for him; as Mr. Colman, then manager of Covent Garden Theatre, protested against the comedy, when as yet he had not struck upon a name for it. Johnson at length stood forth in all his terrors as champion for the piece, and backed by us his client and retainers demanded a fair trial. Colman again protested, but, with that salvo for his own reputation, liberally lent his stage to one of the most eccentric productions that ever found its way to it, and 'She Stoops to Conquer' was put into rehearsal. We were not over-sanguine of success, but perfectly determined to struggle hard for our author; we accordingly assembled our strength at the Shakespeare Tavern in a considerable body for an early dinner, where Samuel Johnson took the chair at the head of a long table, and was the life and soul of the corps; the Poet took post silently by his side with the Burkes, Sir Joshua Reynolds, Fitzherbert, Caleb Whitefoord, and a phalanx of North British predetermined applauders, under the banner of Major Neilly, all good men and true. Our illustrious president was in unimitable glee, and poor Goldsmith that day took all his raillery as patiently and complacently as my friend Boswell any day, or every day of his life. In the meantime we did not forget our duty; and though we had a better comedy going, in which Johnson was chief actor, we betook ourselves in good time to our separate and allotted posts, and waited the awful drawing up of the curtain. As our stations were preconcerted, so were our signals for plaudits arranged and determined upon, in a manner that gave every one his cue, where to look for them, and how to follow them up. We had amongst us a very worthy and efficient member, long since lost to his friends and the world at large, Adam

Drummond, of amiable memory, who was gifted by nature with the most sonorous, and at the same time the most contagious, laugh that ever echoed from the human lungs. The neighing of the horse of the son of Hystaspes was a whisper to it; the whole thunder of the theatre could not drown it. This kind and ingenuous friend fairly forewarned us, that he knew no more when to give his fire than the cannon did that was planted on a battery. He desired therefore to have a flapper at his elbow, and I had the honour to be deputed to that office. I planted him in an upper box, pretty nearly over the stage, in full view of the pit and galleries, and perfectly well situated to give the echo all its play through the hollows and recesses of the theatre. The success of our manœuvres was complete. All eyes were upon Johnson, who sat in a front row of a side box; and, when he laughed, everybody thought themselves warranted to roar. In the meantime my friend followed signals with a rattle so irresistibly comic, that, when he had repeated it several times, the attention of the spectators was so engrossed by his person and performances, that the progress of the play seemed likely to become a secondary object, and I found it prudent to insinuate to him that he might halt his music without any prejudice to the author. But, alas! it was now too late to rein him in: he had laughed upon my signal where he had found no joke, and now unluckily he fancied that he found a joke in almost every thing that was said; so that nothing in nature could be more malapropos than some of his bursts every now and then were. These were dangerous moments, for the pit began to take umbrage; but we carried our play through, and triumphed, not only over Colman's judgment, but our own.

As the life of poor Oliver Goldsmith was now fast approaching to its period, I conclude my account of him with gratitude for the epitaph he bestowed on me in his poem called 'Retaliation.'

It was upon a proposal started by Edmund Burke, that a party of friends, who had dined together at Sir Joshua Reynolds's and my house, should meet at the St. James's Coffeehouse; which accordingly took place, and was occasionally repeated with much festivity and good fellowship. Dr. Bernard, Dean of Derry, a very amiable and old friend of mine, Dr. Douglas, since Bishop of Salisbury, Johnson, David Garrick, Sir Joshua Reynolds, Oliver Goldsmith, Edmund and Richard Burke, Hickey, with two or three others, constituted our party. At one of these meetings, an idea was suggested of extemporary epitaphs upon the parties present; pen and ink were called for, and Garrick off-hand wrote an epitaph with a good deal of humour upon poor Goldsmith, who was the first in jest, as he proved to be in reality, that we committed to the grave. The Dean also gave him an epitaph, and Sir Joshua illuminated the Dean's verses with a sketch of his bust in pen and ink inimitably caricatured. Neither Johnson nor Burke wrote any thing; and when I perceived Oliver was rather sore, and seemed to watch me with that kind of attention which indicated his expectation of something in the same kind of burlesque with theirs, I thought it time to press the joke no further, and wrote a few couplets at a side-table, which when I had finished, and was called on by the company to exhibit, Goldsmith with much agitation besought me to spare him, and I was about to tear them, when Johnson wrested them out of my hand, and in a loud voice read them at the table. I have now lost all recollection of them, and in fact they were little worth remembering; but as they were serious and complimentary, the effect they had upon Goldsmith was the more pleasing for being so entirely unexpected. The concluding line, which is the only one I can call to mind, was, —

'All mourn the poet, I lament the man.'

This I recollect, because he repeated it several times, and seemed much gratified by it. At our next meeting he produced his epitaphs as they stand in the little posthumous poem above mentioned, and this was the last time he ever enjoyed the company of his friends.

As he had served up the company under the similitude of various sorts of meat, I had in the meantime figured them under that of liquor; which little poem I rather think was printed, but of this I am not sure. Goldsmith sickened and died, and we had one concluding meeting at my house, when it was decided to publish his Retaliation, and Johnson at the same time undertook to write an epitaph for our lamented friend, to whom we proposed to erect a monument by subscription in Westminster Abbey. This epitaph Johnson executed; but in the criticism that was attempted against it, and in the Round-Robin signed at Beauclerc's house, I had no part. I had no acquaintance with that gentleman, and was never in his house in my life.

Thus died Oliver Goldsmith, in his chamber in the Temple, at a period of life when his genius was yet in its vigour, and fortune seemed disposed to smile upon him. I have heard Dr. Johnson relate with infinite humour the circumstance of his rescuing him from a ridiculous dilemma by the purchase-money of his Vicar of Wakefield, which he sold on his behalf to Dodsley; and, as I think, for the sum of ten pounds only.* He had run up a debt with his landlady for board and lodging of some few pounds, and was at his wits-end how to wipe off the score and keep a roof over his head, except by closing with a very staggering proposal on her part, and taking his creditor to wife, whose charms were very far from alluring, whilst her demands were extremely urgent. In this crisis of his fate, he was found by Johnson in the act of meditating on the melancholy alternative before him.

He showed Johnson his manuscript of The Vicar of Wakefield, but seemed to be without any plan, or even hope, of raising money upon the disposal of it: when Johnson cast his eye upon it, he discovered something that gave him hope, and immediately took it to Dodsley, who paid down the price above mentioned in ready money, and added an eventual condition upon its future sale. Johnson described the precautions he took in concealing the amount of the sum he had in hand, which he prudently administered to him by a guinea at a time. In the event he paid off the landlady's score, and redeemed the person of his friend from her embraces. Goldsmith had the joy of finding his ingenious work succeed beyond

* £40 to Newbery; see page ciii

his hopes, and from that time began to place a confidence in the resources of his talents, which thenceforward enabled him to keep his station in society, and cultivate the friendship of many eminent persons, who, whilst they smiled at his eccentricities, esteemed him for his genius and good qualities.

NORTHCOTE'S CONVERSATIONS.

Goldsmith and Burke had often violent disputes about politics; the one being a staunch Tory, and the other at that time a Whig and outrageous anti-courtier. One day he came into the room when Goldsmith was there, full of ire and abuse against the late king, and went on in such a torrent of the most unqualified invective that Goldsmith threatened to leave the room. The other, however, persisted; and Goldsmith went out, unable to bear it any longer. So much for Mr. Burke's pretended consistency and uniform loyalty! When Northcote first came to Sir Joshua, he wished very much to see Goldsmith; and one day Sir Joshua, on introducing him, asked why he had been so anxious to see him. 'Because,' said Northcote, 'he is a notable man.' This expression, 'notable,' in its ordinary sense, was so contrary to Goldsmith's character, that they both burst out a laughing very heartily. Goldsmith was two thousand pounds in debt at the time of his death, which was hastened by his chagrin and distressed circumstances; and when 'She Stoops to Conquer' was performed, he was so choked all dinner-time that he could not swallow a mouthful. A party went from Sir Joshua's to support it. The present title was not fixed upon till that morning. Northcote went with Ralph, Sir Joshua's man, into the gallery to see how it went off; and, after the second act, there was no doubt of its success. Northcote says, people had a great notion of the literary parties at Sir Joshua's.

Mrs. G. had certainly a lock of Goldsmith's hair, for she and her sister (Miss Horneck) had wished to have some remembrance of him after his death; and though the coffin was nailed up, it was opened again at their request, (such was the regard Goldsmith was known to have for them!) and a lock of his hair was cut off, which Mrs. G. still has. Northcote said, Goldsmith's death was the severest blow Sir Joshua ever received: he did not paint at all that day. It was proposed to make a grand funeral for him; but Reynolds objected to this, as it would be over in a day, and said it would be better to lay by the money to erect a monument to him in Westminster Abbey; and he went himself and chose the spot. Goldsmith had begun another novel, of which he read the first chapter to the Miss Hornecks a little before his death. Northcote asked what I thought of the Vicar of Wakefield. And I answered, 'What everybody else did.' He said there was that mixture of the ludicrous and the pathetic running through it, which particularly delighted him: it gave a stronger resemblance to nature. He thought this justified Shakespeare in mingling up farce and tragedy together; life itself was a tragi-comedy. Instead of being pure, every thing was chequered. If you went to an execution, you would perhaps see an applewoman in the greatest distress because her stall was overturned, at which you could not help smiling. We then spoke of 'Retaliation,' and praised the character of Burke in particular as a masterpiece. Nothing that he had ever said or done but what was foretold in it; nor was he painted as the principal figure in the foreground with the partiality of a friend, or as the great man of the day, but with a background of history, showing both what he was and what he might have been. Northcote repeated some lines from the 'Traveller,' which were distinguished by a beautiful transparency, by simplicity and originality. He confirmed Boswell's account of Goldsmith, as being about the middle height, rather clumsy, and tawdry in his dress.

Human nature is always the same. It was so with Johnson and Goldsmith. They would allow no one to have any merit but themselves. The very attempt was a piece of presumption, and a trespass upon their privileged rights. I remember a poem that came out, and that was sent to Sir Joshua: his servant Ralph had instructions to bring it in just after dinner. Goldsmith presently got hold of it, and seemed thrown into a rage before he had read a line of it. He then said, 'What wretched stuff is here! what cursed nonsense that is!' and kept all the while marking the passages with his thumb-nail, as if he would cut them in pieces. At last, Sir Joshua, who was provoked, interfered, and said, 'Nay, don't spoil my book, however.'

HAWKINS'S MEMOIRS OF JOHNSON.

Goldsmith is well known by his writings to have been a man of genius and of very fine parts; but of his character and general deportment it is the hardest task any one can undertake to give a description. I will, however, attempt it, trusting to be excused if, in the spirit of a faithful historian, I record as well his singularities as his merits.

There are certain memoirs of him extant, from which we learn that his inclination co-operating with his fortunes, which were but scanty, led him into a course of life little differing from vagrancy, that deprived him of the benefits of regular study: it, however, gratified his humour, stored his mind with ideas and some knowledge, which, when he became settled, he improved by various reading; yet to all the graces of urbanity he was a stranger. With the greatest pretensions to polished manners, he was rude, and, when he most meant the contrary, absurd. He affected Johnson's style and manner of conversation, and when he had uttered, as he often would, a laboured sentence, so tumid as to be scarcely intelligible, would ask if that was not truly Johnsonian; yet he loved not Johnson, but rather envied him for his parts, and once entreated a friend to desist from praising him; 'for in doing so,' said he, 'you harrow up my very soul.'

He had some wit, but no humour, and never told a story but he spoiled it. The following anecdotes will convey some idea of the style and manner of his conversation.

He was used to say he could play on the German flute as well as most men, at other times as well as any man living; and in his poem of the Traveller has hinted at this attainment in the following lines:—

'To kinder skies, where gentler manners reign,
I turn; and France displays her bright domain.
Gay, sprightly land of mirth and social ease,
Pleas'd with thyself, whom all the world can please,
How often have I led thy sportive choir,
With tuneless pipe, beside the murmuring Loire!
Where shading elms along the margin grew,
And, freshen'd from the waves, the zephyrs flew;
And haply, though my harsh touch, faltering still,
But mock'd all tune, and marr'd the dancer's skill,
Yet would the village praise my wondrous power,
And dance forgetful of the noontide hour.'

But, in truth, he understood not the character in which music is written, and played on that instrument, as many of the vulgar do, merely by ear. Roubiliac, the sculptor, a merry fellow, once heard him play, and, minding to put a trick on him, pretended to be charmed with his performance, as also that himself was skilled in the art, and entreated him to repeat the air that he might write it down. Goldsmith readily consenting, Roubiliac called for paper, and scored thereon a few five-lined staves, which having done, Goldsmith proceeded to play and Roubiliac to write; but his writing was only such random notes on the lines and spaces as any one might set down who had ever inspected a page of music. When they had both done, Roubiliac showed the paper to Goldsmith, who, looking it over with seeming great attention, said it was very correct, and that, if he had not seen him do it, he never could have believed his friend capable of writing music after him.

He used frequently to preface a story thus: I will tell you a story of myself, which some people laugh at, and some do not.

At the breaking up of an evening at a tavern, he entreated the company to sit down, and told them if they would call for another bottle, they should hear one of his *bon mots*. They agreed, and he began thus: I was once told that Sheridan the player, in order to improve himself in stage gestures, had looking-glasses to the number of ten hung about his room, and that he practised before them; upon which I said, 'Then there were ten ugly fellows together.' The company were all silent; he asked why they did not laugh, which they not doing, he, without tasting the wine, left the room in anger. In a large company he once said, 'Yesterday I heard an excellent story, and I would relate it now if I thought any of you able to understand it.' The company laughed, and one of them said, 'Doctor, you are very rude;' but he made no apology. He once complained to a friend in these words: 'Mr. Martinelli is a rude man: I said in his hearing, that there were no good writers among the Italians, and he said to one that sat near him, that I was very ignorant.'

'People,' said he, 'are greatly mistaken in me. A notion goes about, that when I am silent I mean to be impudent; but, I assure you, gentlemen, my silence arises from bashfulness.'

Having one day a call to wait on the late duke, then earl of Northumberland, I found Goldsmith waiting for an audience in an outer room. I asked him what had brought him there: he told me an invitation from his lordship. I made my business as short as I could, and, as a reason, mentioned that Dr. Goldsmith was waiting without. The earl asked me if I was acquainted with him: I told him I was, adding what I thought likely to recommend him. I retired, and stayed in the outer room to take him home. Upon his coming out, I asked him the result of his conversation. 'His lordship,' says he, 'told me he had read my poem,' meaning the Traveller, 'and was much delighted with it; that he was going lord-lieutenant of Ireland; and that, hearing that I was a native of that country, he should be glad to do me any kindness.' And what did you answer, asked I, to this gracious offer? 'Why,' said he, 'I could say nothing but that I had a brother there, a clergyman, that stood in need of help; as for myself, I have no dependence on the promises of great men; I look to the booksellers for support, they are my best friends, and I am not inclined to forsake them for others.'

Thus did this idiot, in the affairs of the world, trifle with his fortunes, and put back the hand that was held out to assist him. Other offers of a like kind he either rejected or failed to improve, contenting himself with the patronage of one nobleman, whose mansion afforded him the delights of a splendid table, and a retreat for a few days from the metropolis.

While I was writing the History of Music, he, at the club, communicated to me some curious matter. I desired he would reduce it to writing; he promised me he would, and desired to see me at his chambers: I called on him there; he stepped into a closet, and tore out of a printed book six leaves that contained what he had mentioned to me. As he wrote for the booksellers, we, at the club, looked on him as a mere literary drudge, equal to the task of compiling and translating, but little capable of original, and still less of poetical composition: he had, nevertheless, unknown to us, written and addressed to the countess, afterwards duchess, of Northumberland, one of the finest poems of the lyric kind that our language has to boast of, the ballad, 'Turn, gentle Hermit of the Dale;'* and surprised us with 'The Traveller,' a poem that contains some particulars of his own history. Johnson was supposed to have assisted him in it; but he contributed to the perfection of it only four lines: his opinion of it was, that it was the best written poem since the time of Pope.

Of the booksellers whom he styled his friends, Mr. Newbery was one. This person had apartments in Canonbury-house, where Goldsmith often lay concealed from his creditors. Under a pressing necessity, he there wrote his Vicar of Wakefield, and for it received of Newbery forty pounds.

Of a man named Griffin, a bookseller, in Catherine-street in the Strand, he had borrowed, by two and three guineas at a time, money to the amount of two hundred pounds: to discharge this debt he wrote 'The Deserted Village,' but was

* That this beautiful poem exists we owe to Dr. Chapman, of Sudbury. Soon after he wrote it, Goldsmith showed it to the Doctor, and was by him hardly dissuaded from throwing it into the fire. — *Hawkins.*

two years about it. Soon after its publication, Griffin declared that it had discharged the whole of his debt.

His poems are replete with fine moral sentiment, and bespeak a great dignity of mind; yet he had no sense of the shame, nor dread of the evils, of poverty.

In the latter he was at one time so involved, that, for the clamours of a woman to whom he was indebted for lodging, and for bailiffs that waited to arrest him, he was equally unable, till he had made himself drunk, to stay within doors, or go abroad to hawk among the booksellers a piece of his writing, the title whereof my author does not remember. In this distress he sent for Johnson, who immediately went to one of them, and brought back money for his relief.

In his dealings with the booksellers, he is said to have acted very dishonestly, never fulfilling his engagements. In one year he got of them, and by his plays, the sum of £1,800, which he dissipated by gaming and extravagance. and died poor, in 1774.

He that can account for the inconsistencies of character above noted, otherwise than by showing that wit and wisdom are seldom found to meet in the same mind, will do more than any of Goldsmith's friends were ever able to do. He was buried in the Temple churchyard. A monument was erected for him in the Poet's Corner, in Westminster Abbey, by a subscription of his friends, and is placed over the entrance into St. Blase's Chapel. The inscription thereon was written by Johnson. This I am able to say with certainty, for he showed it to me in manuscript.

THE TRAVELLER;

OR,

A PROSPECT OF SOCIETY.

A POEM.

1

"THE Traveller; or, a Prospect of Society, inscribed to the Rev. Mr. Henry Goldsmith, by Oliver Goldsmith, M. B.," was first published in December, 1764, price 1*s.* 6*d.*, and was the earliest production to which Goldsmith prefixed his name. It went through nine editions in Goldsmith's lifetime, and is here reprinted from the ninth edition, 4to, 1774, compared with the first edition, 4to, 1765, and with the "sixth edition, corrected," 4to, 1770.

This poem is founded on Addison's "Letter from Italy to the Right Honourable Charles Lord Halifax," of which Goldsmith himself says: "Few poems have done more honour to English genius than this. There is in it a strain of political thinking, that was, at that time, [1701,] new in our poetry. Had the harmony of this been equal to that of Pope's versification, it would be incontestably the finest poem in our language; but there is a dryness in the numbers which greatly lessens the pleasure excited both by the parts judgment and imagination." (Beauties of English Poesy, 1767, vol. i. p. 111.)

All that Goldsmith would appear to have received for this poem, was twenty guineas.—*Newberry MSS.*, Prior, ii. 58.—CUNNINGHAM.

DEDICATION.

TO THE REV. HENRY GOLDSMITH.

DEAR SIR, — I am sensible that the friendship between us can acquire no new force from the ceremonies of a dedication; and perhaps it demands an excuse thus to prefix your name to my attempts, which you decline giving with your own. But as a part of this poem was formerly written to you from Switzerland, the whole can now, with propriety, be only inscribed to you. It will also throw a light upon many parts of it, when the reader understands that it is addressed to a man who, despising fame and fortune, has retired early to happiness and obscurity, with an income of forty pounds a year.

I now perceive, my dear brother, the wisdom of your humble choice. You have entered upon a sacred office, where the harvest is great, and the labourers are but few; while you have left the field of ambition, where the labourers are many, and the harvest not worth carrying away.

But of all kinds of ambition, — what from the refinement of the times, from different systems of criticism, and from the divisions of party, — that which pursues poetical fame is the wildest.

Poetry makes a principal amusement among unpolished nations; but in a country verging to the extremes of refinement, painting and music come in for a share. As these offer the feeble mind a less laborious entertainment, they at first rival poetry, and at length supplant her: they engross all that favour once shown to her, and, though but younger sisters, seize upon the elder's birthright.

Yet, however this art may be neglected by the powerful, it is still in greater danger from the mistaken efforts of the learned to improve it. What criticisms have we not heard of late in favour of blank verse and Pindaric odes, choruses, anapests and iambics, alliterative care and happy negligence! Every absurdity has now a champion to defend it; and as he is generally much in the wrong, so he has always much to say; for error is ever talkative.

But there is an enemy to this art still more dangerous—I mean party. Party entirely distorts the judgment, and destroys the taste. When the mind is once infected with this disease, it can only find pleasure in what contributes to increase the distemper. Like the tiger, that seldom desists from pursuing man after having once preyed upon human flesh, the reader, who has once gratified his appetite with calumny, makes, ever after, the most agreeable feast upon murdered reputation. Such readers generally admire some half-witted thing, who wants to be thought a bold man,[1] having lost the character of a wise one. Him they dignify with the name of poet: his tawdry lampoons are called satires; his turbulence is said to be force, and his frenzy fire.

What reception a poem may find, which has neither abuse, party, nor blank verse to support it, I cannot tell, nor am I solicitous to know. My aims are right. Without espousing the cause of any party, I have attempted to moderate the rage of all. I have endeavoured to show, that there may be equal happiness in states that are differently governed from our own; that every state has a particular principle of happiness, and that this principle in each may be carried to a mischievous excess. There are few can judge, better than yourself, how far these positions are illustrated in this poem. I am,

Dear Sir,

Your most affectionate Brother,

OLIVER GOLDSMITH.

[1] Churchill, at whom all this is aimed, died 4th November, 1764, while the first edition of "The Traveller" was passing through the press.—P. C.

THE TRAVELLER.

[1] REMOTE, unfriended, melancholy, slow,
Or by the lazy Scheld, or wandering Po;
Or onward, where the rude Carinthian[2] boor
Against the houseless stranger shuts the door;
Or where Campania's plain forsaken lies,
A weary waste expanding to the skies;
Where'er I roam, whatever realms to see,
My heart untravell'd fondly turns to thee;
Still to my brother turns, with ceaseless pain,
And drags at each remove a lengthening chain.

1 *Remote*] 'Solus, inops, exspes, leto pœnæque relictus.'
Ovid. Metam. xiv. 217.
Exsul, inops erres, alienaque limina lustres,' &c.
Ovid. Ibis. 118.

And compare Petrarch, Son. xxii:
'Solo e pensoso, i più deserti campi
Vo misurando a passi tardi e lenti.'

2 Carinthia was visited by Goldsmith in 1755, and still (1853) retains its character for inhospitality.—P. C.

3 *and drags*] 'When I am with Florimel, it (my heart) is still your prisoner, *it only draws a longer chain after it.*'
Cibber's Com. Lover, p. 249.
'I should of life's weary load complain,
And, drown'd in tears, drag on the encumbering chain.'
Blackmore's Arthur, p. 212.

Eternal blessings crown my earliest friend,
And round his dwelling guardian saints attend;
Blest be that spot, where cheerful guests retire
To pause from toil, and trim their evening fire;
Blest that abode, where want and pain repair,
And every stranger finds a ready chair;
Blest be those feasts with simple plenty crown'd,
Where all the ruddy family around
Laugh at the jests or pranks that never fail,
Or sigh with pity at some mournful tale;
Or press the bashful stranger to his food,
And learn the luxury of doing good.

But me, not destin'd such delights to share,
My prime of life in wandering spent and care;
Impell'd, with steps unceasing, to pursue
Some fleeting good, that mocks me with the view;
That, like the circle bounding earth and skies,
Allures from far, yet, as I follow, flies;
My fortune leads to traverse realms alone,
And find no spot of all the world my own.

Ev'n now, where Alpine solitudes ascend,
I sit me down a pensive hour to spend;
And, plac'd on high above the storm's career,
Look downward where an hundred realms appear

'The farther I travel, I feel the pain of separation with stronger force. Those ties that bind me to my native country and you are still unbroken; by every remove I only drag a greater length of chain.'—*Citizen of the World*, vol. i. lett. 3.

Lakes, forests, cities, plains, extending wide,
The pomp of kings, the shepherd's humbler pride.

When thus creation's charms around combine,
Amidst the store, should thankless pride repine?
Say, should the philosophic mind disdain
That good which makes each humbler bosom vain?
Let school-taught pride dissemble all it can,
These little things are great to little man;
And wiser he, whose sympathetic mind
Exults in all the good of all mankind. [crown'd;
Ye glittering towns, with wealth and splendour
Ye fields, where summer spreads profusion round;
Ye lakes, whose vessels catch the busy gale;
Ye bending swains, that dress the flowery vale;
For me your tributary stores combine:
Creation's heir, the world — the world is mine!

As some lone miser, visiting his store,
Bends at his treasure, counts, recounts it o'er;
Hoards after hoards his rising raptures fill,
Yet still he sighs, for hoards are wanting still:
Thus to my breast alternate passions rise, [plies:
Pleas'd with each good that Heaven to man sup-
Yet oft a sigh prevails, and sorrows fall,
To see the hoard of human bliss so small;
And oft I wish, amidst the scene, to find
Some spot to real happiness consign'd,
Where my worn soul, each wandering hope at rest,
May gather bliss to see my fellows blest.

But where to find that happiest spot below,
Who can direct, when all pretend to know?
The shuddering tenant of the frigid zone
Boldly proclaims that happiest spot his own;
Extols the treasures of his stormy seas,
And his long nights of revelry and ease.
The naked negro, panting at the line,
Boasts of his golden sands and palmy wine,
Basks in the glare, or stems the tepid wave,
And thanks his gods for all the good they gave.
Such is the patriot's boast, where'er we roam,
His first, best country ever is at home.
And yet, perhaps, if countries we compare,
And estimate the blessings which they share,
Though patriots flatter, still shall wisdom find
An equal portion dealt to all mankind;
As different good, by art or nature given,
To different nations makes their blessings even.

Nature, a mother kind alike to all,
Still grants her bliss at labour's earnest call;
With food as well the peasant is supplied
On Idra's cliffs as Arno's shelvy side;
And, though the rocky crested summits frown,
These rocks by custom turn to beds of down.
From art more various are the blessings sent:
Wealth, commerce, honour, liberty, content.
Yet these each other's power so strong contest,
That either seems destructive of the rest. [fails;
Where wealth and freedom reign, contentment

And honour sinks where commerce long prevails.
Hence every state, to one lov'd blessing prone,
Conforms and models life to that alone.
Each to the favourite happiness attends,
And spurns the plan that aims at other ends;
Till, carried to excess in each domain,
This favourite good begets peculiar pain.

But let us try these truths with closer eyes,
And trace them through the prospect as it lies:
Here for a while, my proper cares resign'd,
Here let me sit in sorrow for mankind;
Like yon neglected shrub at random cast,
That shades the steep, and sighs at every blast.

Far to the right, where Apennine ascends,
Bright as the summer, Italy extends;
Its uplands sloping deck the mountain's side,
Woods over woods in gay theatric pride;[4]
While oft some temple's mouldering tops between
With venerable grandeur mark the scene.

Could nature's bounty satisfy the breast,
The sons of Italy were surely blest.

[4] *theatric pride*] *v. Lycophronis, Cass.* v. 600.
Θεατρομόρφωι πρὸς κλίτει γεωλόφωι.
Virg. Æn. v. 288. —'quem collibus undique curvis
Cingebant silvæ, mediaque in valle theatri
Circus erat'—
Senecæ Troades, v. 1125. 'Crescit theatri more.'

Whatever fruits in different climes are found,
That proudly rise, or humbly court the ground;
Whatever blooms in torrid tracts appear,
Whose bright succession decks the varied year;
Whatever sweets salute the northern sky
With vernal lives, that blossom but to die;
These, here disporting, own the kindred soil,
Nor ask luxuriance from the planter's toil;
While sea-born gales their gelid wings expand
To winnow fragrance round the smiling land.

But small the bliss that sense alone bestows,
And sensual bliss is all the nation knows.
In florid beauty groves and fields appear,
Man seems the only growth that dwindles here.
Contrasted faults through all his manners reign;
Though poor, luxurious; though submissive, vain;
Though grave, yet trifling; zealous, yet untrue;
And even in penance planning sins anew.
All evils here contaminate the mind,
That opulence departed leaves behind:
For wealth was theirs; not far remov'd the date,
When commerce proudly flourished through the state;
At her command the palace learnt to rise,
Again the long-fallen column sought the skies;
The canvas glow'd beyond ev'n nature warm,
The pregnant quarry teem'd with human form:
Till, more unsteady than the southern gale,
Commerce on other shores display'd her sail;

While nought remain'd of all that riches gave,
But towns unmann'd, and lords without a slave:
And late the nation found, with fruitless skill,
[5] Its former strength was but plethoric ill.

Yet still the loss of wealth is here supplied
By arts, the splendid wrecks of former pride;
From these the feeble heart and long-fallen mind
An easy compensation seem to find.
Here may be seen, in bloodless pomp array'd,
[6] The pasteboard triumph and the cavalcade;
Processions form'd for piety and love,
A mistress or a saint in every grove.
By sports like these are all their cares beguil'd,
The sports of children satisfy the child;
Each nobler aim, represt by long control,
Now sinks at last, or feebly mans the soul;
While low delights, succeeding fast behind,
In happier meanness occupy the mind:
As in those domes where Cæsars once bore sway,
Defac'd by time and tottering in decay,
There in the ruin, heedless of the dead,
The shelter-seeking peasant builds his shed;

5 *Its*] 'In short, the state resembled one of those bodies bloated with disease, whose bulk is only a symptom of its wretchedness: their former opulence only rendered them more impotent.' — *Cit. of the World*, i. 98.

6 'Where, in the midst of porticos, processions, and cavalcades, abbés turn shepherds; and shepherdesses, without sheep, indulge their innocent divertimenti.' — *Pres. State of Learning*, p. 39.

And, wondering man could want the larger pile,
Exults, and owns his cottage with a smile.

My soul, turn from them; turn we to survey
Where rougher climes a nobler race display;
Where the bleak Swiss their stormy mansion tread,
And force a churlish soil for scanty bread:
No product here the barren hills afford,
But man and steel, the soldier and his sword;
No vernal blooms their torpid rocks array,
But winter lingering chills the lap of May;
No zephyr fondly sues the mountain's breast,
But meteors glare, and stormy glooms invest.

Yet still, even here, content can spread a charm,
Redress the clime, and all its rage disarm.
Though poor the peasant's hut, his feasts tho' small,
He sees his little lot the lot of all;
Sees no contiguous palace rear its head
To shame the meanness of his humble shed;
No costly lord the sumptuous banquet deal
To make him loathe his vegetable meal;
But calm, and bred in ignorance and toil,
Each wish contracting, fits him to the soil.
Cheerful, at morn, he wakes from short repose,
Breasts the keen air, and carols as he goes;
[7] With patient angle trolls the finny deep,
Or drives his venturous ploughshare to the steep;

[7] 'The best manner to draw up the *finny prey.*'
Cit. of the World, ii. 99.

Or seeks the den where snow-tracks mark the way,
[8] And drags the struggling savage into day.
At night returning, every labour sped,
He sits him down, the monarch of a shed;
Smiles by his cheerful fire, and round surveys
His children's looks, that brighten at the blaze;
While his lov'd partner, boastful of her hoard,
Displays her cleanly platter on the board;
And haply too some pilgrim, thither led,
With many a tale repays the nightly bed.

Thus every good his native wilds impart,
Imprints the patriot passion on his heart;
And ev'n those ills, that round his mansion rise,
Enhance the bliss his scanty fund supplies.
Dear is that shed to which his soul conforms,
And dear that hill which lifts him to the storms;
And as a child, when scaring sounds molest,
Clings close and closer to the mother's breast,
So the loud torrent, and the whirlwind's roar,
But bind him to his native mountains more.

Such are the charms to barren states assign'd;
Their wants but few, their wishes all confin'd.
Yet let them only share the praises due,
If few their wants, their pleasures are but few;[9]

8 'Drive the reluctant savage into the toils.'
Cit. of the World, i. 112.

9 See *Citizen of the World*, i. lett. xi. where this position is enlarged on.

[10] For every want that stimulates the breast
Becomes a source of pleasure when redrest.
Whence from such lands each pleasing science flies,
That first excites desire, and then supplies;
Unknown to them, when sensual pleasures cloy,
To fill the languid pause with finer joy;
Unknown those powers that raise the soul to flame,
Catch every nerve, and vibrate through the frame.
Their level life is but a smouldering fire,
Unquench'd by want, unfann'd by strong desire;
Unfit for raptures, or, if raptures cheer
On some high festival of once a year,
In wild excess the vulgar breast takes fire,
Till, buried in debauch, the bliss expire.

But not their joys alone thus coarsely flow:
Their morals, like their pleasures, are but low;
For, as refinement stops, from sire to son,
Unalter'd, unimprov'd, the manners run;
And love's and friendship's finely pointed dart
Fall blunted from each indurated heart.
Some sterner virtues o'er the mountain's breast
May sit, like falcons cowering on the nest;
But all the gentler morals, such as play
Thro' life's more cultur'd walks, and charm the way,
These, far dispers'd, on timorous pinions fly,
To sport and flutter in a kinder sky.

10 *For every want*] 'Every want becomes a means of pleasure in the redressing.' — *Gold. An. Nat.* ii. 123.

To kinder skies, where gentler manners reign,
I turn; and France displays her bright domain.
Gay, sprightly land of mirth and social ease,
Pleas'd with thyself, whom all the world can please,
How often have I led thy sportive choir,
With tuneless pipe, beside the murmuring Loire!
Where shading elms along the margin grew,
And freshen'd from the wave the zephyr flew;
And haply, though my harsh touch faltering still,
But mock'd all tune, and marr'd the dancer's skill;
Yet would the village praise my wondrous power,
And dance, forgetful of the noontide hour.
Alike all ages: dames of ancient days
Have led their children thro' the mirthful maze;
And the gay grandsire, skill'd in gestic lore,
Has frisk'd beneath the burthen of threescore.

So blest a life these thoughtless realms display,
Thus idly busy rolls their world away:
Theirs are those arts that mind to mind endear,
For honour forms the social temper here:
Honour, that praise which real merit gains,
Or even imaginary worth obtains,
Here passes current; paid from hand to hand,
It shifts in splendid traffic round the land;
From courts, to camps, to cottages it strays,
And all are taught an avarice of praise:
They please, are pleas'd, they give to get esteem,
Till, seeming blest, they grow to what they seem.

But while this softer art their bliss supplies,
It gives their follies also room to rise;
For praise too dearly lov'd, or warmly sought,
Enfeebles all internal strength of thought:
And the weak soul, within itself unblest,
Leans for all pleasure on another's breast.
Hence ostentation here, with tawdry art,
Pants for the vulgar praise which fools impart;
Here vanity assumes her pert grimace,
And trims her robes of frieze with copper lace,
Here beggar pride defrauds her daily cheer,
To boast one splendid banquet once a year:
The mind still turns where shifting fashion draws,
Nor weighs the solid worth of self-applause.

To men of other minds my fancy flies,
Embosom'd in the deep where Holland lies.
Methinks her patient sons before me stand,
Where the broad ocean leans against the land,[11]
And, sedulous to stop the coming tide,
Lift the tall rampire's artificial pride.
Onward methinks, and diligently slow,
The firm connected bulwark seems to grow,
Spreads its long arms amidst the watery roar,
Scoops out an empire, and usurps the shore.

11 *v. Statii Theb.* iv. 62: 'Et terris maria inclinata repellit.' And *Dryden, Annus. Mirab.* st. clxiv.:

'And view the ocean leaning on the sky.'

'Bent his breast against the broad wave.' — *Cit. of the World*, ii. 101.

While the pent ocean, rising o'er the pile,
Sees an amphibious world beneath him smile;
The slow canal, the yellow-blossom'd vale,
The willow-tufted bank, the gliding sail,
The crowded mart, the cultivated plain,
[12] A new creation rescued from his reign.

Thus, while around the wave-subjected soil
Impels the native to repeated toil,
Industrious habits in each bosom reign,
And industry begets a love of gain.
Hence all the good from opulence that springs,
With all those ills superfluous treasure brings,
Are here display'd. Their much lov'd wealth im-
Convenience, plenty, elegance, and arts; [parts
But, view them closer, craft and fraud appear;
[13] Even liberty itself is barter'd here.
At gold's superior charms all freedom flies,
The needy sell it, and the rich man buys.
[14] A land of tyrants, and a den of slaves,
Here wretches seek dishonourable graves,
And calmly bent, to servitude conform,
Dull as their lakes that slumber in the storm.

12 *A new*] 'Holland seems to be a conquest upon the sea, and in a manner rescued from its bosom.'
Gold. An. Nat. i. p. 276.

13 *Even liberty*] Slavery was permitted in Holland; children were sold by their parents for a certain number of years.

14 A nation once famous for setting the world an example of freedom is now become *a land of tyrants and a den of slaves.*'
Cit. of the World, i. p. 147.

Heavens! how unlike their Belgic sires of old!
Rough, poor, content, ungovernably bold;
War in each breast, and freedom on each brow;
How much unlike the sons of Britain now!

Fir'd at the sound, my genius spreads her wing,
And flies where Britain courts the western spring;
Where lawns extend that scorn Arcadian pride,
And brighter streams than fam'd Hydaspes glide.
There all around the gentlest breezes stray,
There gentle music melts on every spray;
Creation's mildest charms are there combin'd,
Extremes are only in the master's mind!
Stern o'er each bosom reason holds her state
With daring aims irregularly great;
Pride in their port, defiance in their eye,
I see the lords of human kind pass by;
Intent on high designs, a thoughtful band,
By forms unfashion'd, fresh from nature's hand,
Fierce in their native hardiness of soul,
True to imagin'd right, above control,—
While even the peasant boasts these rights to scan,
And learns to venerate himself as man.

15 So in the *Cit. of the World*, ii. p. 196, in praise of Britain. 'Yet from the vernal softness of the air, the verdure of the fields, the transparency of the streams, and the beauty of the women; here love might sport among painted lawns and warbling groves, and carol upon gales wafting at once both fragrance and harmony.'

Thine, Freedom, thine the blessings pictur'd here,
Thine are those charms that dazzle and endear;
Too blest, indeed, were such without alloy;
But, foster'd even by freedom, ills annoy:
That independence Britons prize too high,
Keeps man from man, and breaks the social tie;
The self-dependent lordlings stand alone,
All claims that bind and sweeten life unknown;
Here, by the bonds of nature feebly held,
Minds combat minds, repelling and repell'd;
[16] Ferments arise, imprison'd factions roar,
Represt ambition struggles round her shore;
Till, over-wrought, the general system feels
Its motions stop, or frenzy fire the wheels.

Nor this the worst. As nature's ties decay,
As duty, love, and honour fail to sway,
Fictitious bonds, the bonds of wealth and law,
Still gather strength, and force unwilling awe.
Hence all obedience bows to these alone,
And talent sinks, and merit weeps unknown;
Till time may come, when, stript of all her charms,
The land of scholars, and the nurse of arms,
Where noble stems transmit the patriot flame,
Where kings have toil'd and poets wrote for fame

16 'It is extremely difficult to induce a number of free beings to co-operate for their mutual benefits: every possible advantage will necessarily be sought, and every attempt to procure it must be attended with a new fermentation.'
Cit. of the World, ii. 228

One sink of level avarice shall lie,
And scholars, soldiers, kings, unhonour'd die.

Yet think not, thus when freedom's ills I state,
[17] I mean to flatter kings, or court the great:
Ye powers of truth, that bid my soul aspire,
Far from my bosom drive the low desire;
And thou, fair Freedom, taught alike to feel
The rabble's rage, and tyrant's angry steel;
Thou transitory flower, alike undone
By proud contempt, or favour's fostering sun,
Still may thy blooms the changeful clime endure
I only would repress them to secure:
For just experience tells, in every soil,
That those who think must govern those that toil;
And all that freedom's highest aims can reach,
Is but to lay proportion'd loads on each.
Hence, should one order disproportion'd grow,
Its double weight must ruin all below.

O then how blind to all that truth requires,
Who think it freedom when a part aspires!
Calm is my soul, nor apt to rise in arms,
Except when fast approaching danger warms:

[17] 'In the things I have hitherto written, I have neither allured the vanity of the great by flattery, nor satisfied the malignity of the vulgar by scandal; but have endeavoured to get an honest reputation by liberal pursuits.'

v. Pref. to Eng. History, p. 398.

But when contending chiefs blockade the throne,
[18] Contracting regal power to stretch their own;
When I behold a factious band agree
To call it freedom when themselves are free;
Each wanton judge new penal statutes draw,
[19] Laws grind the poor, and rich men rule the law;
The wealth of climes, where savage nations roam,
Pillag'd from slaves to purchase slaves at home;
Fear, pity, justice, indignation, start,
Tear off reserve, and bare my swelling heart;
Till, half a patriot, half a coward grown,
[20] I fly from petty tyrants to the throne.

Yes, Brother, curse with me that baleful hour,
When first ambition struck at regal power;

18 'It is not yet decided in politics, whether the diminution of kingly power in England tends to increase the happiness or freedom of the people. For my own part, from seeing the bad effects of the tyranny of the great in those republican states that pretend to be free, I cannot help wishing that our monarchs may still be allowed to enjoy the power of controlling the encroachments of the great at home.'

Goldsmith's Pref. to Hist. of England.

'It is the interest of the great to diminish kingly power as much as possible.' — *Vic. of Wakef.* p. 101.

19 'What they may then expect may be seen by turning our eyes to Holland, Genoa, or Venice, where the laws *govern the poor, and the rich govern the law.'* — *Vic. of Wakef.* cxix.

'There was a time even here when titles softened the rigour of the law; when dignified wretches were suffered to live.'

Cit. of the World, i. 162.

20 *I fly*] 'Marriage may all these *petty tyrants* chase.'

Pope's Ep. to Mrs. Blount.

And thus polluting honour in its source,
Gave wealth to sway the mind with double force.
Have we not seen, round Britain's peopled shore,
Her useful sons exchang'd for useless ore?
Seen all her triumphs but destruction haste,
Like flaring tapers brightening as they waste;
Seen opulence, her grandeur to maintain,
Lead stern depopulation in her train,
And over fields where scatter'd hamlets rose,
In barren, solitary pomp repose?
Have we not seen, at pleasure's lordly call,
The smiling, long frequented village fall?
Beheld the duteous son, the sire decay'd,
The modest matron, and the blushing maid,
Forc'd from their homes, a melancholy train,
To traverse climes beyond the western main;
[21] Where wild Oswego spreads her swamps around,
And Niagara stuns with thundering sound?

Even now, perhaps, as there some pilgrim strays
[22] Thro' tangled forests, and thro' dangerous ways;
[23] Where beasts with man divided empire claim,
And the brown Indian marks with murderous aim;

21 *Where wild*]
'Oh! let me fly a land that spurns the brave,
Oswego's dreary shores shall be my grave.'
Goldsmith's Threnodia Augustalis.

22 *Through tangled*] 'The forests are dark and tangled.'
An. Nat. vol. i. p. 400.

23 *Where beasts*] 'Where man in his savage state owns inferior strength, and the beasts claim divided dominion.'
Gold. An. Nat. vol. ii. p. 9, 12.

There, while above the giddy tempest flies,
And all around distressful yells arise,
The pensive exile, bending with his woe,
To stop too fearful, and too faint to go,
Casts a long look where England's glories shine,
And bids his bosom sympathize with mine.

Vain, very vain, my weary search to find
That bliss which only centres in the mind:
Why have I stray'd from pleasure and repose,
To seek a good each government bestows?
[24] In every government, though terrors reign,
Though tyrant kings or tyrant laws restrain,
How small of all that human hearts endure,
That part which laws or kings can cause or cure!
Still to ourselves in every place consign'd,
Our own felicity we make or find:
With secret course, which no loud storms annoy,
Glides the smooth current of domestic joy.
[25] The lifted axe, the agonizing wheel,

[24] *In every*] 'Every mind seems capable of entertaining a certain quantity of happiness, which no constitutions can increase, no circumstances alter, and entirely independent on fortune.' — *Cit. of the World*, i. p. 185.

[25] *lifted axe*]
'Some the sharp axe, and some the painful wheel.'
v. Blackmore's Eliza, p. 76.

'The lifted axe.' *v. Blackmore's K. Arthur*, p. 220.

'When with her *lifted axe* proud Martha stood.'
v. State Poems, vol. ii. p. 328.

[26] Luke's iron crown, and Damiens'[27] bed of steel,
To men remote from power but rarely known,
Leave reason, faith, and conscience, all our own.[28]

[26] George and Luke Dosa were two brothers who headed an unsuccessful revolt against the Hungarian nobles at the opening of the sixteenth century; and George (not Luke) underwent the torture of the red-hot iron-crown, as a punishment for allowing himself to be proclaimed king of Hungary, 1513, by the rebellious peasants.—See *Biographie Universelle*, xi. 604. The two brothers belonged to one of the native races of Transylvania, called Szecklers or Zecklers.—FORSTER'S *Goldsmith*, i. 395, (ed. 1854.)—P. C.

[27] Robert François Damiens was put to death with revolting barbarity, in the year 1757, for an attempt to assassinate Louis XV. P. C.

[28] Dr. Johnson, being questioned by Boswell, avowed the authorship of the ten concluding verses of The Traveller, (excepting the last couplet but one,) and also of the 420th line:—

"To stop too fearful, and too faint to go."—C.

THE DESERTED VILLAGE.

A POEM.

"The Deserted Village, a Poem by Dr. Goldsmith: London: Printed for W. Griffin, at Garrick's Head, in Catherine Street, Strand, 1770," 4to, was first published in May, 1770, and ran through six editions in the same year in which it was first published. The price was 2*s*. The sum received by Goldsmith for "The Deserted Village," is unknown.—CUNNINGHAM.

DEDICATION.

TO SIR JOSHUA REYNOLDS.

DEAR SIR, — I can have no expectations, in an address of this kind, either to add to your reputation, or to establish my own. You can gain nothing from my admiration, as I am ignorant of that art in which you are said to excel; and I may lose much by the severity of your judgment, as few have a juster taste in poetry than you. Setting interest, therefore, aside, to which I never paid much attention, I must be indulged at present in following my affections. The only dedication I ever made was to my brother, because I loved him better than most other men. He is since dead. Permit me to inscribe this poem to you.

How far you may be pleased with the versification and mere mechanical parts of this attempt, I do not pretend to enquire; but I know you will object (and indeed several of our best and wisest friends concur in the opinion), that the depopulation it deplores is nowhere to be seen, and the disorders it laments are only to be found in the poet's own imagination. To this I can scarce make any other answer than that I sincerely believe what I have written; that I have taken all possible pains, in my country excursions, for these four or five years past, to be certain of what I allege; and that all my views and enquiries have led me to believe those miseries real, which I here attempt to display. But this is not the place to enter into an enquiry, whether the country be depopulating or not: the discussion would take up much room, and I should prove myself, at best, an indifferent politician, to tire the reader with a long preface, when I want his unfatigued attention to a long poem.

In regretting the depopulation of the country, I inveigh against the increase of our luxuries; and here also I expect the shout of modern politicians against me. For twenty or thirty years past, it has been the fashion to consider luxury as one of the greatest national advantages; and all the wisdom of antiquity, in that particular, as erroneous. Still, however, I must remain a professed ancient on that head, and continue to think those luxuries prejudicial to states by which so many vices are introduced, and so many kingdoms have been undone Indeed, so much has been poured out of late on the other side of the question, that, merely for the sake of novelty and variety, one would sometimes wish to be in the right. — I am, dear Sir

Your sincere Friend

and ardent Admirer,

OLIVER GOLDSMITH.

'Sir Joshua Reynolds painted a particularly fine picture in point of expression especially, of Resignation, and dedicated the print taken from it to Dr. Goldsmith, with some lines under it quoted from the "Deserted Village." This seems to have been done by Sir Joshua as a return of the compliment to Goldsmith, who had dedicated the poem to him.' — *v. Northcote's Life of Reynolds*, p. 166.

THE DESERTED VILLAGE.

Sweet Auburn! loveliest village of the plain,
Where health and plenty cheer'd the labouring swain,
Where smiling spring its earliest visit paid,
And parting summer's lingering blooms delay'd:
Dear lovely bowers of innocence and ease,
Seats of my youth, when every sport could please!
How often have I loiter'd o'er thy green,
Where humble happiness endear'd each scene!
How often have I paus'd on every charm,
The shelter'd cot, the cultivated farm,
The never-failing brook, the busy mill,
The decent church that topt the neighbouring hill,
The hawthorn bush, with seats beneath the shade,
For talking age and whispering lovers made!
How often have I blest the coming day,
When toil remitting lent its turn to play,
And all the village train, from labour free,
Led up their sports beneath the spreading tree;
While many a pastime circled in the shade,
The young contending as the old survey'd;

And many a gambol frolick'd o'er the ground,
And sleights of art and feats of strength went round;
And still, as each repeated pleasure tir'd,
Succeeding sports the mirthful band inspir'd;
The dancing pair that simply sought renown,
By holding out, to tire each other down;
The swain mistrustless of his smutted face,
While secret laughter titter'd round the place;
The bashful virgin's sidelong looks of love,
The matron's glance that would those looks reprove:
These were thy charms, sweet village! sports like these,
With sweet succession, taught e'en toil to please;
These round thy bowers their cheerful influence shed,
These were thy charms,—but all these charms are fled.

Sweet smiling village, loveliest of the lawn!
Thy sports are fled, and all thy charms withdrawn;
Amidst thy bowers the tyrant's hand is seen,
And desolation saddens all thy green:
One only master grasps the whole domain,
And half a tillage stints thy smiling plain;
No more thy glassy brook reflects the day,
But, chok'd with sedges, works its weedy way;
Along thy glades, a solitary guest,
[1] The hollow-sounding bittern guards its nest;

1 *The hollow*] 'There is no sound so dismally hollow as the booming of the bittern.'— *Gold. An. Nat.* vi. p. 2.

Amidst thy desert-walks the lapwing flies,
And tires their echoes with unvaried cries.
Sunk are thy bowers in shapeless ruin all,
And the long grass o'ertops the mouldering wall;
And, trembling, shrinking from the spoiler's hand,
Far, far away thy children leave the land.

Ill fares the land, to hastening ills a prey,
[2] Where wealth accumulates, and men decay:
[3] Princes and lords may flourish, or may fade;
A breath can make them, as a breath has made:
But a bold peasantry, their country's pride,
When once destroy'd, can never be supplied.

A time there was, ere England's griefs began,
When every rood of ground maintain'd its man;
For him light labour spread her wholesome store,
Just gave what life requir'd, but gave no more:

[2] *Where*] 'Wealth in all commercial states is found to accumulate; the very laws may contribute to the accumulation of wealth, as when the natural ties that bind the rich and poor together are broken,' &c.— *Vic. of Wakefield*, p. 102.

[3] *Princes*] 'Vespasianus bene intelligit cæteros quidem amicos suos niti iis quæ ab ipso acceperint, quæque ipsi accumulare, et in alios congerere promtum est: Marcellum autem et Crispum attulisse ad amicitiam suam quod non a Principe acceperint, nec accipi possit.'

De Caus. Cor. Eloq. c. viii.

'A kynge may spille, a kynge may save,
A kynge may make a lorde a knave;
And of a knave a lorde also.'

Gower's Conf. Amantis, fol. 152.

His best companions, innocence and health;
And his best riches, ignorance of wealth.

But times are alter'd: trade's unfeeling train
Usurp the land, and dispossess the swain;
Along the lawn, where scatter'd hamlets rose,
Unwieldy wealth and cumbrous pomp repose;
And every want to opulence allied,
And every pang that folly pays to pride.
Those gentle hours that plenty bade to bloom,
[4] Those calm desires that ask'd but little room,
Those healthful sports that grac'd the peaceful scene,
Liv'd in each look, and brighten'd all the green;
These, far departing, seek a kinder shore,
And rural mirth and manners are no more.

Sweet Auburn! parent of the blissful hour,
Thy glades forlorn confess the tyrant's power.
Here, as I take my solitary rounds,
Amidst thy tangling walks and ruin'd grounds,
And, many a year elaps'd, return to view
Where once the cottage stood, the hawthorn grew,
Remembrance wakes, with all her busy train,
Swells at my breast, and turns the past to pain.

In all my wanderings round this world of care,
In all my griefs — and God has given my share —

[4] *Calm desires*] 'Gentle thoughts and *calm desires!*'
Carew's Poems, p. 22.

I still had hopes my latest hours to crown,
Amidst these humble bowers to lay me down:
To husband out life's taper at the close,
And keep the flame from wasting by repose;
I still had hopes — for pride attends us still —
Amidst the swains to show my book-learn'd skill,
Around my fire an evening group to draw,
And tell of all I felt, and all I saw;
And, as a hare, whom hounds and horns pursue,
Pants to the place from whence at first she flew,
I still had hopes, my long vexations past,
Here to return, — and die at home at last.

O blest retirement! friend to life's decline,
Retreat from care, that never must be mine,
How blest is he who crowns in shades like these
A youth of labour with an age of ease;
Who quits a world where strong temptations try,
[5] And, since 'tis hard to combat, learns to fly!
For him no wretches, born to work and weep,
Explore the mine, or tempt the dangerous deep;
No surly porter stands in guilty state,
To spurn imploring famine from the gate:
But on he moves to meet his latter end,
Angels around befriending virtue's friend;
Bends to the grave with unperceiv'd decay,
While Resignation gently slopes the way;

[5] 'By struggling with misfortunes, we are sure to receive some wound in the conflict: the only method to come off victorious is by running away.' — *The Bee*, p. 56.

And, all his prospects brightening to the last,
His heaven commences ere the world be past.

Sweet was the sound, when oft at evening's close
Up yonder hill the village murmur rose;
There, as I past with careless steps and slow,
The mingling notes came soften'd from below;
The swain responsive as the milkmaid sung,
The sober herd that low'd to meet their young;
The noisy geese that gabbled o'er the pool,
The playful children just let loose from school;
The watch-dog's voice that bay'd the whispering wind,
And the loud laugh that spoke the vacant mind.
These all in sweet confusion sought the shade,
[6] And fill'd each pause the nightingale had made.
But now the sounds of population fail,
No cheerful murmurs fluctuate in the gale,
No busy steps the grass-grown footway tread,
But all the bloomy flush of life is fled.
All but yon widow'd, solitary thing,
That feebly bends beside the plashy spring;
She, wretched matron, forc'd in age, for bread,
To strip the brook with mantling cresses spread,
To pick her wintry fagot from the thorn,
To seek her nightly shed, and weep till morn;
She only left of all the harmless train,
The sad historian of the pensive plain.

6 *And filled*] 'The nightingale's pausing song would be the proper epithet for this bird's music.' — *An. Nat.* i. p. 329.

Near yonder copse, where once the garden smil'd,
And still where many a garden flower grows wild,
There, where a few torn shrubs the place disclose,
The village preacher's modest mansion rose.
A man he was to all the country dear,
And passing rich with forty pounds a year;
Remote from towns he ran his godly race,
Nor e'er had chang'd, nor wish'd to change, his place;
Unpractis'd he to fawn, or seek for power,
By doctrines fashion'd to the varying hour;
Far other aims his heart had learn'd to prize,
More skill'd to raise the wretched than to rise.
His house was known to all the vagrant train,
He chid their wanderings, but reliev'd their pain;
The long-remember'd beggar was his guest,
[7] Whose beard descending swept his aged breast;
The ruin'd spendthrift, now no longer proud,
Claim'd kindred there, and had his claims allow'd;
The broken soldier, kindly bade to stay,
Sate by his fire, and talk'd the night away;
Wept o'er his wounds, or tales of sorrow done,
Shoulder'd his crutch, and shew'd how fields were won.
Pleas'd with his guests, the good man learn'd to glow,
And quite forgot their vices in their woe:

[7] *Whose*]
'Stay till my beard shall sweep mine aged breast.'
Hall's Satires, p. 79, ed. Singer.

[8] Careless their merits or their faults to scan,
His pity gave ere charity began.

Thus to relieve the wretched was his pride,
And even his failings lean'd to virtue's side;
But in his duty prompt at every call,
He watch'd and wept, he pray'd and felt for all;
And, as a bird each fond endearment tries
To tempt its new-fledg'd offspring to the skies,
He tried each art, reprov'd each dull delay,
Allur'd to brighter worlds, and led the way.

Beside the bed where parting life was laid,
And sorrow, guilt, and pain, by turns dismay'd,
The reverend champion stood. At his control,
Despair and anguish fled the struggling soul;
Comfort came down the trembling wretch to raise,
And his last faltering accents whisper'd praise.

At church, with meek and unaffected grace,
[9] His looks adorn'd the venerable place;
[10] Truth from his lips prevail'd with double sway,
And fools, who came to scoff, remain'd to pray.

8 'Want pass'd for merit, at her open door.'
Dryden's Elegies, ii. p. 180.

9 'His eyes diffused a venerable grace.'
Dryden's Good Parson, iii. 137.

10 *Truth*]
'For thou e'en sin didst in such words array,
That some who came bad parts, went out good play.'
Jasp. Mayne to the Mem. of B. Jonson.
v. Nicholls' Col. Poems, i. p. 256.

The service past, around the pious man,
With steady zeal, each honest rustic ran;
Even children follow'd, with endearing wile,
And pluck'd his gown, to share the good man's
smile.
His ready smile a parent's warmth exprest,
Their welfare pleas'd him, and their cares distrest;
To them his heart, his love, his griefs, were given,
But all his serious thoughts had rest in heaven.
[11] As some tall cliff that lifts its awful form,
Swells from the vale, and midway leaves the storm,

[11] *As some*]
'As some tall tower, or lofty mountain's brow
Detains the sun, illustrious from its height,
While rising vapours and descending shades,
With damps and darkness drown the spacious vale,
Philander thus augustly rears his head.'
Young's Night Thoughts, b. ii.

And compare the following lines: —

'Below you see, involv'd in guilt and strife,
The vulgar herd tug the gall'd load of life,
While you on nature's highest summit sate,
Unmov'd, regardless of the force of fate;
Olympus thus the rage of heaven divides,
While forky lightning plays around his sides:
Eternally serene, no winter sees,
Nor storms nor tempest interrupt his ease,
Insults the wreck, and higher rears his head
'Midst foaming deluges around him spread.
Hears undisturb'd descending torrents flow,
And spurns the thunder as it lays below.'
Bp. Warburton's Transl. from Claudian on F. M. Theodorus.

Though round its breast the rolling clouds are spread,
Eternal sunshine settles on its head.

Beside yon straggling fence that skirts the way,
With blossom'd furze unprofitably gay,
There, in his noisy mansion, skill'd to rule,
The village master taught his little school.
A man severe he was, and stern to view;
I knew him well, and every truant knew:
Well had the boding tremblers learn'd to trace
The day's disasters in his morning face;
Full well they laugh'd, with counterfeited glee,
At all his jokes, for many a joke had he;
Full well the busy whisper, circling round,
Convey'd the dismal tidings when he frown'd
Yet he was kind, or, if severe in aught,
The love he bore to learning was in fault.
The village all declar'd how much he knew;
'Twas certain he could write, and cipher too;
Lands he could measure, terms and tides presage,
And even the story ran that he could gauge;
In arguing, too, the parson own'd his skill,
For even though vanquish'd he could argue still;
While words of learned length and thundering sound
Amaz'd the gazing rustics rang'd around;
And still they gaz'd, and still the wonder grew,
That one small head could carry all he knew.

But past is all his fame. The very spot,
Where many a time he triumph'd, is forgot.
Near yonder thorn, that lifts its head on high,
Where once the sign-post caught the passing eye,
Low lies that house where nut-brown draughts
inspir'd,
Where gray-beard mirth and smiling toil retir'd,
Where village statesmen talk'd with looks profound,
And news much older than their ale went round.
Imagination fondly stoops to trace
The parlour splendours of that festive place:
The whitewash'd wall, the nicely sanded floor,
The varnish'd clock that click'd behind the door;
The chest contriv'd a double debt to pay,
A bed by night, a chest of drawers by day;
The pictures plac'd for ornament and use,
The twelve good rules, the royal game of goose;
The hearth, except when winter chill'd the day,
With aspen boughs, and flowers and fennel gay;
While broken teacups, wisely kept for show,
Rang'd o'er the chimney, glisten'd in a row.

Vain, transitory splendours! could not all
Reprieve the tottering mansion from its fall?
Obscure it sinks, nor shall it more impart
An hour's importance to the poor man's heart;
Thither no more the peasant shall repair
To sweet oblivion of his daily care;
No more the farmer's news, the barber's tale,
No more the woodman's ballad shall prevail;

No more the smith his dusky brow shall clear,
Relax his ponderous strength, and lean to hear;
The host himself no longer shall be found
Careful to see the mantling bliss go round;
Nor the coy maid, half willing to be prest,
Shall kiss the cup to pass it to the rest.

Yes! let the rich deride, the proud disdain,
These simple blessings of the lowly train;
To me more dear, congenial to my heart,
One native charm, than all the gloss of art.
Spontaneous joys, where nature has its play,
The soul adopts, and owns their first-born sway;
Lightly they frolic o'er the vacant mind,
Unenvied, unmolested, unconfin'd:
But the long pomp, the midnight masquerade,
With all the freaks of wanton wealth array'd,—
In these, ere triflers half their wish obtain,
The toiling pleasure sickens into pain;
And, even while fashion's brightest arts decoy,
The heart, distrusting, asks if this be joy.

Ye friends to truth, ye statesmen, who survey
The rich man's joys increase, the poor's decay,
'Tis yours to judge, how wide the limits stand
[12] Between a splendid and a happy land.
Proud swells the tide with loads of freighted ore,

[12] 'Too much commerce may injure a nation as well as too little; and there is a wide difference between a conquering and a flourishing empire.' — *Cit. of the World*, i. 98.

And shouting Folly hails them from her shore;
Hoards e'en beyond the miser's wish abound,
And rich men flock from all the world around.
Yet count our gains. This wealth is but a name,
That leaves our useful products still the same.
Not so the loss. The man of wealth and pride
[13] Takes up a space that many poor supplied;
Space for his lake, his park's extended bounds,
Space for his horses, equipage, and hounds:
The robe that wraps his limbs in silken sloth
Has robb'd the neighbouring fields of half their growth;
His seat, where solitary sports are seen,
Indignant spurns the cottage from the green;
Around the world each needful product flies,
For all the luxuries the world supplies:
While thus the land, adorn'd for pleasure all,
In barren splendour feebly waits the fall.

[14] As some fair female, unadorn'd and plain,
Secure to please while youth confirms her reign,
Slights every borrow'd charm that dress supplies,
Nor shares with art the triumph of her eyes;

13 *Takes*] 'Abstulerat miseris tecta superbus ager.'
Martial, Ep. 1, 2, 3.

14 'Veil'd in a simple robe, their best attire,
Beyond the pomp of dress; for loveliness
Needs not the foreign aid of ornament,
But is, when unadorn'd, adorn'd the most.'
Thomson, Autumn, l. 202.

But when those charms are past, — for charms
are frail, —
When time advances, and when lovers fail,
She then shines forth, solicitous to bless,
In all the glaring impotence of dress:
Thus fares the land, by luxury betray'd,
In nature's simplest charms at first array'd;
But, verging to decline, its splendours rise,
Its vistas strike, its palaces surprise;
While, scourged by famine from the smiling land.
The mournful peasant leads his humble band;
[15] And while he sinks, without one arm to save,
The country blooms — a garden and a grave.

Where then, ah where, shall poverty reside,
To 'scape the pressure of contiguous pride?
If to some common's fenceless limits stray'd,
He drives his flock to pick the scanty blade,
Those fenceless fields the sons of wealth divide,
And even the bare-worn common is denied.
If to the city sped, what waits him there?
[16] To see profusion that he must not share;
To see ten thousand baneful arts combin'd
To pamper luxury, and thin mankind;
To see those joys the sons of pleasure know
Extorted from his fellow-creature's woe.

15 *And while*] 'Sinks the poor babe, without a hand to save.' *Roscoe's Nurse*, p. 69.

16 *To see profusion*] 'He only guards those luxuries he is not fated to share.' — *An. Nat.* iv. p. 43.

Here while the courtier glitters in brocade,
There the pale artist plies the sickly trade;
Here while the proud their long-drawn pomps
display,
There the black gibbet glooms beside the way.
The dome where Pleasure holds her midnight reign,
Here, richly deck'd, admits the gorgeous train;
Tumultuous grandeur crowds the blazing square,
The rattling chariots clash, the torches glare.
Sure scenes like these no troubles e'er annoy!
Sure these denote one universal joy! [eyes
Are these thy serious thoughts? Ah! turn thine
[17] Where the poor houseless shivering female lies.
She once, perhaps, in village plenty blest,
Has wept at tales of innocence distrest;
Her modest looks the cottage might adorn,
Sweet as the primrose peeps beneath the thorn:
Now lost to all, her friends, her virtue fled,
Near her betrayer's door she lays her head,
And, pinch'd with cold, and shrinking from the
shower,
With heavy heart deplores that luckless hour,
When idly first, ambitious of the town,
She left her wheel, and robes of country brown.

17 'These poor shivering females have once seen happier days, and been flattered into beauty. They have been prostituted to the gay and luxurious villain, and now turned out to meet the severity of the winter. Perhaps now lying at the doors of their betrayers, they sue to wretches whose hearts are insensible.' — *Cit. of the World*, ii. 211. See also *The Bee. The City Night Piece*, p. 126.

Do thine, sweet Auburn, thine, the loveliest
train,
Do thy fair tribes participate her pain?
Even now, perhaps, by cold and hunger led,
At proud men's doors they ask a little bread.

Ah, no! To distant climes, a dreary scene,
Where half the convex world intrudes between,
Through torrid tracts with fainting steps they go,
Where wild Altama* murmurs to their woe.
Far different there from all that charm'd before,
The various terrors of that horrid shore:
Those blazing suns that dart a downward ray,
And fiercely shed intolerable day;
Those matted woods where birds forget to sing,
But silent bats in drowsy clusters cling;
Those pois'nous fields with rank luxuriance crown'd,
Where the dark scorpion gathers death around;
Where at each step the stranger fears to wake
The rattling terrors of the vengeful snake;
[18] Where crouching tigers wait their hapless prey,
And savage men more murderous still than they;
While oft in whirls the mad tornado flies,
Mingling the ravag'd landscape with the skies.
Far different these from every former scene,
The cooling brook, the grassy-vested green,

* [The Altamaha, in Georgia, is referred to.]

18 'To savage beasts who on the weaker prey,
Or human savages more wild than they!'
Sir W. Temple. v. Nicholls' Poems, ii. 80.

The breezy covert of the warbling grove,
[19] That only shelter'd thefts of harmless love

Good Heaven! what sorrows gloom'd that parting day
That call'd them from their native walks away;
When the poor exiles, every pleasure past,
[20] Hung round the bowers, and fondly look'd their last,
And took a long farewell, and wish'd in vain
For seats like these beyond the western main;
And, shuddering still to face the distant deep,
Return'd and wept, and still return'd to weep!
[21] The good old sire the first prepar'd to go
To new-found worlds, and wept for others' woe;
But for himself, in conscious virtue brave,
He only wish'd for worlds beyond the grave.

19 *That only*] ——— 'Thy shady groves
Only relieve the heats, and cover loves,
Sheltering no other thefts or cruelties.'
v. Nicholls' Poems, ii. 80.
'Often in amorous thefts of lawless love!'
v. Nicholls' Poems, ii. 278.

20 Compare *Quinctiliani Declam.* xiii. p. 272. 'Quod cives pascebat, nunc divitis unius hortus est. Æquatæ solo villæ, et excisa patria sacra, et cum conjugibus, parvisque liberis, respectantes patrium larem migraverunt veteres coloni,' &c.

21 *good old sire*] 'The good old sire!'
v. Dryden's Ovid, vol. iii. p. 302.
And, 'The good old sire, unconscious of decay!
The modest matron clad in homespun gray.'
v Threnod. August.

His lovely daughter, lovelier in her tears,
The fond companion of his helpless years,
Silent went next, neglectful of her charms,
And left a lover's for a father's arms.
With louder plaints the mother spoke her woes,
And bless'd the cot where every pleasure rose;
And kiss'd her thoughtless babes with many a tear,
And clasp'd them close, in sorrow doubly dear;
Whilst her fond husband strove to lend relief
In all the silent manliness of grief.

O Luxury! thou curst by Heaven's decree,
How ill exchang'd are things like these for thee!
How do thy potions, with insidious joy,
Diffuse their pleasures only to destroy!
Kingdoms by thee, to sickly greatness grown,
Boast of a florid vigour not their own.
At every draught more large and large they grow,
A bloated mass of rank unwieldy woe;
Till sapp'd their strength, and every part unsound,
Down, down they sink, and spread a ruin round.

Even now the devastation is begun,
And half the business of destruction done;
Even now, methinks, as pondering here I stand,
I see the rural virtues leave the land.
Down where yon anchoring vessel spreads the sail
That idly waiting flaps with every gale,
Downward they move, a melancholy band,
Pass from the shore, and darken all the strand.

Contented toil, and hospitable care,
And kind connubial tenderness, are there;
And piety with wishes plac'd above,
And steady loyalty, and faithful love.
And thou, sweet Poetry, thou loveliest maid,
Still first to fly where sensual joys invade;
Unfit, in these degenerate times of shame,
To catch the heart, or strike for honest fame;
Dear charming nymph, neglected and decried,
My shame in crowds, my solitary pride;
Thou source of all my bliss and all my woe,
That found'st me poor at first, and keep'st me so;
Thou guide, by which the nobler arts excel,
Thou nurse of every virtue, fare thee well!
Farewell; and oh! where'er thy voice be tried,
On Torno's cliffs, or Pambamarca's side,[22]
Whether where equinoctial fervours glow,
Or winter wraps the polar world in snow,
Still let thy voice, prevailing over time,
Redress the rigours of the inclement clime;
Aid slighted truth with thy persuasive strain;
Teach erring man to spurn the rage of gain;
Teach him, that states of native strength possest,
Though very poor, may still be very blest;
That trade's proud empire hastes to swift decay,
As ocean sweeps the labour'd mole away;

[22] The river Tornea falls into the Gulf of Bothnia. Pam bamarca is a mountain near Quito.—P. C.

While self-dependent power can time defy,
As rocks resist the billows and the sky.[23]

[23] "Dr. Johnson favoured me at the same time by marking the lines which he furnished to Goldsmith's Deserted Village, which are only the last four." Boswell, by Croker, p. 174.—P. C.

EDWIN AND ANGELINA.

(THE HERMIT.)

A BALLAD.

"Written 1764, and privately printed the same year, 'for the amusement of the Countess of Northumberland,'—and first published in 1766, in The Vicar of Wakefield, vol. i. pp. 70–77. The text here given is that of The Vicar of Wakefield, compared with the poem as printed by Goldsmith in 1767, in his Poems for Young Ladies, and the edition of Goldsmith's Miscellaneous Works, published in 1801, under the unacknowledged superintendence of Bishop Perry."—CUNNINGHAM.

THE FOLLOWING LETTER,

ADDRESSED TO THE PRINTER OF THE ST. JAMES'S CHRONICLE, APPEARED IN THAT PAPER IN JULY, M.DCC.LXVII.

SIR, — As there is nothing I dislike so much as newspaper controversy, particularly upon trifles, permit me to be as concise as possible in informing a correspondent of yours, that I recommended Blainville's Travels, because I thought the book was a good one; and I think so still. I said, I was told by the bookseller that it was then first published; but in that, it seems, I was misinformed, and my reading was not extensive enough to set me right.

Another correspondent of yours accuses me of having taken a ballad, I published some time ago, from one[1] by the ingenious Mr. Percy. I do not think there is any great resemblance between the two pieces in question. If there be any, his ballad is taken from mine. I read it to Mr. Percy some years ago; and he (as we both

[1] 'The Friar of Orders Gray.' — *Reliq. of Anc. Poetry*, vol. i. p. 243.

considered these things as trifles at best) told me with his usual good humour, the next time I saw him, that he had taken my plan to form the fragments of Shakespeare into a ballad of his own. He then read me his little Cento, if I may so call it, and I highly approved it. Such petty anecdotes as these are scarcely worth printing; and, were it not for the busy disposition of some of your correspondents, the public should never have known that he owes me the hint of his ballad, or that I am obliged to his friendship and learning for communications of a much more important nature.

I am, Sir, yours, &c.

Oliver Goldsmith.

EDWIN AND ANGELINA.[1]

'TURN, gentle Hermit of the dale,
And guide my lonely way
To where yon taper cheers the vale
With hospitable ray.

'For here forlorn and lost I tread,
With fainting steps and slow;
Where wilds, immeasurably spread,
Seem lengthening as I go.'

'Forbear, my son,' the Hermit cries,
'To tempt the dangerous gloom;
For yonder faithless phantom flies
To lure thee to thy doom.

'Here to the houseless child of want
My door is open still;
And though my portion is but scant,
I give it with good will.

'Then turn to-night, and freely share
Whate'er my cell bestows;
My rushy couch and frugal fare,
My blessing and repose.

[1] See the Vicar of Wakefield, cap. viii.

'No flocks that range the valley free
To slaughter I condemn;
Taught by that Power that pities me,
I learn to pity them:

'But from the mountain's grassy side
A guiltless feast I bring;
A scrip with herbs and fruits supplied,
And water from the spring.

'Then, pilgrim, turn, thy cares forego;
All earth-born cares are wrong:
[2] Man wants but little here below,
Nor wants that little long.'

Soft as the dew from heaven descends,
His gentle accents fell:
The modest stranger lowly bends,
And follows to the cell.

Far in a wilderness obscure
The lonely mansion lay;
A refuge to the neighbouring poor,
And strangers led astray.

No stores beneath its humble thatch
Requir'd a master's care:

[2] "The running brook, the herbs of the field, can amply satisfy nature; man wants but little, nor that little long."—*The Citizen of the World*, Letter lxvii.—P. C.

'Man wants but little, nor that little long.'
Young's Night 4th.

The wicket, opening with a latch,
  Receiv'd the harmless pair.

And now, when busy crowds retire
  To take their evening rest,
The Hermit trimm'd his little fire,
  And cheer'd his pensive guest;

And spread his vegetable store,
  And gaily prest and smil'd;
And, skill'd in legendary lore,
  The lingering hours beguil'd.

Around, in sympathetic mirth,
  Its tricks the kitten tries;
The cricket chirrups in the hearth;
  The crackling fagot flies.

But nothing could a charm impart
  To soothe the stranger's woe;
For grief was heavy at his heart,
  And tears began to flow.

His rising cares the Hermit spied,
  With answering care opprest:
'And whence, unhappy youth,' he cried,
  'The sorrows of thy breast?

'From better habitations spurn'd,
  Reluctant dost thou rove?
Or grieve for friendship unreturn'd,
  Or unregarded love?

'Alas! the joys that fortune brings
Are trifling, and decay;
And those who prize the paltry things,
More trifling still than they.

'And what is friendship but a name,
A charm that lulls to sleep;
A shade that follows wealth or fame,
But leaves the wretch to weep?

'And love is still an emptier sound,
The modern fair-one's jest;
On earth unseen, or only found
To warm the turtle's nest.

'For shame, fond youth! thy sorrows hush,
And spurn the sex,' he said;
But, while he spoke, a rising blush
His lovelorn guest betray'd.

Surpris'd, he sees new beauties rise,
Swift mantling to the view;
Like colours o'er the morning skies,
As bright, as transient too.

The bashful look, the rising breast,
Alternate spread alarms:
The lovely stranger stands confest
A maid in all her charms.

'And, ah! forgive a stranger rude,
  A wretch forlorn,' she cried;
'Whose feet unhallow'd thus intrude
  Where heaven and you reside.

'But let a maid thy pity share,
  Whom love has taught to stray;
Who seeks for rest, but finds despair
  Companion of her way.

'My father liv'd beside the Tyne,
  A wealthy lord was he,
And all his wealth was mark'd as mine;
  He had but only me.

'To win me from his tender arms,
  Unnumber'd suitors came;
Who prais'd me for imputed charms,
  And felt, or feign'd, a flame.

'Each hour a mercenary crowd
  With richest proffers strove:
Among the rest young Edwin bow'd,
  But never talk'd of love.

'In humble, simplest habit clad,
  No wealth or power had he;
Wisdom and worth were all he had,
  But these were all to me.

'[8] And when beside me in the dale
He caroll'd lays of love,
His breath lent fragrance to the gale,
And music to the grove.

'The blossom opening to the day,
The dews of heaven refin'd,
Could nought of purity display
To emulate his mind.

'The dew, the blossom on the tree,
With charms inconstant shine;
Their charms were his, but, woe to me
Their constancy was mine.

'For still I tried each fickle art,
Importunate and vain;
And while his passion touch'd my heart,
I triumph'd in his pain:

'Till, quite dejected with my scorn,
He left me to my pride;
And sought a solitude forlorn,
In secret, where he died.

'But mine the sorrow, mine the fault,
And well my life shall pay;
I'll seek the solitude he sought,
And stretch me where he lay.

[8] *And when beside me*] This stanza communicated by Richard Archdall, Esq to whom it was given by Goldsmith.

'And there forlorn, despairing, hid,
I'll lay me down and die;
'Twas so for me that Edwin did,
And so for him will I.'

'Forbid it, Heaven!' the Hermit cried,
And clasp'd her to his breast:
The wondering fair one turn'd to chide, —
'Twas Edwin's self that prest.

'Turn, Angelina, ever dear,
My charmer, turn to see
Thy own, thy long-lost Edwin here,
Restor'd to love and thee.

'Thus let me hold thee to my heart,
And every care resign:
And shall we never, never part,
My life — my all that's mine?

'No, never from this hour to part,
We'll live and love so true:
The sigh that rends thy constant heart
Shall break thy Edwin's too.'

[4] RAIMOND ET ANGELINE.

'ENTENS ma voix gémissante,
Habitant de ces vallons!
Guide ma marche tremblante,
Qui se perd dans les buissons.

[4] From 'Les deux Habitants de Lozanne.' See *Monthly Review*, Sept. 1797, and *European Magazine*, 1802.

N'est-il pas quelque chaumière,
  Dans le fond de ce réduit,
Où je vois une lumière
  Percer l'ombre de la nuit.'

'Mon fils,' dit le solitaire,
  'Crains ce feu qui te séduit;
C'est une vapeur légère,
  Elle égare qui le suit.
Viens dans ma cellule obscure:
  Je l'offrirai de bon cœur,
Mon pain noir, ma couche dure,
  Mon repos et mon bonheur.'

Ces accens faisant sourire
  Le voyageur attendri,
Un secret penchant l'attire
  Vers le bienfaisant abri:
Un toit de chaume le couvre,
  Et l'hermite hospitalier
Pause au loquet qui les ouvre
  L'humble porte du foyer.

Devant lui son chien folâtre,
  Et partage sa gaîté;
Le grillon chante dans l'atre,
  Etincelant de clarté.
Mais hélas! rien n'a de charmes
  Pour son hôte malheureux;
Rien ne peut tenir les larmes
  Qui s'échappent de ses yeux.

L'hermite voit sa tristesse,
  Et voudroit la soulager,
D'où vient l'ennui qui te presse?'
  Dit-il au jeune étranger.
'Est-ce une amitié trahie,
  Est-ce un amour dédaigné?
Ou la misère ennemie
  Qui te rende infortuné?

'Hélas! tous les biens du monde
Sont peu dignes de nos vœux;
Et l'insensé qui s'en confonde
Est plus méprisable qu'eux.
L'amitié, s'il en est une,
N'est qu'une fantôme imposteur,
Une voix qui suit la fortune,
Et s'éloigne du malheur.

'L'amour est plus vain encore,
C'est un éclat emprunté;
Un nom faux dont se décore
L'ambitieuse beauté;
On ne voit l'amour fidelle,
S'il daigne quitter les cieux,
Qu'en aide de la tourterelle
Qu'il échauffe de ses feux.

'Va, crois-moi, deviens plus sage,
Méprise un sexe trompeur;'—
L'hôte, ému de ce langage,
S'embellit par sa rougeur.
Son front où la candeur brille,
Les yeux, sa bouche, et son sein,
Font reconnoître une belle
Dans la charmante pélerin.

'Voyez,' dit-elle, 'une amante,
Qui cherche en vain le repos;
Voyez une fille errante,
Dont l'amour cause les maux.
Long-tems, superbe, inhumaine,
Ignorant la prix d'un cœur,
A fuir une tendre chaine
J'avois mit tout mon bonheur.

'Dans cette faute volage
Qui renoît grossir mon cœur,
Raimond m'offrit son hommage,
Sans m'oser parler d'amour.

Le ciel étoit dans son âme;
  Le lis qui s'ouvre au matin
N'est plus pur que la flamme
  Que j'allumois dans son sein.

'Sa naissance étoit commune,
  Raimond, sans bien, sans emploi,
N'avoit qu'un cœur pour fortune,
  Mais ce cœur fut tout à moi.
Las de mon ingratitude,
  Il me quitte pour toujours,
Et dans une solitude
  Il alla finir ses jours.

'Maintenant désespérée,
  Victime d'un fol orgueil,
Je m'en vais dans la contrée
  Qui renferme son cercueil;
Là je n'ai plus d'autre envie
  Que de mourir à ses pieds,
Payant des jours de ma vie
  Ceux qu'il m'a sacrifiés.'

'Non, non,' dit Raimond lui-même,
  En la serrant dans ses bras;
'Non, celui qui ton cœur aime
  N'a point subi le trépas.
Regarde, O mon Angéline!
  Cher object de mes regrets,
Regarde, O fille divine!
  Cet amant que tu pleurais.'

Angéline est dans l'ivresse,
  Sa transport coupe sa voix;
'Ah!' dit-elle avec tendresse,
  'Est-ce toi que je revois?
Vivons, mourons, l'un pour l'autre;
  Il ne faut plus vous quittor;
Qu'un seul trépas soit le nôtre;
  Qu'aurons nous à regretter?'

THE

HAUNCH OF VENISON.

A POETICAL EPISTLE TO LORD CLARE.

"The Haunch of Venison," written, it is believed, in 1771, was first published in 1776, two years after Goldsmith's death. It is here printed from the second edition, 1776, containing ten additional lines and numerous emendations, said to be taken from the *last* transcript of its author.—CUNNINGHAM.

THE Lord Clare to whom this poem is addressed, was Robert Nugent of Carlanstown, Westmeath, created, 1766, Viscount Clare, and, in 1776, Earl Nugent. He died at Dublin, in 1788, and was buried at Gosfield, in Essex. He was a poet, and a stanza from his Ode to Pulteney has been quoted by Gibbon in his character of Brutus:—

"What! though the good, the brave, the wise,
With adverse force undaunted rise
To break th' eternal doom;
Though Cato liv'd, though Tully spoke,
Though Brutus dealt the godlike stroke,—
Yet perished fatal Rome."

He was thrice married; was a big, jovial, voluptuous Irishman, with a loud voice, a strong Irish accent, and a ready, though coarse wit.—CUNNINGHAM.

"The leading idea of 'Haunch of Venison' is taken from Boileau's third Satire, (which itself was no doubt suggested by Horace's raillery of the banquet of Nasidienus;) and two or three of the passages which one would *à priori* have pronounced the most original and natural, are closely copied from the French poet."—CROKER.

THE HAUNCH OF VENISON

THANKS, my lord, for your venison, for finer or fatter
Never rang'd in a forest, or smok'd in a platter;
The haunch was a picture for painters to study,
[a] The fat was so white, and the lean was so ruddy;
Though my stomach was sharp, I could scarce help regretting
To spoil such a delicate picture by eating;
I had thoughts, in my chambers to place it in view,
To be shown to my friends as a piece of virtù;
As in some Irish houses, where things are so-so,
One gammon of bacon hangs up for a show;
But, for eating a rasher of what they take pride in,
They'd as soon think of eating the pan it is fried in.
But hold,—let me pause,—don't I hear you pronounce,
This tale of the bacon a damnable bounce?
Well, suppose it a bounce—sure a poet may try,
By a bounce, now and then, to get courage to fly.
But, my lord, it's no bounce: I protest in my turn
It's a truth, and your lordship may ask Mr. Byrne.[1]

[1] Lord Clare's nephew.

VARIATIONS (First Edition.)

[a] The white was so white, and the red was so ruddy!

To go on with my tale: as I gaz'd on the haunch,
I thought of a friend that was trusty and staunch,
So I cut it, and sent it to Reynolds undrest,
To paint it, or eat it, just as he lik'd best.
Of the neck and the breast I had next to dispose;
'Twas a neck and a breast that might rival Monroe's:
But in parting with these I was puzzled again,
With the how, and the who, and the where, and the when.
[b] There's Howard, and Coley, and H—rth, and Hiff,
I think they love venison — I know they love beef.
There's my countryman Higgins — oh! let him alone
For making a blunder, or picking a bone.
But hang it—to poets [c]who seldom can eat,
Your very good mutton 's a very good treat;
Such dainties to them [d]their health it might hurt,
It's like sending them ruffles, when wanting a shirt.

While thus I debated, in reverie center'd
An acquaintance, a friend as he call'd himself, enter'd;
[e] An under-bred, fine spoken fellow was he,
And he smil'd as he look'd at the venison and me.

VARIATIONS.

b There's Coley, and Williams, and Howard, and Hiff—,

c that

d ——— It would look like a flirt,
Like sending 'em ruffles ——

e A fine spoken customhouse officer he,
Who smil'd as he gaz'd on the venison and me.

'What have we got here? Why, this is good eating!
Your own, I suppose — or is it in waiting?'
'Why, whose should it be?' cried I with a flounce:
'I get these things often;' — but that was a bounce:
'Some lords, my acquaintance, that settle the nation,
Are pleas'd to be kind — but I hate ostentation.'

'If that be the case, then,' cried he, very gay,
'I'm glad I have taken this house in my way.
To-morrow you take a poor dinner with me;
No words — I insist on't — precisely at three:
We'll have Johnson and Burke, all the wits will
be there;
My acquaintance is slight, or I'd ask my lord Clare.
And now that I think on't, as I am a sinner!
We wanted this venison to [f] make out the dinner.
What say you — a pasty? — it shall, and it must,
And my wife, little Kitty, is famous for crust.
Here, porter — this venison with me to Mile-end;
[g] No stirring — I beg — my dear friend — my dear
friend!' [wind,
Thus, [h] snatching his hat, he brush'd off like the
And the porter and eatables follow'd behind.

Left alone to reflect, having emptied my shelf,

VARIATIONS.

f ——— make up the dinner,
I'll take no denial — you shall, and you must.

g No words, my dear Goldsmith! my very good friend!

h seizing

And 'nobody with me at sea but myself;'[2]
Tho' I could not help thinking my gentleman hasty,
Yet Johnson and Burke, and a good venison pasty,
Were things that I never dislik'd in my life,
Though clogg'd with a coxcomb, and Kitty his wife.
So next day in due splendour to make my approach,
I drove to his door in my own hackney-coach.

When come to the place where we all were to dine
(A chair-lumber'd closet just twelve feet by nine),
My friend bade me welcome, but struck me quite dumb
With tidings that Johnson and Burke [i] would not come;
'For I knew it,' he cried, 'both eternally fail,
The one [k] with his speeches, and t'other with Thrale;
But no matter, I'll warrant we'll make up the party,
With two full as clever, and ten times as hearty.
The one is a Scotchman, the other a Jew;
[l] They're both of them merry, and authors like you;
The one writes the Snarler, the other the Scourge;
Some thinks he writes Cinna: he owns to Panurge.'
While thus he describ'd them by trade and by name,
They enter'd, and dinner was serv'd as they came.

2 See the letters that passed between his Royal Highness Henry Duke of Cumberland, and Lady Grosvenor,—12mo, 1769.

VARIATIONS.

i could

k ——— at the house,
But, I warrant for me, we shall make up the party.

l Who dabble and write in the papers—like you.

At the top, a fried liver and bacon were seen;
At the bottom was tripe, in a swingeing tureen;
At the sides there was spinage and pudding made hot;
In the middle a place where the [m] pasty—was not.
Now, my lord, as for tripe, it's my utter aversion,
And your bacon I hate like a Turk or a Persian;
So there I sat stuck, like a horse in a pound,
While the bacon and liver went merrily round:
But what vex'd me most was that damn'd Scottish rogue,
With his long-winded speeches, his smiles and his brogue,
And, 'Madam,' quoth he, 'may this bit be my poison.
[n] A prettier dinner I never set eyes on;
Pray a slice of your liver, though, may I be curst,
But I've eat of your tripe till I'm ready to burst.'
[o] 'The tripe!' quoth the Jew, with his chocolate cheek,
'I could dine on this tripe seven days in a week:
I like these here dinners, so pretty and small;
But your friend there, the doctor, eats nothing at all.'
'O—ho!' quoth my friend, 'he'll come on in a trice,
He's keeping a corner for something that's nice:

VARIATIONS.

[m] venison

[n] If a prettier dinner I ever set eyes on!

[o] 'Your tripe!' quoth the Jew, 'If the truth I may speak,
I could eat of this tripe seven days in the week!'

[p] There's a pasty'—'A pasty!' repeated the Jew;
I don't care if I keep a corner for 't too.'
'What the de'il, mon, a pasty!' re-echoed the Scot;
'Though splitting, I'll still keep a corner for that.'
'We'll all keep a corner,' the lady cried out;
'We'll all keep a corner,' was echo'd about.
While thus we resolv'd, and the pasty delay'd,
With looks [q] that quite petrified, enter'd the maid:
A visage so sad, and so pale with affright,
Wak'd Priam in drawing his curtains by night.
But [r] we quickly found out,—for who could mistake her?—
That she came with some terrible news from the baker:
And so it fell out, for that negligent sloven
Had shut out the pasty on shutting his oven.
Sad Philomel thus—but let similes drop—
And now that I think on't, the story may stop.
To be plain, my good lord, it's but labour misplac'd
To send such good verses to one of your taste;
You've got an odd something—a kind of discerning—
A relish—a taste—sicken'd over by learning;
At least, it's your temper, as very well known,
That you think very slightly of all that's your own:
So, perhaps, in your habits of thinking amiss,
You may make a mistake, and think slightly of this.

VARIATIONS.

p 'There's a pasty.' 'A pasty!' returned the Scot;
'I don't care if I keep a corner for thot.'

q looks quite astonishing

r too soon we

RETALIATION.

A POEM.

"As the cause of writing the following printed poem called Retaliation, has not yet been fully explained, a person concerned in the business begs leave to give the following just and minute account of the whole affair.

At a meeting[1] of a company of gentlemen, who were well known to each other, and diverting themselves, among many other things, with the peculiar oddities of Dr. Goldsmith, who never would allow a superior in any art, from writing poetry down to dancing a hornpipe, the Dr. with great eagerness insisted upon trying his epigrammatic powers with Mr. Garrick, and each of them was to write the other's epitaph. Mr. Garrick immediately said that his epitaph was finished, and spoke the following distich extempore:

Here lies Nolly Goldsmith, for shortness call'd Noll,
Who wrote like an angel, but talk'd like poor Poll.

Goldsmith, upon the company's laughing very heartily, grew very thoughtful, and either would not, or could not, write any thing at that time; however, he went to work, and some weeks after produced the following printed poem called Retaliation, which has been much admired, and gone through several editions. The publick in general have been mistaken

[1] At the St. James's Coffee-House in St. James's Street. See Art. 'James's (St.) Coffee House,' in Cunningham's Hand-Book of London, 2d ed. 1850, p. 254.

in imagining that this poem was written in anger by the Doctor; it was just the contrary; the whole on all sides was done with the greatest good humour; and the following poems in manuscript were written by several of the gentlemen on purpose to provoke the Doctor to an answer, which came forth at last with great credit to him in Retaliation."—D. GARRICK, [MS.]

"For this highly interesting account, (now first printed, or even referred to by any biographer or editor of Goldsmith,) I am indebted to my friend Mr. George Daniel, of Islington, who allowed me to transcribe it from the original in Garrick's own handwriting discovered among the Garrick papers, and evidently designed as a preface to a collected edition of the poems which grew out of Goldsmith's trying his epigrammatic powers with Garrick. I may observe also that Garrick's epitaph or distich on Goldsmith is (through this very paper) for the first time printed as it was spoken by its author.

"Retaliation was the last work of Goldsmith, and a posthumous publication—appearing for the first time on the 18th or April, 1774."

CUNNINGHAM.

RETALIATION.

Of old, when Scarron his companions invited,
Each guest brought his dish, and the feast was
united;
If our [1] landlord supplies us with beef and with fish,
Let each guest bring himself, and he brings the
best dish:
Our [2] dean shall be venison, just fresh from the
plains; [brains;
Our [3] Burke shall be tongue, with the garnish of
Our [4] Will shall be wildfowl, of excellent flavour,
And [5] Dick with his pepper shall heighten the
savour: [tain,
Our [6] Cumberland's sweetbread its place shall ob-

1 The master of the St. James's Coffee-house, where the Doctor, and the friends he has characterised in this poem, occasionally dined.

2 Doctor Barnard, Dean of Derry, in Ireland.

3 Mr. Edmund Burke.

4 Mr. William Burke, late secretary to General Conway, and member for Bedwin.

5 Mr. Richard Burke, collector of Grenada.

6 Mr. Richard Cumberland, author of the 'West Indian,' 'Fashionable Lover,' 'The Brothers,' and other dramatic pieces.

And [7] Douglas is pudding, substantial and plain;
Our [8] Garrick 's a salad; for in him we see
Oil, vinegar, sugar, and saltness agree:
To make out the dinner, full certain I am
That [9] Ridge is anchovy, and [10] Reynolds is lamb;
That [11] Hickey 's a capon, and, by the same rule,
Magnanimous Goldsmith a gooseberry fool.
At a dinner so various, at such a repast,
Who 'd not be a glutton, and stick to the last?
Here, waiter, more wine! let me sit while I'm able,
Till all my companions sink under the table;
Then, with chaos and blunders encircling my head,
Let me ponder, and tell what I think of the dead.

[12] Here lies the good dean,[13] reunited to earth,
Who mixt reason with pleasure, and wisdom with mirth:

7 Doctor Douglas, canon of Windsor, an ingenious Scotch gentleman, who has no less distinguished himself as a citizen of the world, than a sound critic, in detecting several literary mistakes (or rather forgeries) of his countrymen; particularly Lauder on Milton, and Bower's History of the Popes.

8 David Garrick, Esq.

9 Counsellor John Ridge, a gentleman belonging to the Irish Bar.

10 Sir Joshua Reynolds.

11 An eminent attorney, whose hospitality and good humour acquired him in his club the title of 'honest Tom Hickey.'

12 *Here lies the good dean*] See a poem by Dean Barnard to Sir J. Reynolds, in Northcote's Life of Reynolds, p. 130.

13 Vide page 77.

If he had any faults, he has left us in doubt,
At least in six weeks I could not find 'em out;
Yet some have declar'd, and it can't be denied 'em,
That slyboots was cursedly cunning to hide 'em.

Here lies our good [14] Edmund, whose genius was such,
We scarcely can praise it or blame it too much;
Who, born for the universe, narrow'd his mind,
And to party gave up what was meant for mankind.
Though fraught with all learning, yet straining his throat
To persuade [15] Tommy Townshend to lend him a vote;
Who, too deep for his hearers, still went on refining,
And thought of convincing, while they thought of dining:
Though equal to all things, for all things unfit;
Too nice for a statesman, too proud for a wit;
For a patriot too cool; for a drudge disobedient;
And too fond of the *right* to pursue the *expedient.*
In short, 'twas his fate, unemploy'd or in place, sir,
To eat mutton cold, and cut blocks with a razor.

Here lies honest [16] William, whose heart was a mint,
While the owner ne'er knew half the good that was in't;

[14] Vide page 77.
[15] Mr. T. Townshend, member for Whitchurch.—See *H. Walpole's Letter to Lord Hertford,* p. 6.
[16] Vide page 77.

The pupil of impulse, it forc'd him along,
His conduct still right, with his argument wrong;
Still aiming at honour, yet fearing to roam,
The coachman was tipsy, the chariot drove home:
Would you ask for his merits? alas! he had none;
What was good was spontaneous, his faults were
his own.

Here lies honest Richard, whose fate I must
sigh at;
Alas that such frolic should now be so quiet!
What spirits were his! what wit and what whim,
[17] Now breaking a jest, and now breaking a limb;
Now wrangling and grumbling to keep up the ball,
Now teasing and vexing, yet laughing at all!
In short, so provoking a devil was Dick,
That we wish'd him full ten times a day at Old
Nick;
But, missing his mirth and agreeable vein,
As often we wish'd to have Dick back again.

Here [18] Cumberland lies, having acted his parts,
The Terence of England, the mender of hearts;
A flattering painter, who made it his care
To draw men as they ought to be, not as they are.

17 Mr. Richard Burke; vide page 77. This gentleman having slightly fractured one of his arms and legs, at different times, the doctor has rallied him on those accidents, as a kind of retributive justice for breaking his jests upon other people.

18 Vide p. 77.

His gallants are all faultless, his women divine,
And comedy wonders at being so fine;
Like a tragedy queen he has dizen'd her out,
Or rather like tragedy giving a rout.
His fools have their follies so lost in a crowd
Of virtues and feelings, that folly grows proud;
And coxcombs, alike in their failings alone,
Adopting his portraits, are pleas'd with their own.
Say, where has our poet this malady caught,
Or wherefore his characters thus without fault?
Say, was it that vainly directing his view
To find out men's virtues, and finding them few,
Quite sick of pursuing each troublesome elf,
He grew lazy at last, and drew from himself?

Here [19] Douglas retires from his toils to relax,
The scourge of impostors, the terror of quacks:
Come, all ye quack bards, and ye quacking di-
vines,
Come, and dance on the spot where your tyrant
reclines:
When satire and censure encircled his throne,
I fear'd for your safety, I fear'd for my own;
But now he is gone, and we want a detector,
Our [20] Dodds shall be pious, our [21] Kenricks shall
lecture;

19 Vide p. 78.

20 The Rev. Dr. Dodd.

21 Dr. Kenrick, who read lectures at the Devil Tavern, under the title of 'The School of Shakespeare.'

[22] Macpherson write bombast, and call it a style;
Our [23] Townshend make speeches, and I shall compile;
New [24] Lauders and Bowers the Tweed shall cross over,
No countryman living their tricks to discover;
Detection her taper shall quench to a spark,
[25] And Scotchman meet Scotchman, and cheat in the dark.

Here lies [26] David Garrick, describe me who can,
An abridgment of all that was pleasant in man;
As an actor, confest without rival to shine;
As a wit, if not first, in the very first line:
Yet, with talents like these, and an excellent heart,
The man had his failings, a dupe to his art.
Like an ill-judging beauty, his colours he spread,
And beplaster'd with rouge his own natural red.
On the stage he was natural, simple, affecting;
'Twas only that when he was off, he was acting.
With no reason on earth to go out of his way,
He turn'd and he varied full ten times a day:
Though secure of our hearts, yet confoundedly sick
If they were not his own by finessing and trick.
He cast off his friends, as a huntsman his pack;
For he knew, when he pleas'd, he could whistle them back.

[22] James Macpherson, Esq. who lately, from the mere force of his style, wrote down the first poet of all antiquity.

[23] Vide page 79. [24] Vide page 78. [26] Vide page 78.

[25] 'And gods meet gods, and jostle in the dark.'
See *Farquhar's Love in a Bottle*, vol. i. p. 150.

Of praise a mere glutton, he swallow'd what came,
And the puff of a dunce he mistook it for fame;
Till his relish grown callous, almost to disease,
Who pepper'd the highest was surest to please.
But let us be candid, and speak out our mind,
If dunces applauded, he paid them in kind.
Ye [27] Kenricks, ye [28] Kellys, and [29] Woodfalls so grave,
What a commerce was yours, while you got and you gave!
How did Grub-street re-echo the shouts that you rais'd,
While he was be-Roscius'd and you were beprais'd!
But peace to his spirit, wherever it flies,
To act as an angel, and mix with the skies.
Those poets who owe their best fame to his skill,
Shall still be his flatterers, go where he will;
Old Shakespeare receive him with praise and with love,
And Beaumonts and Bens be his Kellys above.[30]

27 Vide page 81.

28 Mr. Hugh Kelly, author of 'False Delicacy,' 'Word to the Wise,' 'Clementina,' 'School for Wives,' &c. &c.

29 Mr. William Woodfall, printer of the Morning Chronicle.

30 The following poems, by Mr. Garrick, may in some measure account for the severity exercised by Dr. Goldsmith in respect to that gentleman: —

JUPITER AND MERCURY.

A FABLE.

Here, Hermes, says Jove, who with nectar was mellow,
Go fetch me some clay, — I will make an odd fellow.
Right and wrong shall be jumbled, much gold and some dross;
Without cause be he pleas'd, without cause be he cross:

Here [31] Hickey reclines, a most blunt, pleasant
creature,
And slander itself must allow him good nature;
He cherish'd his friend, and he relish'd a bumper;
Yet one fault he had, and that one was a thumper.
Perhaps you may ask if the man was a miser:
I answer, No, no, for he always was wiser.
Too courteous, perhaps, or obligingly flat?
His very worst foe can't accuse him of that.
Perhaps he confided in men as they go,
And so was too foolishly honest? Ah, no!

Be sure, as I work, to throw in contradictions;
A great love of truth, yet a mind turn'd to fictions.
Now mix these ingredients, which, warm'd in the baking,
Turn to learning and gaming, religion and raking.
With the love of a wench, let his writings be chaste;
Tip his tongue with strange matter, his pen with fine taste.
That the rake and the poet o'er all may prevail,
Set fire to the head, and set fire to the tail.
For the joy of each sex, on the world I'll bestow it,
This scholar, rake, Christian, dupe, gamester, and poet.
Though a mixture so odd, he shall merit great fame,
And among brother mortals be Goldsmith his name.
When on earth this strange meteor no more shall appear,
You, Hermes, shall fetch him to make us sport here.

ON DR. GOLDSMITH'S CHARACTERISTICAL COOKERY.

A JEU D'ESPRIT.

Are these the choice dishes the Doctor has sent us?
Is this the great poet whose works so content us?
This Goldsmith's fine feast, who has written fine books?
Heaven sends us good meat, but the devil sends cooks.

---

[31] Vide page 78.

Then what was his failing? come, tell it, and
burn ye:
He was — could he help it? — a special attorney.

Here [82] Reynolds is laid, and, to tell you my mind,
He has not left a wiser or better behind.
His pencil was striking, resistless, and grand;
His manners were gentle, complying, and bland:
Still born to improve us in every part,
His pencil our faces, his manners our heart.
To coxcombs averse, yet most civilly steering,
When they judg'd without skill, he was still hard
of hearing:
When they talk'd of their Raphaels, Correggios,
and stuff,
He shifted his [83] trumpet, and only took snuff.

[82] Vide page 78.

[83] Sir Joshua Reynolds was so remarkably deaf as to be under the necessity of using an ear-trumpet in company.—See La Vie de Le Sage, p. xiii. "Il faisait usage d'un cornet qu'il appeloit son bienfaiteur. Quand je trouve, disoit-il, des visages nouveaux, et que j'espère rencontrer des gens d'esprit, je tire mon cornet; quand ce sont des sots, je le resserre et je les défie de m'ennuyer."

POSTSCRIPT.

AFTER the fourth edition of this poem was printed, the publisher received the following epitaph on Mr. Whitefoord,[34] from a friend of the late Dr. Goldsmith: —

HERE Whitefoord reclines, and deny it who can,
Though he merrily liv'd, he is now a [35] grave man:
Rare compound of oddity, frolic, and fun!
Who relish'd a joke, and rejoic'd in a pun;
Whose temper was generous, open, sincere;
A stranger to flattery, a stranger to fear;
Who scatter'd around wit and humour at will;
Whose daily *bon mots* half a column might fill:
A Scotchman, from pride and from prejudice free;
A scholar, yet surely no pedant was he.

What pity, alas! that so liberal a mind
Should so long be to newspaper essays confin'd!
Who perhaps to the summit of science could soar,
Yet content 'if the table he set in a roar;'
Whose talents to fill any station were fit,
Yet happy if [36] Woodfall confess'd him a wit.

34 Mr. Caleb Whitefoord, author of many humorous essays.

35 Mr. W. was so notorious a punster, that Doctor Goldsmith used to say it was impossible to keep him company, without being infected with the itch of punning.

36 Mr. H. S. Woodfall, printer of the Public Advertiser.

Ye newspaper witlings! ye pert scribbling folks!
Who copied his squibs, and re-echoed his jokes:
Ye tame imitators, ye servile herd, come,
Still follow your master, and visit his tomb:
To deck it, bring with you festoons of the vine,
And copious libations bestow on his shrine;
Then strew all around it (you can do no less)
[87] *Cross readings, ship news*, and *mistakes of the press.*

Merry Whitefoord, farewell! for thy sake I admit
That a Scot may have humour, I had almost said wit:
This debt to thy memory I cannot refuse,
[88] 'Thou best humour'd man with the worst humour'd muse.'

[87] Mr. Whitefoord has frequently indulged the town with humorous pieces under those titles in the Public Advertiser. On C. Whitefoord, see *Smith's Life of Nollekens*, vol. i. p. 338—340. See his poem to Sir Joshua Reynolds, 'Admire not, dear knight,' in Northcote's Life of Reynolds, p. 128.

[88] 'When you and Southern, Moyle, and Congreve meet,
The best good men, with the best natured wit.'
C. Hopkins. v. Nicholls' Col. Poems, ii. p. 207.

THE CAPTIVITY.

AN ORATORIO.

IN THREE ACTS.

"Written in 1764, but never set to music, or even published by its author. It is here printed from the original manuscript, in Goldsmith's handwriting, in the possession of Mr. Murray, of Albemarle Street, compared with the copy printed by Messrs. Prior and Wright, in 1837. I have adopted the most poetical readings of both copies.

"For this Oratorio Goldsmith received at least ten guineas. In Mr. Murray's collection is the following receipt in Goldsmith's handwriting:—

'Received from Mr. Dodsley ten guineas for an Oratorio, which he and Mr. Newbery are to share.

OLIVER GOLDSMITH.'

October 31*st*, 1764.

"Mr. Murray's MS. is the copy sold by Goldsmith to James Dodsley."

P. C.

DRAMATIS PERSONÆ.[1]

FIRST ISRAELITISH PROPHET.
SECOND ISRAELITISH PROPHET.
ISRAELITISH WOMAN.
FIRST CHALDEAN PRIEST.
SECOND CHALDEAN PRIEST.
CHALDEAN WOMAN.
CHORUS OF YOUTHS AND VIRGINS.

SCENE.—*The Banks of the Euphrates, near Babylon*

[1] The *Dramatis Personæ* is not in the MS.

THE CAPTIVITY.

ACT I.

Scene I.—ISRAELITES *sitting on the Banks of the Euphrates.*

First PROPHET.

Recitative.

YE captive tribes, that hourly work and weep,
Where flows Euphrates, murmuring to the deep—
Suspend awhile the task, the tear suspend,
And turn to God, your father and your friend:
Insulted, chain'd, and all the world a foe,
Our God alone is all we boast below.

Chorus of ISRAELITES.

Our God is all we boast below,
To Him we turn our eyes;
And every added weight of woe
Shall make our homage rise.

And though no temple richly drest,
Nor sacrifice is here;
We'll make His temple in our breast,
And offer up a tear.

Recitative.

That strain once more: it bids remembrance rise,
And calls my long-lost country to mine eyes.
Ye fields of Sharon, dress'd in flowery pride;
Ye plains where Jordan rolls its glassy tide;
Ye hills of Lebanon, with cedars crown'd;
Ye Gilead groves, that fling perfumes around:
These hills how sweet! those plains how wondrous fair!
But sweeter still, when Heaven was with us there.

Air.

O Memory, thou fond deceiver!
Still importunate and vain;
To former joys recurring ever,
And turning all the past to pain;

Hence, deceiver, most distressing,
Seek the happy and the free;
They who want each other blessing,
Ever want a friend in thee.[1]

First PROPHET.

Recitative.

Yet, why repine? What, though by bonds confin'd,
Should bonds enslave the vigour of the mind?

[1] *Variation.*—"Thou, like the world, opprest oppressing,
Thy smiles increase the wretch's woe;
And he who wants each other blessing,
In thee must ever find a foe."

Have we not cause for triumph, when we see
Ourselves alone from idol-worship free?
Are not this very day those rites begun,
Where prostrate folly hails the rising sun?
Do not our tyrant lords this day ordain
For superstitious rites and mirth profane?
And should we mourn? Should coward Virtue fly,
When impious Folly rears her front on high?
No; rather let us triumph still the more,
And as our fortune sinks, our wishes soar.

Air.

The triumphs that on vice attend
Shall ever in confusion end;
The good man suffers but to gain,
And every virtue springs from pain:

As aromatic plants bestow
No spicy fragrance while they grow,
But crush'd or trodden to the ground,
Diffuse their balmy sweets around.

Second PROPHET.

Recitative.

But hush, my sons! our tyrant lords are near;
The sound of barbarous mirth offends mine ear;
Triumphant music floats along the vale;
Near, nearer still, it gathers on the gale;
The growing note their near approach declares;—
Desist, my sons, nor mix the strain with theirs.

Enter CHALDEAN PRIESTS, *attended.*

First PRIEST.

Air.

Come on, my companions, the triumph display;
Let rapture the minutes employ;
The sun calls us out on this festival day,
And our monarch partakes of our joy.

Second PRIEST.

Like the sun, our great monarch all pleasure supplies;
Both similar blessings bestow;
The sun with his splendour illumines the skies,
And our monarch enlivens below.

Chaldean WOMAN.

Air.

Haste, ye sprightly sons of pleasure;
Love presents its brightest treasure,
Leave all other joys for me.

Chaldean ATTENDANT.

Or rather Love's delights despising,
Haste to raptures ever rising;
Wine shall bless the brave and free.

Second PRIEST.

Wine and beauty thus inviting,
Each to different joys exciting,
Whither shall my choice incline?

But if, rebellious to his high command,
You spurn the favours offer'd at his hand;
Think, timely think, what ills remain behind;
Reflect, nor tempt to rage the royal mind.

Second PRIEST.

Air.

Fierce is the whirlwind howling
O'er Afric's sandy plain,
And fierce the tempest rolling
Along the furrow'd main:
But storms that fly,
To rend the sky,
Every ill presaging,
Less dreadful show
To worlds below
Than angry monarch's raging.

ISRAELITISH WOMAN.

Recitative.

Ah, me! what angry terrors round us grow;
How shrinks my soul to meet the threaten'd blow!
Ye prophets, skill'd in Heaven's eternal truth,
Forgive my sex's fears, forgive my youth!
If shrinking thus, when frowning power appears,
I wish for life, and yield me to my fears.
Let us one hour, one little hour obey;
To-morrow's tears may wash our stains away.

Air.

To the last moment of his breath,
  On hope the wretch relies;
And even the pang preceding death
  Bids expectation rise.[1]

Hope, like the gleaming taper's light,
  Adorns and cheers our way;
And still, as darker grows the night,
  Emits a brighter ray.[2]

Second Priest.

Recitative.

Why this delay? At length for joy prepare;
I read your looks, and see compliance there.
Come raise the strain and grasp the full-ton'd lyre;
The time, the theme, the place, and all conspire.

1 "The wretch condemn'd with life to part,
  Still, still on hope relies;
And every pang that rends the heart
  Bids expectation rise."—*Orig. MS.*

2 "Fatigued with life, yet loth to part,
  On hope the wretch relies;
And every blow that sinks the heart,
  Bids the deluder rise.

"Hope, like the taper's gleamy light,
  Adorns the wretch's way;
And still, as darker grows the night,
  Emits a brighter ray."—*Orig. MS.*

CHALDEAN WOMAN.

Air.

See the ruddy morning smiling,
Hear the grove to bliss beguiling;
Zephyrs through the valley playing,
Streams along the meadow straying.

First PRIEST.

While these a constant revel keep,
Shall Reason only bid me weep?
Hence, intruder! we'll pursue
Nature, a better guide than you.

Second PRIEST.

Air.

Every moment, as it flows,
Some peculiar pleasure owes;
Then let us, providently wise,
Seize the debtor as it flies.

Think not to-morrow can repay
The pleasures that we lose to-day;
To-morrow's most unbounded store
Can but pay its proper score.

First PRIEST.

Recitative.

But, hush! see foremost of the captive choir,
The master-prophet grasps his full-ton'd lyre.

Mark where he sits, with executing art,
Feels for each tone, and speeds it to the heart.
See inspiration fills his rising form,
Awful as clouds that nurse the growing storm;
And now his voice, accordant to the string,
Prepares our monarch's victories to sing.

First PROPHET.

Air.

From north, from south, from east, from west,
  Conspiring foes shall come;
Tremble thou vice-polluted breast,
  Blasphemers, all be dumb.

The tempest gathers all around,
  On Babylon it lies;
Down with her! down—down to the ground,
  She sinks, she groans, she dies.

Second PROPHET.

Down with her, Lord, to lick the dust,
  Ere yonder setting sun;
Serve her as she has serv'd the just!
  'Tis fix'd—it shall be done.

First PRIEST.

Recitative.

No more! when slaves thus insolent presume,
The king himself shall judge, and fix their doom.

Short-sighted wretches! have not you and all,
Beheld our power in Zedekiah's fall?
To yonder gloomy dungeon turn your eyes;
See where dethron'd your captive monarch lies,
Depriv'd of sight and rankling in his chain;
He calls on Death to terminate his pain.
Yet know, ye slaves, that still remain behind
More ponderous chains, and dungeons more confin'd.

Chorus.

Arise, all potent ruler, rise,
And vindicate thy people's cause;
Till every tongue in every land
Shall offer up unfeign'd applause.

[*Exeunt*

ACT III.

Scene as before.

First PRIEST.

Recitative.

Yes, my companions, Heaven's decrees are past,
And our fix'd empire shall forever last;
In vain the maddening prophet threatens woe,
In vain Rebellion aims her secret blow;
Still shall our fame and growing power be spread,
And still our vengeance crush the guilty head.

Air.

Coeval with man
Our empire began,
And never shall fall
Till ruin shakes all:
With the ruin of all
Shall Babylon fall.

PROPHET.

Recitative.

'Tis thus that pride triumphant rears the head,
A little while, and all her power is fled;
But ha! what means yon sadly plaintive train,
That this way slowly bends along the plain?
And now, methinks, to yonder bank they bear
A pallid corse, and rest the body there.
Alas! too well mine eyes indignant trace
The last remains of Judah's royal race:
Our monarch falls, and now our fears are o'er,
And wretched Zedekiah is no more!

Air.

Ye wretches who, by fortune's hate,
  In want and sorrow groan;
Come ponder his severer fate,
  And learn to bless your own.

You vain, whom youth and pleasure guide,
  Awhile the bliss suspend;
Like yours, his life began in pride,
  Like his, your lives shall end.

Second PROPHET.

Behold his squalid corse with sorrow worn,
His wretched limbs with ponderous fetters torn;
Those eyeless orbs that shock with ghastly glare,
These ill-becoming rags—that matted hair.
And shall not Heaven for this its terrors show,
Grasp the red bolt, and lay the guilty low?[1]
How long, how long, Almighty God of all,
Shall wrath vindictive threaten ere it fall!

ISRAELITISH WOMAN.

Air.

As panting flies the hunted hind,
  Where brooks refreshing stray;
And rivers through the valley wind,
  That stop the hunter's way.

Thus we, O Lord, alike distrest,
  For streams of mercy long;
Those streams which cheer the sore opprest,
  And overwhelm the strong.

First PROPHET.

Recitative.

But, whence that shout? Good heavens! amazement all!
See yonder tower just nodding to the fall;

[1] "And shall not Heaven for this its terror show,
And deal its angry vengeance on the foe?"—*Orig. MS.*

See where an army covers all the ground,
Saps the strong wall, and pours destruction round!
The ruin smokes, destruction pours along,
How low the great, how feeble are the strong!
The foe prevails, the lofty walls recline—
O God of hosts, the victory is Thine!

Chorus of ISRAELITES.

Down with them, Lord, to lick the dust,
  Thy vengeance be begun:
Serve them as they have serv'd the just,
  And let thy will be done.

First PRIEST.

Recitative.

All, all is lost. The Syrian army fails,
Cyrus, the conqueror of the world, prevails!
The ruin smokes, the torrent pours along,—
How low the proud, how feeble are the strong!
Save us, O Lord! to thee, though late, we pray,
And give repentance but an hour's delay.

First and Second PRIEST.

Thrice happy, who in happy hour
  To heaven their praise bestow,
And own his all-consuming power
  Before they feel the blow.

First PROPHET.

Recitative.

Now, now's our time! ye wretches bold and blind,
Brave but to God, and cowards to mankind;
Too late you seek that power unsought before,
Your wealth, your pride, your kingdom, are no more.

Air.

O Lucifer, thou son of morn,
Alike of Heaven and man the foe;
Heaven, men, and all,
Now press thy fall,
And sink thee lowest of the low.

First PROPHET.

O Babylon, how art thou fallen!
Thy fall more dreadful from delay!
Thy streets forlorn
To wilds shall turn,
Where toads shall pant and vultures prey.

Second PROPHET.

Recitative.

Such be her fate! But listen! from afar
The clarion's note proclaims the finish'd war.
Cyrus, our great restorer, is at hand,
And this way leads his formidable band.
Give, give your songs of Zion to the wind,
And hail the benefactor of mankind:

He comes pursuant to divine decree,
To chain the strong, and set the captive free.

Chorus of YOUTHS.

Rise to transports past expressing,
Sweeter from remember'd woes;
Cyrus comes, our wrongs redressing,
Comes to give the world repose.

Chorus of VIRGINS.

Cyrus comes, the world redressing,
Love and pleasure in his train;
Comes to heighten every blessing,
Comes to soften every pain.

Semi-Chorus.

Hail to him with mercy reigning,
Skill'd in every peaceful art;
Who from bonds our limbs unchaining,
Only binds the willing heart.

Last Chorus.

But chief to Thee, our God, defender, friend,
Let praise be given to all eternity;
O Thou, without beginning, without end,
Let us, and all, begin and end in Thee.

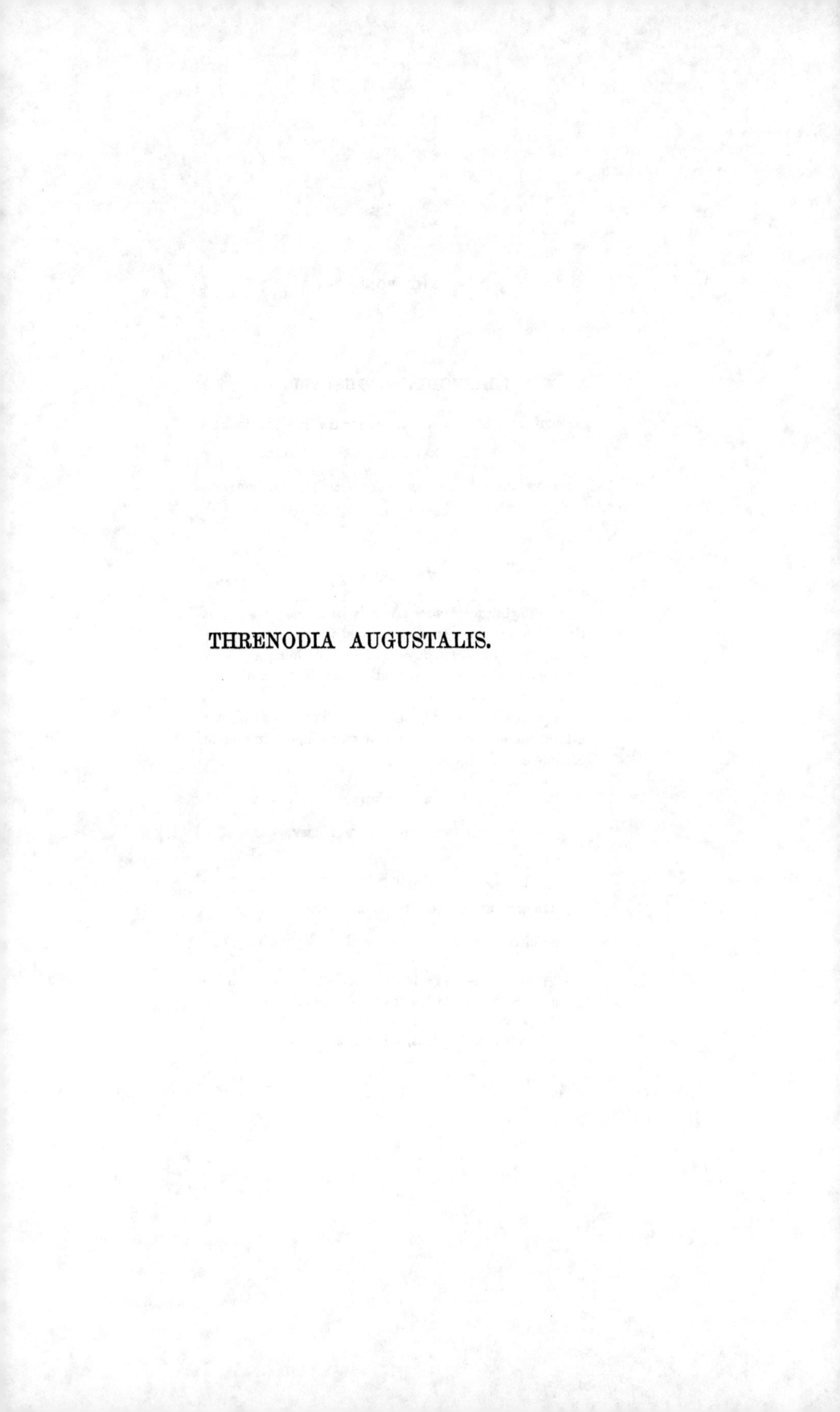

THRENODIA AUGUSTALIS.

THRENODIA AUGUSTALIS.[1]

SACRED TO THE MEMORY OF HER LATE ROYAL HIGHNESS

THE PRINCESS DOWAGER OF WALES.

SPOKEN AND SUNG IN THE GREAT ROOM IN SOHO SQUARE,

THURSDAY, FEB. 20, 1772.

ADVERTISEMENT.

THE following may more properly be termed a compilation than a poem. It was prepared for the composer in little more than two days; and may therefore rather be considered as an industrious effort of gratitude than of genius.

In justice to the composer, it may likewise be right to inform the public that the music was adapted in a period of time equally short.

SPEAKERS.

MR. LEE AND MRS. BELLAMY.

SINGERS.

MR. CHAMPNES, MR. DINE, AND MISS JAMESON.

The music prepared and adapted by Signor Vento.

1 This poem was first printed by Mr. Chalmers from a copy given by Goldsmith to his friend, Joseph Cradock, Esq. of Gumley, author of Zobeide, &c., and lent to Mr. Chalmers by Mr. Nicholls. *v. Br. Poets*, vol. xvi. p. 509.

THRENODIA AUGUSTALIS.

OVERTURE — A SOLEMN DIRGE. AIR — TRIO.

ARISE, ye sons of worth, arise,
And waken every note of woe!
When truth and virtue reach the skies,
'Tis ours to weep the want below.

CHORUS.

When truth and virtue, &c.

MAN SPEAKER.

The praise attending pomp and power,
The incense given to kings,
Are but the trappings of an hour,
Mere transitory things.
The base bestow them; but the good agree
To spurn the venal gifts as flattery.
But when to pomp and power are join'd
An equal dignity of mind;
When titles are the smallest claim;
When wealth, and rank, and noble blood,
But aid the power of doing good,
Then all their trophies last — and flattery turns
to fame.

Blest spirit thou, whose fame, just born to bloom,
Shall spread and flourish from the tomb,
How hast thou left mankind for heaven!
Even now reproach and faction mourn,
And, wondering how their rage was born,
Request to be forgiven!
Alas! they never had thy hate:
Unmov'd in conscious rectitude,
Thy towering mind self-centred stood,
Nor wanted man's opinion to be great.
In vain, to charm thy ravish'd sight,
A thousand gifts would fortune send;
In vain, to drive thee from the right,
A thousand sorrows urged thy end:
Like some well-fashion'd arch thy patience stood,
And purchased strength from its increasing load;
Pain met thee like a friend to set thee free;
Affliction still is virtue's opportunity!

SONG. BY A MAN—AFFETUOSO.

Virtue, on herself relying,
Every passion hush'd to rest,
Loses every pain of dying
In the hopes of being blest.
Every added pang she suffers
Some increasing good bestows,
And every shock that malice offers
Only rocks her to repose.

WOMAN SPEAKER.

Yet, ah! what terrors frown'd upon her fate,—
Death with its formidable band,
Fever, and pain, and pale consumptive care,
Determined took their stand.
Nor did the cruel ravagers design
To finish all their efforts at a blow;
But, mischievously slow,
They robb'd the relic and defac'd the shrine.
With unavailing grief,
Despairing of relief,
Her weeping children round
Beheld each hour
Death's growing power,
And trembled as he frown'd.
As helpless friends who view from shore
The labouring ship, and hear the tempest roar,
While winds and waves their wishes cross,—
They stood, while hope and comfort fail,
Not to assist, but to bewail
The inevitable loss.
Relentless tyrant, at thy call
How do the good, the virtuous, fall!
Truth, beauty, worth, and all that most engage,
But wake thy vengeance, and provoke thy rage.

SONG. BY A MAN — BASSO, STACCATO, SPIRITUOSO.

When vice my dart and scythe supply,
How great a king of terrors I!
If folly, fraud, your hearts engage,
Tremble, ye mortals, at my rage!

Fall, round me fall, ye little things,
Ye statesmen, warriors, poets, kings!
If virtue fail her counsel sage,
Tremble, ye mortals, at my rage!

MAN SPEAKER.

Yet let that wisdom, urged by her example,
Teach us to estimate what all must suffer:
Let us prize death as the best gift of nature;
As a safe inn, where weary travellers,
When they have journey'd through a world of cares,
May put off life, and be at rest for ever.
Groans, weeping friends, indeed, and gloomy sables,
May oft distract us with their sad solemnity:
The preparation is the executioner.
Death, when unmask'd, shows me a friendly face,
And is a terror only at a distance:
For as the line of life conducts me on
To Death's great court, the prospect seems more fair.
'Tis nature's kind retreat, that's always open
To take us in when we have drain'd the cup
Of life, or worn our days to wretchedness.
In that secure, serene retreat,
Where all the humble, all the great,
Promiscuously recline;
Where, wildly huddled to the eye,
The beggar's pouch and prince's purple lie;
May every bliss be thine!

And ah! blest spirit, wheresoe'er thy flight,
Through rolling worlds, or fields of liquid light,
May cherubs welcome their expected guest;
May saints with songs receive thee to their rest;
May peace, that claim'd, while here, thy warmest
love, —
May blissful, endless peace be thine above!

SONG. BY A WOMAN — AMOROSO.

Lovely, lasting Peace below,
Comforter of every woe,
Heavenly born, and bred on high,
To crown the favourites of the sky, —
Lovely, lasting Peace, appear!
This world itself, if thou art here,
Is once again with Eden blest,
And man contains it in his breast.

WOMAN SPEAKER.

Our vows are heard! Long, long to mortal eyes,
Her soul was fitting to its kindred skies:
Celestial-like her bounty fell,
Where modest want and patient sorrow dwell;
Want pass'd for merit at her door,
Unseen the modest were supplied,
Her constant pity fed the poor, —
Then only poor, indeed, the day she died.
And oh! for this, while sculpture decks thy shrine,
And art exhausts profusion round,
The tribute of a tear be mine,

A simple song, a sigh profound.
[1] There Faith shall come, a pilgrim gray,
To bless the tomb that wraps thy clay;
And calm Religion shall repair
To dwell a weeping hermit there.
Truth, Fortitude, and Friendship shall agree
To blend their virtues while they think of thee.

AIR. CHORUS — POMPOSO.

Let us, let all the world, agree,
To profit by resembling thee.

PART II.

OVERTURE — PASTORALE.

MAN SPEAKER.

FAST by that shore where Thames' translucent stream
Reflects new glories on his breast,
Where, splendid as the youthful poet's dream,
He forms a scene beyond Elysium blest;
Where sculptur'd elegance and native grace
Unite to stamp the beauties of the place;
While, sweetly blending, still are seen
The wavy lawn, the sloping green;

1 These four lines, with some alteration, taken from Collins's Ode in the year 1746.

While novelty, with cautious cunning,
Through every maze of fancy running,
From China borrows aid to deck the scene:
There, sorrowing by the river's glassy bed,
Forlorn, a rural band complain'd.
[2] All whom Augusta's bounty fed,
All whom her clemency sustain'd;
The good old sire, unconscious of decay,
The modest matron, clad in homespun gray,
The military boy, the orphan'd maid,
The shatter'd veteran, now first dismay'd,—
These sadly join beside the murmuring deep,
And, as they view the towers of Kew,
Call on their mistress, now no more, and weep.

CHORUS — AFFETUOSO, LARGO.

Ye shady walks, ye waving greens,
Ye nodding towers, ye fairy scenes,
Let all your echoes now deplore,
That she who form'd your beauties is no more.

MAN SPEAKER.

First of the train the patient rustic came,
Whose callous hand had form'd the scene,
Bending at once with sorrow and with age,
With many a tear, and many a sigh between:

[2] All that on Granta's fruitful plain
Rich streams of regal bounty pour'd.
Gray's Inst. Ode, st. iv.

'And where,' he cried, 'shall now my babes have
Or how shall age support its feeble fire? [bread,
No lord will take me now, my vigour fled,
Nor can my strength perform what they require:
Each grudging master keeps the labourer bare,
A sleek and idle race is all their care.
My noble mistress thought not so:
Her bounty, like the morning dew,
Unseen, though constant, used to flow,
And as my strength decay'd, her bounty grew.'

WOMAN SPEAKER.

In decent dress, and coarsely clean,
The pious matron next was seen,
Clasp'd in her hand a godly book was borne,
By use and daily meditation worn;
That decent dress, this holy guide,
Augusta's care had well supplied.
'And ah!' she cries, all woebegone,
'What now remains for me?
Oh! where shall weeping want repair
To ask for charity?
Too late in life for me to ask,
And shame prevents the deed,
And tardy, tardy are the times
To succour, should I need.
But all my wants, before I spoke,
Were to my mistress known;
She still reliev'd, nor sought my praise,
Contented with her own.

But every day her name I'll bless,
My morning prayer, my evening song;
I'll praise her while my life shall last,
A life that cannot last me long.'

SONG — BY A WOMAN.

Each day, each hour, her name I'll bless,
My morning and my evening song;
And when in death my vows shall cease,
My children shall the note prolong.

MAN SPEAKER.

The hardy veteran after struck the sight,
Scarr'd, mangled, maim'd in every part,
Lopp'd of his limbs in many a gallant fight,
In nought entire — except his heart:
Mute for a while, and sullenly distress'd,
At last the impetuous sorrow fired his breast.
'Wild is the whirlwind rolling
O'er Afric's sandy plain,
And wild the tempest howling
Along the billow'd main:
But every danger felt before,
The raging deep, the whirlwind's roar,
Less dreadful struck me with dismay
Than what I feel this fatal day.
Oh, let me fly a land that spurns the brave!
Oswego's dreary shores shall be my grave;
I'll seek that less inhospitable coast,
And lay my body where my limbs were lost.'

SONG. BY A MAN — BASSO SPIRITUOSO.

[8] Old Edward's sons, unknown to yield,
Shall crowd from Cressy's laurell'd field,
To do thy memory right:
For thine and Britain's wrongs they feel,
Again they snatch the gleamy steel,
And wish the avenging fight.

WOMAN SPEAKER.

In innocence and youth complaining,
Next appear'd a lovely maid;
Affliction, o'er each feature reigning,
Kindly came in beauty's aid:
Every grace that grief dispenses,
Every glance that warms the soul,
In sweet succession charm'd the senses,
While pity harmonized the whole.
'The garland of beauty' ('tis thus she would say)
'No more shall my crook or my temples adorn;
I'll not wear a garland, — Augusta 's away, —
I'll not wear a garland until she return.
But, alas! that return I never shall see:
The echoes of Thames shall my sorrows proclaim.
There promised a lover to come; but, oh me!
'Twas death, 'twas the death of my mistress, that
came.
But ever, for ever, her image shall last,

[8] These lines altered from Collins's Ode on the Death of Col. Ross.

I'll strip all the spring of its earliest bloom;
On her grave shall the cowslip and primrose be cast,
And the new-blossom'd thorn shall whiten her tomb.'

SONG. BY A WOMAN — PASTORALE.

With garlands of beauty the Queen of the May
No more will her crook or her temples adorn;
For who'd wear a garland when she is away,
When she is remov'd, and shall never return?

On the grave of Augusta these garlands be plac'd,
We'll rifle the spring of its earliest bloom,
And there shall the cowslip and primrose be cast,
And the new-blossom'd thorn shall whiten her tomb.

CHORUS — ALTRO MODO.

[4] On the grave of Augusta this garland be plac'd,
We'll rifle the spring of its earliest bloom,
And there shall the cowslip and primrose be cast,
And the tears of her country shall water her tomb.

[4] 'Each opening sweet of earliest bloom,
And rifle all the breathing spring.'
Collins's Dirge in Cymbeline.

MISCELLANIES.

THE DOUBLE TRANSFORMATION.[1]

A TALE.

SECLUDED from domestic strife,
Jack Bookworm led a college life
A fellowship at twenty-five
Made him the happiest man alive;
He drank his glass, and crack'd his joke,
And freshmen wonder'd as he spoke.[a]

Such pleasures, unalloy'd with care,
Could any accident impair?
Could Cupid's shaft at length transfix
Our swain, arriv'd at thirty-six?
Oh, had the archer ne'er come down
To ravage in a country town;
Or Flavia been content to stop
At triumphs in a Fleet-street shop!
Oh, had her eyes forgot to blaze;
Or Jack had wanted eyes to gaze!
Oh! —— but let exclamation cease,

[1] Printed in Goldsmith's Essays (the xxvi.) in 1765.

VARIATIONS.

[a] Without politeness, aim'd at breeding,
And laugh'd at pedantry and reading.

Her presence banish'd all his peace.[b]
So with decorum all things carried;
Miss frown'd, and blush'd, and then was—married.

Need we expose to vulgar sight
The raptures of the bridal night?
Need we intrude on hallow'd ground,
Or draw the curtains clos'd around?
Let it suffice that each had charms:
He clasp'd a goddess in his arms;
And though she felt his usage[c] rough,
Yet in a man 'twas well enough.

The honeymoon like lightning flew,
The second brought its transports too;
A third, a fourth, were not amiss,
The fifth was friendship mix'd with bliss:
But, when a twelvemonth pass'd away,
Jack found his goddess made of clay;
Found half the charms that deck'd her face
Arose from powder, shreds, or lace;

VARIATIONS.

[b] Our alter'd parson now began
To be a perfect ladies' man;
Made sonnets, lisp'd his sermons o'er,
And told the tales he told before,
Of bailiffs pump'd, and proctors bit;
At college how he show'd his wit;
And, as the fair one still approv'd,
He fell in love — or thought he lov'd.

[c] visage

But still the worst remain'd behind,
That very face had robb'd her mind.

Skill'd in no other arts was she,
But dressing, patching, repartee;
And, just as humour rose or fell,
By turns a slattern or a belle.
'Tis true she dress'd with modern grace,
Half-naked at a ball or race;
But when at home, at board or bed,
Five greasy nightcaps wrapp'd her head.
Could so much beauty condescend
To be a dull, domestic friend?
Could any curtain-lectures bring
To decency so fine a thing?
In short, by night 'twas fits or fretting;
By day 'twas gadding or coquetting.
Fond to be seen, she kept a bevy [d]
Of powder'd coxcombs at her levee;
The 'squire and captain took their stations,
And twenty other near relations;
Jack suck'd his pipe, and often broke
A sigh in suffocating smoke; [e]
While all their hours were pass'd [f] between
Insulting repartee or spleen.

VARIATIONS.

d Now tawdry madam kept a bevy.
e She in her turn became perplexing,
And found substantial bliss in vexing.
f Thus every hour was pass'd.

Thus as her faults each day were known,[g]
He thinks her features coarser grown;
He fancies every vice she shows
Or thins her lip, or points her nose
Whenever rage or envy rise,
How wide her mouth, how wild her eyes!
He knows not how, but so it is,
Her face is grown a knowing phiz;
And, though her fops are wondrous civil,
He thinks her ugly as the devil.

Now,[h] to perplex the ravell'd noose,
As each a different way pursues,
While sullen or loquacious strife
Promis'd to hold them on for life,
That dire disease, whose ruthless power
Withers the beauty's transient flower,—
Lo! the smallpox, with horrid glare,
Levell'd its terrors at the fair;
And, rifling every youthful grace,
Left but the remnant of a face.

The glass, grown hateful to her sight,
Reflected now a perfect fright:
Each former art she vainly tries
To bring back lustre to her eyes.

VARIATIONS.

g Each day the more her faults were known.
h Thus.

In vain she tries her paste[1] and creams,
To smooth her skin, or hide its seams;
Her country beaux and city cousins,
Lovers no more, flew off by dozens;
The 'squire himself was seen to yield,
And e'en the captain quit the field.

Poor madam now condemn'd to hack
The rest of life with anxious Jack,
Perceiving others fairly flown,
Attempted pleasing him alone.
Jack soon was dazzled to behold
Her present face surpass the old:
With modesty her cheeks are dyed,
Humility displaces pride;
For tawdry finery is seen
A person ever neatly clean;
No more presuming on her sway,
She learns good-nature every day;
Serenely gay, and strict in duty,
Jack finds his wife a perfect beauty.

VARIATION.

[1] pastes.

A NEW SIMILE.[1]

IN THE MANNER OF SWIFT.

[a] LONG had I sought in vain to find
A likeness for the scribbling kind;
The modern scribbling kind, who write
In wit, and sense, and nature's spite:
Till reading, I forget what day on,
A chapter out of Tooke's Pantheon,
I think I met with something there
To suit my purpose to a hair.
But let us not proceed too furious, —
First please to turn to god Mercurius:
You'll find him pictur'd at full length
In book the second, page the tenth:
The stress of all my proofs on him I lay,
And now proceed we to our simile.

Imprimis, pray observe his hat,
Wings upon either side, — mark that.
Well! what is it from thence we gather?
Why, these denote a brain of feather.

[1] Printed among the Essays (the xxvii.)

VARIATIONS.

[a] I long had rack'd my brains to find.

A brain of feather! very right,
With wit that's flighty, learning light;
Such as to modern bard 's decreed:
A just comparison, — proceed.

In the next place, his feet peruse,
Wings grow again from both his shoes;
Design'd, no doubt, their part to bear,
And waft his godship through the air:
And here my simile unites;
For in the modern poet's flights,
I'm sure it may be justly said,
His feet are useful as his head.

Lastly, vouchsafe t' observe his hand,
Fill'd with a snake-encircled wand,
By classic authors term'd caduceus,
And highly fam'd for several uses:
To wit, — most wondrously endued,
No poppy water half so good;
For let folks only get a touch,
Its soporific virtue 's such,
Though ne'er so much awake before,
That quickly they begin to snore.
Add, too, what certain writers tell,
With this he drives men's souls to hell.

Now to apply, begin we then:
His wand 's a modern author's pen;
The serpents, round about it twin'd,

Denote him of the reptile kind;
Denote the rage with which he writes,
His frothy slaver, venom'd bites;
An equal semblance still to keep,
Alike, too, both conduce to sleep.
This difference only, as the god
Drove souls to Tartarus with his rod,
With his goosequill the scribbling elf,
Instead of others, damns himself.

And here my simile almost tript,
Yet grant a word by way of postscript.
Moreover, Mercury had a failing:
Well! what of that? out with it — stealing;
In which all modern bards[b] agree,
Being each as great a thief as he.
But e'en this deity's existence
Shall lend my simile assistance:
Our modern bards! why, what a pox
Are they but senseless stones and blocks?

VARIATIONS.

[b] our scribbling bards

THE LOGICIANS REFUTED.[1]

IN IMITATION OF DEAN SWIFT.

LOGICIANS have but ill defin'd
As rational the human mind:
Reason, they say, belongs to man;
But let them prove it if they can.
Wise Aristotle and Smiglecius,
By ratiocinations specious,
Have strove to prove, with great precision,
With definition and division,
Homo est ratione preditum;
But for my soul I cannot credit 'em;
And must in spite of them maintain,
That man and all his ways are vain;
And that this boasted lord of nature
Is both a weak and erring creature;
That instinct is a surer guide
Than reason, boasting mortals' pride;
And that brute beasts are far before 'em;
Deus est anima brutorum.
Who ever knew an honest brute
At law his neighbour prosecute,
Bring action for assault and battery,
Or friend beguile with lies and flattery?

1 From *The Busy Body*, No. 5.

O'er plains they ramble unconfin'd,
No politics disturb their mind;
They eat their meals, and take their sport,
Nor know who's in or out at court.
They never to the levee go
To treat as dearest friend a foe:
They never importune his Grace,
Nor ever cringe to men in place;
Nor undertake a dirty job,
Nor draw the quill to write for Bob.[1]
Fraught with invective, they ne'er go
To folks at Paternoster Row:
No judges, fiddlers, dancing-masters,
No pickpockets or poetasters,
Are known to honest quadrupeds;
No single brute his fellows leads.
Brutes never meet in bloody fray,
Nor cut each others' throats for pay.
Of beasts, it is confess'd, the ape
Comes nearest us in human shape;
Like man he imitates each fashion,
And malice is his ruling passion:
But, both in malice and grimaces,
A courtier any ape surpasses.
Behold him humbly cringing wait
Upon the minister of state;
View him soon after to inferiors,
Aping the conduct of superiors:

[1] Sir Robert Walpole.

He promises with equal air,
And to perform takes equal care.
He in his turn finds imitators:
At court, the porters, lacqueys, waiters,
Their masters' manners still contract,
And footmen lords and dukes can act.
Thus, at the court, both great and small
Behave alike, for all ape all.

AN ELEGY ON THE DEATH OF A MAD DOG.[1]

Good people all, of every sort,
  Give ear unto my song;
And if you find it wondrous short,
  It cannot hold you long.

In Islington there was a man
  Of whom the world might say,
That still a godly race he ran,
  Whene'er he went to pray.

A kind and gentle heart he had,
  To comfort friends and foes:
The naked every day he clad,
  When he put on his clothes.

And in that town a dog was found,
  As many dogs there be,
Both mongrel, puppy, whelp, and hound,
  And curs of low degree.

[1] See Vicar of Wakefield, c. xvii.

In the Citizen of the World, vol. ii. lett. lxvi. is a paper on the '*Epidemic Terror, the dread of mad dogs*, which now prevails: the whole nation is now actually groaning under the malignity of its influence.'

This dog and man at first were friends;
  But when a pique began,
The dog, to gain his private ends,
  Went mad, and bit the man.

Around from all the neighbouring streets
  The wondering people ran,
And swore the dog had lost his wits,
  To bite so good a man.

The wound it seem'd both sore and sad
  To every Christian eye;
And while they swore the dog was mad,
  They swore the man would die.

But soon a wonder came to light,
  That show'd the rogues they lied;
The man recover'd of the bite;
  The dog it was that died.

AN ELEGY ON THE GLORY OF HER SEX, MRS. MARY BLAIZE.[1]

Good people all, with one accord,
  Lament for Madam Blaize,
Who never wanted a good word —
  From those who spoke her praise.

The needy seldom pass'd her door,
  And always found her kind:
She freely lent to all the poor —
  Who left a pledge behind.

She strove the neighbourhood to please,
  With manners wondrous winning;
And never follow'd wicked ways —
  Unless when she was sinning.

At church, in silks and satins new,
  With hoop of monstrous size,
She never slumber'd in her pew —
  But when she shut her eyes.

Her love was sought, I do aver,
  By twenty beaux and more;
The king himself has follow'd her —
  When she has walk'd before.

1 See *The Bee*, No. iv.

But now, her wealth and finery fled,
  Her hangers-on cut short all;
The doctors found, when she was dead —
  Her last disorder mortal.

Let us lament in sorrow sore;
  For Kent-street well may say,
That had she liv'd a twelvemonth more —
  She had not died to-day.[2]

[2] This poem [as well as the *Elegy on the Death of a Mad Dog*] is an imitation of the chanson called 'Le fameux la Galisse, homme imaginaire,' in fifty stanzas, printed in the *Ménagiana*, iv. 191:—

'Messieurs, vous plait-il d'ouir
  L'air du fameux la Galisse,
Il pourra vous réjouir,
  Pourvû qu'il vous divertisse

* * * *

'Bien instruit dès le berceau
  Jamais, tant il fut honnête,
Il se mettoit son chapeau
  Qu'il ne se couvrît la tête.

* * * *

'On dit que dans ses amours
  Il fut caressé des belles,
Qui le suivirent toujours,
  Tant qu'il marche devant elles.

* * * *

'Il fut, par un triste sort,
  Blessé d'une main cruelle;
On croit, puisqu'il est mort,
  Que la plaie était mortelle.

'Regretté de ses soldats,
  Il mourut digne d'envie,
Et le jour de son trépas
  Fut le dernier de sa vie.'

* * *

THE CLOWN'S REPLY.

John Trott was desir'd by two witty peers
To tell them the reason why asses had ears.
'An't please you,' quoth John, 'I'm not given to letters,
Nor dare I pretend to know more than my betters:
Howe'er, from this time I shall ne'er see your graces, —
As I hope to be sav'd! — without thinking on asses.'

Edinburgh, 1753.

ON A BEAUTIFUL YOUTH STRUCK BLIND BY LIGHTNING.

IMITATED FROM THE SPANISH.[1]

Sure 'twas by Providence design'd,
  Rather in pity than in hate,
That he should be, like Cupid, blind,
  To save him from Narcissus' fate.

STANZAS ON THE TAKING OF QUEBEC.[2]

Amidst the clamour of exulting joys,
  Which triumph forces from the patriot heart,
Grief dares to mingle her soul-piercing voice,
  And quells the raptures which from pleasures start.

O Wolfe! to thee a streaming flood of woe,
  Sighing we pay, and think e'en conquest dear:
Quebec in vain shall teach our breast to glow,
  Whilst thy sad fate extorts the heart-wrung tear.

Alive the foe thy dreadful vigour fled,
  And saw thee fall with joy-pronouncing eyes:
Yet they shall know thou conquerest, tho' dead!
  Since from thy tomb a thousand heroes rise.

[1] See *The Bee*, No. i.
[2] First printed in *The Busy Body*, 1759.—P. C.

THE GIFT

TO IRIS, IN BOW STREET, COVENT GARDEN.[1]

Say, cruel Iris, pretty rake,
  Dear mercenary beauty,
What annual offering shall I make
  Expressive of my duty?

My heart, a victim to thine eyes,
  Should I at once deliver,
Say, would the angry fair one prize
  The gift, who slights the giver?

A bill, a jewel, watch, or toy,
  My rivals give, — and let 'em:
If gems or gold impart a joy,
  I'll give them — when I get 'em.

I'll give — but not the full-blown rose,
  Or rosebud, more in fashion;
Such short-liv'd offerings but disclose
  A transitory passion.

[1] See *The Bee*, No. ii.

I'll give thee something yet unpaid,
Not less sincere than civil;
I'll give thee — ah! too charming maid,
I'll give thee — to the devil.[2]

[2] This poem is taken from *Ménagiana*, vol. iv. 200.

'ÉTRENNE À IRIS.

'Pour témoignage de ma flamme,
Iris, du meilleur de mon âme
Je vous donne à ce nouvel an,
Non pas dentelle, ni ruban,
Non pas essence, ni pommade,
Quelques boîtes de marmalade,
Un mouchoir, des gans, un bouquet,
Non pas fleures, ni chapelet.
Quoi donc? attendez, je vous donne,
O fille plus belle que bonne,
Qui m'avez toujours refusé,
Le point si souvent proposé,
Je vous donne — Ah! le puis-je dire?
Oui: c'est trop souffrir le martyre,
Il est temps de m'émanciper,
Patience va m'échapper.
Fussiez-vous cent fois plus aimable,
Belle Iris, je vous donne — au diable.'

A DESCRIPTION OF AN AUTHOR'S BEDCHAMBER.[1]

WHERE the Red Lion, staring o'er the way,
Invites each passing stranger that can pay;
Where Calvert's butt, and Parson's black champagne,
Regale the drabs and bloods of Drury-lane;
There, in a lonely room, from bailiffs snug,
The Muse found Scroggen stretch'd beneath a rug:
A window, patch'd with paper, lent a ray,
That dimly show'd the state in which he lay;
The sanded floor that grits beneath the tread;
The humid wall with paltry pictures spread;
The royal game of goose was there in view,
And the twelve rules the royal martyr drew;[2]

1 First printed in *The Citizen of the World*, Letter xxx., and afterwards inserted, with a few variations, in *The Deserted Village*, 1770.—P. C. [See, *post*, the extract from a letter to the Rev. Henry Goldsmith.]

2 Viz: "1. Urge no healths; 2. Profane no divine ordinances; 3. Touch no state matters; 4. Reveal no secrets; 5. Pick no quarrels; 6. Make no comparisons; 7. Maintain no ill opinions; 8. Keep no bad company; 9. Encourage no vice; 10. Make no long meals; 11. Repeat no grievances· 12. Lay no wagers."—P. C.

The seasons, fram'd with listing, found a place,
And brave prince William[8] show'd his lampblack face.
The morn was cold; he views with keen desire
The rusty grate unconscious of a fire:
With beer and milk arrears the frieze was scor'd,
And five crack'd teacups dress'd the chimney board;
A nightcap deck'd his brows instead of bay,
A cap by night,—a stocking all the day!

[8] William, Duke of Cumberland, the hero of Culloden, d. 1765.—P. C.

EPITAPH ON DR. PARNELL.[1]

THIS tomb inscrib'd to gentle Parnell's name,
May speak our gratitude, but not his fame.
What heart but feels his sweetly moral lay,
That leads to truth thro' pleasure's flowery way?
Celestial themes confess'd his tuneful aid;
And Heaven, that lent him genius, was repaid.
Needless to him the tribute we bestow,
The transitory breath of fame below:
More lasting rapture from his works shall rise,
While converts thank their poet in the skies.

EPITAPH ON EDWARD PURDON.[2]

HERE lies poor Ned Purdon, from misery freed,
  Who long was a bookseller's hack;
He led such a damnable life in this world,
  I don't think he'll wish to come back.

1 From *The Haunch of Venison*, &c. 1776.—P. C.

2 This gentleman was educated at Trinity College, Dublin; but, having wasted his patrimony, he enlisted as a foot soldier. Growing tired of that employment, he obtained his discharge, and became a scribbler in the newspapers. [This epitaph is an imitation of the French, (*La Mort du Sieur Etienne*,) or of an epigram in Swift's *Miscellanies*, xiii. 372.—FORSTER.]

STANZAS ON WOMAN.[1]

WHEN lovely woman stoops to folly,
  And finds too late that men betray,
What charm can soothe her melancholy?
  What art can wash her guilt away?

The only art her guilt to cover,
  To hide her shame from every eye,
To give repentance to her lover,
  And wring his bosom, is—to die.

[1] See Vicar of Wakefield, c. xxiv.

SONG.

INTENDED TO HAVE BEEN SUNG IN THE COMEDY OF 'SHE STOOPS TO CONQUER.'[1]

Ah me! when shall I marry me?
Lovers are plenty, but fail to relieve me.
He, fond youth, that could carry me,
Offers to love, but means to deceive me.
But I will rally, and combat the ruiner:
Not a look, not a smile shall my passion discover.
She that gives all to the false one pursuing her,
Makes but a penitent, and loses a lover.

[1] Sir, — I send you a small production of the late Dr. Goldsmith, which has never been published, and which might perhaps have been totally lost, had I not secured it. He intended it as a song in the character of Miss Hardcastle, in his admirable comedy of 'She Stoops to Conquer;' but it was left out, as Mrs. Bulkley, who played the part, did not sing. He sung it himself in private companies very agreeably. The tune is a pretty Irish air, called 'The Humours of Balamagairy,' to which he told me he found it very difficult to adapt words; but he has succeeded very happily in these few lines. As I could sing the tune, and was fond of them, he was so good as to give me them, about a year ago, just as I was leaving London, and bidding him adieu for that season, little apprehending that it was a last farewell. I preserve this little relic, in his own handwriting, with an affectionate care. — I am, Sir,

Your humble Servant,

James Boswell.

A SONNET.[1]

WEEPING, murmuring, complaining,
  Lost to every gay delight;
Myra, too sincere for feigning,
  Fears th' approaching bridal night.

Yet why impair thy bright perfection
  Or dim thy beauty with a tear?
Had Myra followed my direction,
  She long had wanted cause of fear.

SONG.[2]

THE wretch condemn'd with life to part,
  Still, still on hope relies;
And every pang that rends the heart
  Bids expectation rise.

Hope, like the glimmering taper's light,
  Adorns and cheers the way;
And still, as darker grows the night,
  Emits a brighter ray.

[1] See *The Bee*, No. iii. Imitated from the French of Saint Pavin, whose poems were collectively edited in 1759.—P. C.

[2] [See the Oratorio of *The Captivity*.]

SONG.[1]

O MEMORY! thou fond deceiver,
  Still importunate and vain;
To former joys recurring ever,
  And turning all the past to pain;

Thou, like the world, the opprest oppressing,
  Thy smiles increase the wretch's woe!
And he who wants each other blessing,
  In thee must ever find a foe.

[1] See the Oratorio of *The Captivity.*

SONG.[1]

LET schoolmasters puzzle their brain
  With grammar, and nonsense, and learning:
Good liquor, I stoutly maintain,
  Gives *genus* a better discerning.
Let them brag of their heathenish gods,
  Their Lethes, their Styxes, and Stygians;
Their quis, and their quæs, and their quods,
  They're all but a parcel of pigeons.
    Toroddle, toroddle, toroll.

When methodist preachers come down,
  A preaching that drinking is sinful,
I'll wager the rascals a crown,
  They always preach best with a skinful.
But when you come down with your pence
  For a slice of their scurvy religion,
I'll leave it to all men of sense,
  But you, my good friend, are the pigeon.
    Toroddle, toroddle, toroll.

Then come, put the jorum about,
  And let us be merry and clever;
Our hearts and our liquors are stout;
  Here's the Three Jolly Pigeons for ever.

1 From 'She Stoops to Conquer.'

Let some cry up woodcock or hare,
  Your bustards, your ducks, and your widgeons;
But of all the birds in the air,
  Here's a health to the three jolly pigeons.
    Toroddle, toroddle, toroll.

NOTE. — We drank tea with the ladies, and Goldsmith sung Tony Lumpkins' song in his comedy, and a very pretty one, to an Irish tune (The Humours of Ballanagairy), which he had designed for Miss Hardcastle; but as Mrs. Bulkley, who played the part, could not sing, it was left out. He afterwards wrote it down for me, by which means it was preserved, and now appears among his poems.

Boswell's Johnson, v. ii. p. 217

VERSES.

IN REPLY TO AN INVITATION TO DINNER AT DR. BAKER'S.[1]

"This *is* a poem! This *is* a copy of verses!"

YOUR mandate I got,
You may all go to pot;
Had your senses been right,
You'd have sent before night;
As I hope to be saved,
I put off being shaved;
For I could not make bold,
While the matter was cold,
To meddle in suds,
Or to put on my duds;
So tell Horneck and Nesbitt,
And Baker and his bit,
And Kauffman beside,
And the Jessamy bride,[2]
With the rest of the crew,
The Reynoldses two,

[1] Written about the year 1769, in reply to an invitation to dinner at Dr. afterwards Sir George Baker's (d. 1809,) to meet the Misses Horneck, Angelica Kauffman, Miss Reynolds, Sir Joshua Reynolds, and others. For the above verses, first published in 1837, the reader is indebted to Major General Sir Henry Bunbury, Bart. P. C.

[2] Miss Mary Horneck, afterwards Mrs. Gwyn. She died in 1840, aged 88. P. C.

Little Comedy's[1] face,
And the Captain in lace.[2]
(By the bye you may tell him,
I have something to sell him;
Of use I insist,
When he comes to enlist.
Your worships must know
That a few days ago,
An order went out
For the foot guards so stout
To wear tails in high taste,
Twelve inches at least:
Now I've got him a scale
To measure each tail,
To lengthen a short tail,
And a long one to curtail.)—

Yet how can I when vext,
Thus stray from my text?
Tell each other to rue
Your Devonshire crew,
For sending so late
To one of my state.
But 'tis Reynolds's way
From wisdom to stray,

[1] Miss Catherine Horneck, afterwards (1771) Mrs. Bunbury. Her portrait by Sir Joshua, one of his finest works, is now at Bowood.

[2] Ensign (afterwards General) Horneck, son of Mrs. Horneck, widow of Captain Kane Horneck.

And Angelica's whim
To be frolick like him,
But, alas! your good worships, how could they be wiser,
When both have been spoil'd in to-day's *Advertiser?*[1]

OLIVER GOLDSMITH.

[1] The following is the compliment alluded to:—

"While fair Angelica, with matchless grace,
Paints Conway's lovely form and Stanhope's face;
Our hearts to beauty willing homage pay,
We praise, admire, and gaze our souls away.
But when the likeness she hath done for thee,
O Reynolds! with astonishment we see,
Forced to submit, with all our pride we own,
Such strength, such harmony excell'd by none,
And thou art rivall'd by thyself alone."

LETTER,

IN PROSE AND VERSE, TO MRS. BUNBURY.[1]

MADAM: I read your letter with all that allowance which critical candour could require, but after all find so much to object to, and so much to raise my indignation, that I cannot help giving it a serious answer. I am not so ignorant, Madam, as not to see there are many sarcasms contained in it, and solecisms also, (solecism is a word that comes from the town of Soleis in Attica among the Greeks, built by Solon, and applied as we use the word Kidderminster for curtains from a town also of that name; but this is learning you have no taste for.)—I say, Madam, there are sarcasms in it and solecisms also. But, not to seem an ill-natured critic, I'll take leave to quote your own words, and give you my remarks upon them as they occur. You begin as follows:—

"I hope, my good Doctor, you soon will be here,
And your spring velvet coat very smart will appear,
To open our ball the first day in the year."

Pray, Madam, where did you ever find the

[1] See note 1, p. 152. An invitation from Mr. and Mrs. Bunbury, in a rhyming and jocular strain, to spend some time with them at their seat at Barton in Suffolk, brought from the Poet the above reply, printed for the first time in 1837 by Messrs. Prior and Wright, though written in 1772. P. C.

epithet "good" applied to the title of Doctor? Had you called me learned Doctor, or grave Doctor, or noble Doctor, it might be allowable, because they belong to the profession. But, not to cavil at trifles, you talk of my spring velvet coat, and advise me to wear it the first day in the year, that is in the middle of winter;—a spring velvet in the middle of winter!!! That would be a solecism indeed; and yet, to increase the inconsistence, in another part of your letter you call me a beau: now, on one side or other, you must be wrong. If I am a beau, I can never think of wearing a spring velvet in winter; and if I am not a beau—why—then—that explains itself. But let me go on to your two next strange lines:—

> "And bring with you a wig that is modish and gay,
> To dance with the girls that are making of hay."

The absurdity of making hay at Christmas you yourself seem sensible of; you say your sister will laugh, and so indeed she well may. The Latins have an expression for a contemptuous sort of laughter, *Naso contemnere adunco;* that is, to laugh with a crooked nose; she may laugh at you in the manner of the ancients if she thinks fit.—But now I am come to the most extraordinary of all extraordinary propositions, which is, to take your and your sister's advice in playing at loo. The presumption of the offer raises my indignation beyond the bounds of prose; it inspires me at once with verse and resentment. I take advice! And from whom? You shall hear.

First let me suppose, what may shortly be true,
The company set and the word to be—loo;
All smirking and pleasant and big with adventure,
And ogling the stake which is fixed in the centre.
Round and round go the cards, while I inwardly
damn,
At never once finding a visit from pam;
I lay down my stake apparently cool,
While the harpies about me all pocket the pool;
I fret in my gizzard, get cautious and sly,
I wish all my friends may be bolder than I;
Yet still they sit snug; not a creature will aim,
By losing their money, to venture at fame.
'Tis in vain that at niggardly caution I scold,
'Tis in vain that I flatter the brave and the bold;
All play their own way, and they think me an ass;
What does Mrs. Bunbury? I, Sir? I pass.
Pray what does Miss Horneck? Take courage,
come, do!
Who, I? Let me see, Sir; why I must pass too.
Mrs. Bunbury frets, and I fret like the Devil,
To see them so cowardly, lucky, and civil;
Yet still I sit snug, and continue to sigh on,
Till made by my losses as bold as a lion.
I venture at all; while my avarice regards
The whole pool as my own. Come, give me five
cards.

Well done! cry the ladies; ah! Doctor, that's good,
The pool's very rich. Ah! the Doctor is loo'd.
Thus foil'd in my courage, on all sides perplext,
I ask for advice from the lady that's next.
Pray, Ma'am, be so good as to give your advice;
Don't you think the best way is to venture for 't
twice?
I advise, cries the lady, to try it I own;
Ah! the Doctor is loo'd. Come Doctor, put down.
Thus playing and playing I still grow more eager,
And so bold and so bold, I'm at last a bold beggar.
Now, ladies, I ask if law matters you're skilled in,
Whether crimes such as yours should not come
before Fielding;
For giving advice that is not worth a straw,
May well be called picking of pockets in law;
And picking of pockets with which I now charge
ye,
Is by *Quinto* Elizabeth, death without clergy.
What justice, when both to the Old Bailey brought!
By the gods I'll enjoy it, tho' 'tis but in thought!
Both are placed at the bar with all proper decorum,
With bunches of fennel and nosegays before 'em;
Both cover their faces with mobs and all that,
But the Judge bids them angrily take off their hat.
When uncover'd, a buzz of inquiry goes round,
Pray what are their crimes? They've been pil-
fering found.
But, pray whom have they pilfer'd? A Doctor,
I hear;

What, yon solemn-faced odd-looking man that
stands near?
The same. What a pity! How does it surprise
one!
Two handsomer culprits I never set eyes on!
Then their friends all come round me with cringing and leering,
To melt me to pity and soften my swearing.
First Sir Charles advances with phrases well
strung,
Consider, dear Doctor, the girls are but young.
The younger the worse, I return him again,
It shows that their habits are all dyed in grain;
But then they're so handsome, one's bosom it
grieves:
What signifies handsome when people are thieves!
But where is your justice? Their cases are hard;
What signifies justice?—I want the reward.

There's the parish of Edmonton offers forty pounds—There's the parish of St. Leonard, Shoreditch, offers forty pounds—There's the parish of Tyburn, from the Hog in the Pound to St. Giles's Watchhouse, offers forty pounds—I shall have all that if I convict them.—

But consider their case, it may yet be your own,
And see how they kneel; is your heart made of
stone?
This moves; so at last I agree to relent,
For ten pounds in hand and ten pounds to be spent.

I challenge you all to answer this. I tell you, you cannot. It cuts deep; but now for the rest of the letter; and next—but I want room.—So I believe I shall battle the rest out at Barton some day next week.—I don't value you all.

O. G.

A PROLOGUE WRITTEN AND SPOKEN BY THE POET LABERIUS,

A ROMAN KNIGHT, WHOM CÆSAR FORCED UPON THE STAGE.

PRESERVED BY MACROBIUS.[1]

WHAT! no way left to shun th' inglorious stage,
And save from infamy my sinking age!
Scarce half alive, oppress'd with many a year,
What in the name of dotage drives me here?
A time there was, when glory was my guide,
Nor force nor fraud could turn my steps aside;
Unaw'd by power, and unappall'd by fear,
With honest thrift I held my honour dear:
But this vile hour disperses all my store,
And all my hoard of honour is no more;
For, ah! too partial to my life's decline,
Cæsar persuades, submission must be mine;
Him I obey, whom Heaven itself obeys,
Hopeless of pleasing, yet inclin'd to please.
Here then at once I welcome every shame,
And cancel at threescore a life of fame:

1 This translation was first printed in one of our author's earliest works: 'The Present State of Polite Learning in Europe,' 12mo. 1759.

No more my titles shall my children tell,
The old buffoon will fit my name as well;
This day beyond its term my fate extends,
For life is ended when our honour ends.[2]

[2] See Macrobii Saturn. lib. ii. c. vii. p. 369, ed. Zeunii Goldsmith has translated, or rather imitated, only the first fifteen lines of the Prologus, ending, —

'Uno plus vixi mihi quam vivendum fuit.'

I venture to add the remainder: —

Too lavish still in good or evil hour,
To show to man the empire of thy power,
If, Fortune, at thy wild impetuous sway,
The blossoms of my fame must drop away,
Then was the time the obedient plant to strain
When life was warm in every vigorous vein,
To mould young nature to thy plastic skill,
And bend my pliant boyhood to thy will.
So might I hope applauding crowds to hear,
Catch the quick smile, and HIS attentive ear.
But, ah! for what hast thou reserv'd my age?
Say, how can I expect the approving stage?
Fled is the bloom of youth — the manly air —
The vigorous mind that spurn'd at toil and care;
Gone is the voice, whose clear and silver tone
The enraptur'd theatre would love to own.
As clasping ivy chokes the encumber'd tree,
So age with foul embrace has ruin'd me.
Thou, and the tomb, Laberius, art the same,
Empty within, what hast thou but a name?

PROLOGUE TO ZOBEIDE.

A TRAGEDY.

SPOKEN BY MR. QUICK, IN THE CHARACTER OF A SAILOR.

In these bold times, when learning's sons explore
The distant climates, and the savage shore;
When wise astronomers to India steer,
And quit for Venus many a brighter here;
While botanists, all cold to smiles and dimpling,
Forsake the fair, and patiently—go simpling;
When every bosom swells with wondrous scenes,
Priests, cannibals, and *hoity-toity* queens,
Our bard into the general spirit enters,
And fits his little frigate for adventures.
With Scythian stores, and trinkets deeply laden,
He this way steers his course, in hopes of trading;
Yet, ere he lands, he has order'd me before
To make an observation on the shore.
Where are we driven? our reckoning sure is lost!
This seems a rocky and a dangerous coast.
Lord, what a sultry climate am I under!
Yon ill-foreboding cloud seems big with thunder.
(*Upper gallery.*)
There mangroves spread, and larger than I've seen 'em— (*Pit.*)
Here trees of stately size—and turtles in 'em;
(*Balconies.*)

Here ill-conditioned oranges abound—
(*Stage.*)
And apples, bitter apples, strew the ground:
(*Tasting them.*)
The place is uninhabited I fear;
I heard a hissing—there are serpents here!
Oh there the natives are, a dreadful race;
The men have tails, the women paint the face.
No doubt they're all barbarians.—Yes, 'tis so;
I'll try to make palaver with them though.
(*Making signs.*)
'Tis best, however, keeping at a distance.
"Good savages, our Captain craves assistance.
Our ship's well stor'd—in yonder creek we've laid her,
His honour is no mercenary trader.
This is his first adventure, lend him aid,
Or you may chance to spoil a thriving trade.
His goods, he hopes, are prime, and brought from far,
Equally fit for gallantry and war."
What, no reply to promises so ample?
I'd best step back, and order up a sample.[1]

[1] *Zobeide*, a Tragedy, by Joseph Cradock, Esq., was first represented at Covent Garden, on the 10th of December, 1771, and was well received. The text here given is that of the third edition of *Zobeide*, 1772."—P. C.

EPILOGUE SPOKEN BY MR. LEE LEWES,

IN THE CHARACTER OF HARLEQUIN, AT HIS BENEFIT.

HOLD! prompter, hold! a word before your non-
 sense:
I'd speak a word or two, to ease my conscience.
My pride forbids it ever should be said,
My heels eclips'd the honours of my head;
That I found humour in a pyebald vest,
Or ever thought that jumping was a jest.
[*Takes off his mask.*
Whence, and what art thou, visionary birth?
Nature disowns, and reason scorns, thy mirth;
In thy black aspect every passion sleeps,
The joy that dimples, and the woe that weeps.
How hast thou fill'd the scene with all thy brood
Of fools pursuing, and of fools pursu'd!
Whose ins and outs no ray of sense discloses;
Whose only plot it is to break our noses;
Whilst from below the trapdoor demons rise,
And from above the dangling deities:
And shall I mix in this unhallow'd crew?
May rosin'd lightning blast me if I do!
No — I will act, I'll vindicate the stage:
Shakespeare himself shall feel my tragic rage.
Off! off, vile trappings! a new passion reigns;
The maddening monarch revels in my veins.

Oh! for a Richard's voice to catch the theme:
'Give me another horse! bind up my wounds! — soft — 'twas but a dream.'
Ay, 'twas but a dream, for now there 's no retreating:
If I cease Harlequin, I cease from eating.
'Twas thus that Æsop's stag, a creature blameless,
Yet something vain, like one that shall be nameless,
Once on the margin of a fountain stood,
And cavill'd at his image in the flood.
'The deuce confound,' he cries, 'these drumstick shanks!
They never have my gratitude nor thanks;
They 're perfectly disgraceful! strike me dead!
But for a head, yes, yes, I have a head:
How piercing is that eye! how sleek that brow!
My horns — I'm told horns are the fashion now.'
Whilst thus he spoke, astonish'd, to his view,
Near, and more near, the hounds and huntsmen drew.
'Hoicks! hark forward!' came thundering from behind:
He bounds aloft, outstrips the fleeting wind;
He quits the woods, and tries the beaten ways;
He starts, he pants, he takes the circling maze.
At length his silly head, so priz'd before,
Is taught his former folly to deplore;
Whilst his strong limbs conspire to set him free,
And at one bound he saves himself — like me.

[*Taking a jump through the stage-door.*

EPILOGUE TO THE COMEDY OF THE SISTER.[1]

WHAT? five long acts—and all to make us wiser!
Our authoress sure has wanted an adviser.
Had she consulted me, she should have made
Her moral play a speaking masquerade;
Warm'd up each bustling scene, and, in her rage,
Have emptied all the green room on the stage.
My life on't, this had kept her play from sinking;
Have pleas'd our eyes, and sav'd the pain of thinking.
Well, since she thus has shown her want of skill,
What if I give a masquerade?—I will.
But how? ay, there's the rub! [*pausing*]—I've got my cue:
The world 's a masquerade! the masquers, you, you, you. [*To Boxes, Pit, and Gallery.*
Lud! what a group the motley scene discloses!
False wits, false wives, false virgins, and false spouses!
Statesmen with bridles on; and, close beside 'em,
Patriots in party-colour'd suits that ride 'em.

[1] *The Sister*] A comedy by Mrs. Charlotte Lennox, 1769, taken from the authoress's own novel, 'Henrietta.' It was performed only one night. The author of the *Biographia Dramatica* says that 'this epilogue is the best that has appeared the last thirty years.'

There Hebes, turn'd of fifty, try once more
To raise a flame in Cupids of threescore;
These in their turn, with appetites as keen,
Deserting fifty, fasten on fifteen.
Miss, not yet full fifteen, with fire uncommon,
Flings down her sampler, and takes up the woman;
The little urchin smiles, and spreads her lure,
And tries to kill, ere she's got power to cure.
Thus 'tis with all: their chief and constant care
Is to seem every thing — but what they are.
Yon broad, bold, angry spark, I fix my eye on,
Who seems to have robb'd his vizor from the lion;
Who frowns, and talks, and swears, with round parade,
Looking, as who should say, — Dam'me! who's afraid? [*Mimicking.*
Strip but this vizor off, and sure I am
You'll find his lionship a very lamb.
Yon politician, famous in debate,
Perhaps, to vulgar eyes, bestrides the state;
Yet, when he deigns his real shape t' assume,
He turns old woman, and bestrides a broom.
Yon patriot, too, who presses on your sight,
And seems, to every gazer, all in white,
If with a bribe his candour you attack,
He bows, turns round, and whip — the man's in black!
Yon critic, too, — but whither do I run?
If I proceed, our bard will be undone!
Well, then, a truce, since she requests it too:
Do you spare her, and I'll for once spare you.

EPILOGUE TO THE GOOD-NATURED MAN.[1]

SPOKEN BY MRS. BULKLEY.

As puffing quacks some caitiff wretch procure
To swear the pill, or drop, has wrought a cure,
Thus, on the stage, our playwrights still depend
For Epilogues and Prologues on some friend,
Who knows each art of coaxing up the town,
And makes full many a bitter pill go down.
Conscious of this, our bard has gone about,
And teas'd each rhyming friend to help him out.
'An Epilogue,—things can't go on without it;
It could not fail, would you but set about it.'
'Young man,' cries one, (a bard laid up in clover,)
'Alas, young man, my writing days are over;
Let boys play tricks, and kick the straw, not I;
Your brother Doctor there, perhaps, may try.'
'What, I! dear Sir,' the Doctor interposes;
'What, plant my thistle, Sir, among his roses!
No, no, I've other contests to maintain;
To-night I head our troops at Warwick-lane.[2]

1 The author, in expectation of an Epilogue from a friend at Oxford, deferred writing one himself till the very last hour. What is here offered owes all its success to the graceful manner of the actress who spoke it.—*Goldsmith.*

2 Where the College of Physicians then stood.

Go ask your manager.'—'Who, me! Your pardon:
These things are not our forte at Covent-Garden.'
Our author's friends, thus plac'd at happy distance,
Give him good words indeed, but no assistance.
As some unhappy wight at some new play,
At the pit door stands elbowing away,
While oft, with many a smile, and many a shrug,
He eyes the centre, where his friends sit snug;
His simpering friends, with pleasure in their eyes,
Sink as he sinks, and as he rises rise;
He nods, they nod; he cringes, they grimace;
But not a soul will budge to give him place.
Since then, unhelp'd, our bard must now conform
"To bide the pelting of this pitiless storm,"
Blame where you must, be candid where you can,
And be each critic the *Good-natur'd Man.*

EPILOGUE TO THE COMEDY OF 'SHE STOOPS TO CONQUER.'

WELL, having *stoop'd to conquer* with success,
And gain'd a husband without aid from dress,
Still, as a barmaid, I could wish it too,
As I have conquer'd him, to conquer you:
And let me say, for all your resolution,
That pretty barmaids have done execution.
Our life is all a play, compos'd to please;
'We have our exits and our entrances.'
The first act shows the simple country maid,
Harmless and young, of every thing afraid;
Blushes when hir'd, and, with unmeaning action,
'I hope as how to give you satisfaction.'
Her second act displays a livelier scene,—
Th' unblushing barmaid of a country-inn,
Who whisks about the house, at market caters,
Talks loud, coquets the guests, and scolds the waiters.
Next the scene shifts to town, and there she soars,
The chop-house toast of ogling connoisseurs.
On 'squires and cits she there displays her arts,
And on the gridiron broils her lovers' hearts;
And as she smiles, her triumphs to complete,
Even common-councilmen forget to eat.

The fourth act shows her wedded to the 'squire,
And madam now begins to hold it higher;
Pretends to taste, at operas cries *caro!*
And quits her Nancy Dawson for *Che Faro.*
Dotes upon dancing, and, in all her pride,
Swims round the room, the Heinel[1] of Cheapside;
Ogles and leers with artificial skill,
Till, having lost in age the power to kill,
She sits all night at cards, and ogles at spadille.
Such, through our lives, the eventful history!
The fifth and last act still remains for me:
The barmaid now for your protection prays,
Turns female barrister, and pleads for bays.

[1] Madame Heinel was a favorite dancer in London when this Epilogue was spoken.—P. C.

INTENDED EPILOGUE TO "SHE STOOPS TO CONQUER."

Enter Mrs. Bulkley, who curtsies very low, as beginning to speak. Then enter Miss Catley, who stands full before her, and curtsies to the audience.

MRS. BULKLEY.

Hold, Ma'am, your pardon. What's your business here?

MISS CATLEY.

The Epilogue.

MRS. BULKLEY.

The Epilogue?

MISS CATLEY.

Yes, the Epilogue, my dear.

MRS. BULKLEY.

Sure you mistake, Ma'am. The Epilogue, *I* bring it.

MISS CATLEY.

Excuse me, Ma'am. The author bid *me* sing it.

RECITATIVE.

Ye beaux and belles, that form this splendid ring,
Suspend your conversation while I sing.

MRS. BULKLEY.

Why, sure the girl 's beside herself: an Epilogue
of singing?
A hopeful end indeed to such a blest beginning.
Besides, a singer in a comic set!
Excuse me, Ma'am, I know the etiquette.

MISS CATLEY.

What if we leave it to the House?

MRS. BULKLEY.

The House! — Agreed.

MISS CATLEY.

Agreed.

MRS. BULKLEY.

And she, whose party 's largest, shall proceed.
And first, I hope, you'll readily agree
I've all the critics and the wits for me.
They, I am sure, will answer my commands:
Ye candid judging few, hold up your hands.
What! no return? I find, too late, I fear,
That modern judges seldom enter here.

MISS CATLEY.

I'm for a different set, — old men, whose trade is
Still to gallant and dangle with the ladies.

RECITATIVE.

Who mump their passion, and who, grimly smiling,
Still thus address the fair with voice beguiling:

AIR — COTILLON.

Turn, my fairest, turn, if ever
Strephon caught thy ravish'd eye;
Pity take on your swain so clever,
Who without your aid must die.
    Yes, I shall die, hu, hu, hu, hu!
    Yes, I must die, ho, ho, ho, ho!
Da Capo.

MRS. BULKLEY.

Let all the old pay homage to your merit;
Give me the young, the gay, the men of spirit.
Ye travell'd tribe, ye macaroni train,
Of French friseurs, and nosegays, justly vain,
Who take a trip to Paris once a year
To dress, and look like awkward Frenchmen here;
Lend me your hands — Oh! fatal news to tell:
Their hands are only lent to the Heinel.[1]

MISS CATLEY.

Ay, take your travellers — travellers indeed!
Give me my bonny Scot, that travels from the Tweed.
Where are the chiels? Ah! ah, I well discern
The smiling looks of each bewitching bairn.

AIR — *A bonny young lad is my Jockey.*

I'll sing to amuse you by night and by day,
And be unco merry when you are but gay;

1 [A favorite dancer.]

When you with your bagpipes are ready to play,
My voice shall be ready to carol away
With Sandy, and Sawney, and Jockey,
With Sawney, and Jarvie, and Jockey.

MRS. BULKLEY.

Ye gamesters, who, so eager in pursuit,
Make but of all your fortune one *va toute:*
Ye jockey tribe, whose stock of words are few,
'I hold the odds.—Done, done, with you, with you:'
Ye barristers, so fluent with grimace,—
'My Lord, your Lordship misconceives the case:'
Doctors, who cough and answer every misfortuner,
'I wish I'd been call'd in a little sooner;'
Assist my cause with hands and voices hearty,
Come, end the contest here, and aid my party.

AIR—BALLINAMONY.

MISS CATLEY.

Ye brave Irish lads, hark away to the crack,
Assist me, I pray, in this woful attack;
For sure I don't wrong you, you seldom are slack,
When the ladies are calling, to blush, and hang back.
For you're always polite and attentive,
Still to amuse us inventive,
And death is your only preventive:
Your hands and your voices for me.

MRS. BULKLEY.

Well, Madam, what if, after all this sparring,
We both agree, like friends, to end our jarring?

MISS CATLEY.

And that our friendship may remain unbroken,
What if we leave the Epilogue unspoken?

MRS. BULKLEY.

Agreed.

MISS CATLEY.

Agreed.

MRS. BULKLEY.

And now, with late repentance,
Unepilogued the poet waits his sentence.
Condemn the stubborn fool who can't submit
To thrive by flattery, though he starves by wit.
[*Exeunt.*

ANOTHER INTENDED EPILOGUE TO "SHE STOOPS TO CONQUER."

TO BE SPOKEN BY MRS. BULKLEY.

THERE is a place — so Ariosto sings —
A treasury for lost and missing things;
Lost human wits have places there assign'd them,
And they who lose their senses, there may find
them.
But where's this place, this storehouse of the age?
The moon, says he; — but I affirm, the stage:
At least, in many things, I think I see
His lunar and our mimic world agree.
Both shine at night; for, but at Foote's alone,
We scarce exhibit till the sun goes down;
Both prone to change, no settled limits fix,
And sure the folks of both are lunatics.
But, in this parallel, my best pretence is,
That mortals visit both to find their senses.
To this strange spot, rakes, macaronies, cits,
Come thronging to collect their scattered wits.
The gay coquette, who ogles all the day,
Comes here at night, and goes a prude away.
Hither the affected city dame advancing,
Who sighs for operas, and dotes on dancing,
Taught by our art her ridicule to pause on,
Quits the Ballet, and calls for *Nancy Dawson*.
The gamester, too, whose wit's all high or low,
Oft risks his fortune on one desperate throw,

Come here to saunter, having made his bets,
Finds his lost senses out, and pays his debts.
The Mohawk, too, with angry phrases stor'd,
As 'Dam'me, sir,' and 'Sir, I wear a sword,'
Here lesson'd for a while, and hence retreating,
Goes out, affronts his man, and takes a beating.
Here come the sons of scandal and of news,
But find no sense — for they had none to lose.
Of all the tribe here wanting an adviser,
Our author 's the least likely to grow wiser;
Has he not seen how you your favour place
On sentimental queens and lords in lace?
Without a star, a coronet, or garter,
How can the piece expect or hope for quarter?
No high-life scenes, no sentiment: the creature
Still stoops among the low to copy nature.
Yes, he's far gone: — and yet some pity fix;
The English laws forbid to punish lunatics.[1]

[1] Presented in MS., among other papers, to Dr. Percy, by the Poet, and first printed in *Miscellaneous Works*, 1801.—P. C.

POEMS

EXTRACTED FROM THE PROSE WORKS OF GOLDSMITH.

(See Citizen of the World, L. 85.) It is the business of the stage-poet to watch the appearance of every new player at his own house, and so come out next day with a flaunting copy of newspaper verses. In these, nature and the actor may be set to run races, the player always coming off victorious; or nature may mistake him for herself; or old Shakespeare may put on his winding-sheet, and pay him a visit; or the tuneful Nine may strike up their harps in his praise; or, should it happen to be an actress, Venus, the beauteous Queen of Love, and the naked Graces, are ever in waiting. The lady must be herself a goddess bred and born; she must —— but you shall have a specimen of one of these poems, which may convey a more precise idea: —

ON SEEING MRS. —— PERFORM IN THE CHARACTER OF ——.

For you, bright fair, the Nine address their lays,
And tune my feeble voice to sing thy praise.
The heartfelt power of every charm divine,
Who can withstand their all-commanding shine?
See how she moves along with every grace,
While soul-brought tears steal down each shining face.

She speaks! 'tis rapture all, and nameless bliss,
Ye gods! what transport e'er compar'd to this!
As when, in Paphian groves, the Queen of Love
With fond complaint address'd the listening Jove;
'Twas joy and endless blisses all around,
And rocks forgot their hardness at the sound.
Then first, at last even Jove was taken in,
And felt her charms, without disguise, within.

(V. Citizen of the World, L. 106.) I am amazed that none have yet found out the secret of flattering the worthless, and yet of preserving a safe conscience. I have often wished for some method by which a man might do himself and his deceased patron justice, without being under the hateful reproach of self-conviction. After long lucubration, I have hit upon such an expedient, and send you the specimen of a poem upon the decease of a great man, in which the flattery is perfectly fine, and yet the poet perfectly innocent.

ON THE DEATH OF THE RIGHT HON. ——.

Ye Muses, pour the pitying tear
For Pollio snatch'd away;
Oh! had he liv'd another year,—
He had not died to-day.

Oh! were he born to bless mankind
In virtuous times of yore,
Heroes themselves had fallen behind—
Whene'er he went before.

How sad the groves and plains appear,
  And sympathetic sheep!
Even pitying hills would drop a tear, —
  If hills could learn to weep.

His bounty, in exalted strain,
  Each bard might well display;
Since none implor'd relief in vain —
  That went reliev'd away.

And hark! I hear the tuneful throng
  His obsequies forbid:
He still shall live, shall live as long —
  As ever dead man did.

These verses seem to have been the first rough sketch, afterwards altered and improved into the Elegy on Mrs. Mary Blaize.

(V. Citizen of the World, L. 113.) The weapon chiefly used in the present contest is epigram, and certainly never was a keener made use of. They have discovered surprising sharpness on both sides. The first that came out upon this occasion was a kind of new composition in this way, and might more properly be called an epigrammatic thesis than an epigram. It consists, first, of an argument in prose; next follows a motto from Roscommon; then comes the epigram; and, lastly, notes serving to explain the epigram. But you shall have it with all its decorations: —

AN EPIGRAM,

ADDRESSED TO THE GENTLEMEN REFLECTED ON IN THE ROSCIAD, A POEM, BY THE AUTHOR.

Worried with debts, and past all hopes of bail,
His pen he prostitutes t' avoid a gaol.

ROSCOM.

LET not the hungry Bavius' angry stroke
Awake resentment, or your rage provoke;
But, pitying his distress, let virtue[1] shine,
And giving each your bounty,[2] *let him dine.*
For thus retain'd, as learned counsel can,
Each case, however bad, he 'll new japan;
And, by a quick transition, plainly show
'Twas no defect of yours, but *pocket low,*
That caus'd his *putrid kennel* to o'erflow.

The last lines are certainly executed in a very masterly manner: it is of that species of argumentation called the perplexing. It effectually flings the antagonist into a mist; there's no answering it: the laugh is raised against him, while he is endeavouring to find out the jest. At once he shows that the author has a kennel, and that this kennel is putrid, and that this putrid kennel overflows. But why does it overflow? It overflows because the author happens to have low pockets.

---

1 Charity.

2 Settled at one shilling, the price of the poem.

There was also another new attempt in this way, a prosaic epigram, which came out upon this occasion. This is so full of matter, that a critic might split it into fifteen epigrams, each properly fitted with its sting. You shall see it: —

TO G. C. AND R. L.

'Twas you, or I, or he, or all together,
'Twas one, both, three of them, they know not
whether;
This, I believe, between us great or small,
You, I, he, wrote it not — 'twas Churchill's all.

There, there is a perplex! I could have wished to have made it quite perfect; the author, as in the case before, had added notes. Almost every word admits a scholium, and a long one too. I, YOU, HE. Suppose a stranger should ask, And who are you? Here are three obscure persons spoken of, that may in a short time be utterly forgotten. Their names should consequently have been written in notes at the bottom; but when the reader comes to the words *great* and *small*, the maze is inextricable. Here the stranger may dive for a mystery, without ever reaching the bottom. Let him know, then, that *small* is a word poorly introduced to make good rhyme, and *great* was a very proper word to keep *small* company.

This was denoted against the triumvirate of friends, Churchill, Colman, and Lloyd.

(V. Cit. of the World, L. 116.) Even in the sultry wilds of Southern America, the lover is not satisfied with possessing his mistress's person, without having her mind.

In all my Enna's beauties blest,
   Amidst profusion still I pine;
For though she gives me up her breast,
   Its panting tenant is not mine.

"You should have given me your opinion of the design of the heroi-comical poem which I sent you; you remember I intended to introduce the hero of the poem as lying in a paltry ale-house. You may take the following specimen of the manner, which I flatter myself is quite original. The room in which he lies may be described somewhat in this way:—

THE window, patch'd with paper, lent a ray,
That feebly show'd the state in which he lay.
The sanded floor that grits beneath the tread,
The humid wall with paltry pictures spread;
The game of goose was there exposed to view,
And the twelve rules the royal martyr drew;
The seasons, fram'd with listing, found a place,
And Prussia's monarch show'd his lampblack face.
The morn was cold; he views with keen desire
A rusty grate, unconscious of a fire:
An unpaid reckoning on the frieze was scor'd,
And five crack'd teacups dress'd the chimney board.

And now imagine, after his soliloquy, the landlord to make his appearance, in order to dun him for the reckoning:—

Not with that face, so servile and so gay,
That welcomes every stranger that can pay;
With sulky eye he smok'd the patient man,
Then pull'd his breeches tight, and thus began:[1]

[1] Letter to the Rev. Henry Goldsmith.

Addison, in some beautiful Latin lines inserted in the Spectator, is entirely of opinion that birds observe a strict chastity of manners, and never admit the caresses of a different tribe. — (*v.* vol. vi. No. 412.)

CHASTE are their instincts, faithful is their fire,
No foreign beauty tempts to false desire;
The snow-white vesture, and the glittering crown,
The simple plumage, or the glossy down,
Prompt not their loves — the patriot bird pursues
His well-acquainted tints, and kindred hues.
Hence through their tribes no mix'd polluted flame,
No monster breed to mark the groves with shame;
But the chaste blackbird, to its partner true,
Thinks black alone is beauty's favourite hue.
The nightingale, with mutual passion blest,
Sings to its mate, and nightly charms the rest.
While the dark owl to court its partner flies,
And owns its offspring in their yellow eyes.[1]

[1] See Goldsmith's An. Nat. vol. v. p. 212.

LINES ATTRIBUTED TO DR. GOLDSMITH,

INSERTED IN THE MORNING CHRONICLE OF APRIL 3, 1800.

E'ER have you seen, bath'd in the morning dew,
  The budding rose its infant bloom display:
When first its virgin tints unfold to view,
  It shrinks, and scarcely trusts the blaze of day.

So soft, so delicate, so sweet she came,
  Youth's damask glow just dawning on her cheek;
I gaz'd, I sigh'd, I caught the tender flame,
  Felt the fond pang, and droop'd with passion weak.

VIDA'S GAME OF CHESS,

AS IT HAS BEEN FOUND TRANSCRIBED IN THE HANDWRITING

OF

OLIVER GOLDSMITH.

NOW FIRST PRINTED FROM THE ORIGINAL MS.

IN THE POSSESSION OF

BOLTON CORNEY, ESQ.

Of the MS. of this translation, Mr. Forster, who has drawn largely and importantly from it, gives the following account: "It is a small quarto manuscript of thirty-four pages, containing 679 lines, to which a fly-leaf is appended, in which Goldsmith notes the differences of nomenclature between Vida's chessmen and our own. It has occasional interlineations and corrections, but rather such as would occur in transcription, than in a first or original copy. Sometimes, indeed, choice appears to have been made (as at page 29) between two words equally suitable to the sense and verse, as 'to' for 'toward;' but the insertions and erasures refer almost wholly to words or lines accidentally omitted and replaced. The triplet is always carefully marked; and though it is seldom found in any other of Goldsmith's poems, I am disposed to regard its frequent recurrence, here, as even helping in some degree to explain the motive which had led him to the trial of an experiment in rhyme comparatively new to him. If we suppose him, half consciously it may be, taking up the manner of the great master of translation, Dryden, who was at all times so much a favourite with him, he would at least be less apt to fall short in so marked a peculiarity, than to err perhaps a little on the side of excess; though I am far from thinking such to be the result in the present instance. The effect of the whole translation is very pleasing to me, and the mock heroic effect I think not a little assisted by the reiterated use of the triplet and Alexandrine. As to any evidences of authorship derivable from the appearance of the manu script, I will only add another word. The lines in the translation have been carefully counted, and the number is marked in Goldsmith's hand at the close of his transcription. Such a fact is, of course, only to be taken in aid of other proof; but a man is not generally at the pains of counting,—still less, I should say, in such a case as Goldsmith's, of elaborately transcribing, lines which are not his own."—*Forster's Goldsmith*, ii. 265.

There had been an earlier translation of the poem by George Jeffreys, (4to. 1736,) but it is very inferior to the translation which Mr. Cornev has now enabled me to reprint.

Cunningham.

VIDA'S GAME OF CHESS.

TRANSLATED.

ARMIES of box that sportively engage,
And mimic real battles in their rage,
Pleased I recount; how, smit with glory's charms,
Two mighty monarchs met in adverse arms,
Sable and white: assist me to explore,
Ye Serian Nymphs, what ne'er was sung before.
No path appears; yet resolute I stray
Where youth undaunted bids me force my way.
O'er rocks and cliffs while I the task pursue,
Guide me, ye Nymphs, with your unerring clue.
For you the rise of this diversion know,
You first were pleased in Italy to show
This studious sport; from Scacchis was its name,
The pleasing record of your sister's fame.
When Jove through Ethiopia's parch'd extent
To grace the nuptials of old Ocean went,
Each god was there; and mirth and joy around
To shores remote diffused their happy sound.
Then when their hunger and their thirst no more
Claim'd their attention, and the feast was o'er,
Ocean, with pastime to divert the thought,
Commands a painted table to be brought.

Sixty-four spaces fill the chequer'd square;
Eight in each rank eight equal limits share.
Alike their form, but different are their dyes;
They fade alternate, and alternate rise,
White after black; such various stains as those
The shelving backs of tortoises disclose.
Then to the Gods that mute and wondering sate,
"You see," says he, "the field prepared for fate.
Here will the little armies please your sight,
With adverse colours hurrying to the fight,
On which so oft, with silent sweet surprise,
The Nymphs and Nereids used to feast their eyes,
And all the neighbours of the hoary deep,
When calm the sea, and winds were lull'd asleep.
But see, the mimic heroes tread the board."
He said, and straightway from an urn he pour'd
The sculptured box, that neatly seem'd to ape
The graceful figure of a human shape:—
Equal the strength and number of each foe,
Sixteen appear'd like jet, sixteen like snow.
As their shape varies various is the name,
Different their posts, nor is their strength the same.
There might you see two Kings with equal pride
Gird on their arms, their consorts by their side;
Here the Foot-warriors glowing after fame,
There prancing Knights and dexterous Archers came,
And Elephants, that on their backs sustain
Vast towers of war, and fill and shake the plain.

And now both hosts, preparing for the storm
Of adverse battle, their encampments form.
In the fourth space, and on the farthest line,
Directly opposite the monarchs shine;
The swarthy on white ground, on sable stands
The silver King; and thence they send commands.
Nearest to these the Queens exert their might;
One the left side, and t'other guards the right:
Where each, by her respective armour known,
Chooses the colour that is like her own.
Then the young Archers, two that snowy-white
Bend the tough yew, and two as black as night;
(Greece call'd them Mars's favourites heretofore,
From their delight in war, and thirst of gore.)
These on each side the Monarch and his Queen
Surround obedient; next to these are seen
The crested Knights in golden armour gay;
Their steeds by turns curvet, or snort or neigh.
In either army, on each distant wing
Two mighty Elephants their castles bring,
Bulwarks immense! and then at last combine
Eight of the Foot to form the second line,
The vanguard to the King and Queen; from far
Prepared to open all the fate of war.
So moved the boxen hosts, each double-lined,
Their different colours floating in the wind:
As if an army of the Gauls should go,
With their white standards, o'er the Alpine snow
To meet in rigid fight on scorching sands
The sun-burnt Moors and Memnon's swarthy bands.

Then Father Ocean thus: "You see them here,
Celestial Powers, what troops, what camps appear.
Learn now the sev'ral orders of the fray,
For ev'n these arms their stated laws obey.
To lead the fight, the Kings from all their bands
Choose whom they please to bear their great commands.
Should a black hero first to battle go,
Instant a white one guards against the blow;
But only one at once can charge or shun the foe.
Their gen'ral purpose on one scheme is bent,
So to besiege the King within the tent,
That there remains no place by subtle flight
From danger free; and that decides the fight.
Meanwhile, howe'er, the sooner to destroy
Th' imperial prince, remorseless they employ
Their swords in blood; and whosoever dare
Oppose their vengeance, in the ruin share.
Fate thins their camp; the parti-coloured field
Widens apace, as they o'ercome or yield:
But the proud victor takes the captive's post,
There fronts the fury of th' avenging host
One single shock, and (should he ward the blow,)
May then retire at pleasure from the foe.
The Foot alone (so their harsh laws ordain)
When they proceed can ne'er return again.
But neither all rush on alike to prove
The terror of their arms: the Foot must move
Directly on, and but a single square;
Yet may these heroes, when they first prepare

To mix in combat on the bloody mead,
Double their sally, and two steps proceed;
But when they wound, their swords they subtly guide
With aim oblique, and slanting pierce his side.
But the great Indian beasts, whose backs sustain
Vast turrets arm'd, when on the redd'ning plain
They join in all the terror of the fight,
Forward or backward, to the left or right,
Run furious, and impatient of confine
Scour through the field, and threat the farthest line.
Yet must they ne'er obliquely aim their blows;
That only manner is allow'd to those
Whom Mars has favour'd most, who bend the stubborn bows.
These glancing sidewards in a straight career,
Yet each confined to their respective sphere,
Or white or black, can send th' unerring dart
Wing'd with swift death to pierce through ev'ry part.
The fiery steed, regardless of the reins,
Comes prancing on; but sullenly disdains
The path direct, and boldly wheeling round,
Leaps o'er a double space at ev'ry bound,
And shifts from white or black to diff'rent colour'd ground.
But the fierce Queen, whom dangers ne'er dismay,
The strength and terror of the bloody day,
In a straight line spreads her destruction wide,
To left or right, before, behind, aside.

Yet may she never with a circling course
Sweep to the battle like the fretful Horse;
But unconfined may at her pleasure stray,
If neither friend nor foe block up the way:
For to o'erleap a warrior, 'tis decreed
Those only dare who curb the snorting steed.
With greater caution and majestic state
The warlike Monarchs in the scene of fate
Direct their motions, since for these appear
Zealous each hope, and anxious ev'ry fear.
While the King's safe, with resolution stern
They clasp their arms; but should a sudden turn
Make him a captive, instantly they yield,
Resolved to share his fortune in the field.
He moves on slow; with reverence profound
His faithful troops encompass him around,
And oft, to break some instant fatal scheme,
Rush to their fates, their sov'reign to redeem:
While he, unanxious where to wound the foe,
Need only shift and guard against a blow.
But none, however, can presume t' appear
Within his reach, but must his vengeance fear;
For he on ev'ry side his terror throws;
But when he changes from his first repose,
Moves but one step, most awfully sedate,
Or idly roving, or intent on fate.
These are the sev'ral and establish'd laws:
Now see how each maintains his bloody cause."
    Here paused the God, but (since whene'er they wage
War here on earth the Gods themselves engage

In mutual battle as they hate or love,
And the most stubborn war is oft above,)
Almighty Jove commands the circling train
Of Gods from fav'ring either to abstain,
And let the fight be silently survey'd;
And added solemn threats if disobey'd.
Then call'd he Phœbus from among the Powers
And subtle Hermes, whom in softer hours
Fair Maia bore: youth wanton'd in their face;
Both in life's bloom, both shone with equal grace.
Hermes as yet had never wing'd his feet;
As yet Apollo in his radiant seat
Had never driv'n his chariot through the air,
Known by his bow alone and golden hair.
These Jove commission'd to attempt the fray,
And rule the sportive military day;
Bid them agree which party each maintains,
And promised a reward that's worth their pains.
The greater took their seats; on either hand
Respectful the less Gods in order stand,
But careful not to interrupt their play,
By hinting when t' advance or run away.
  Then they examine, who shall first proceed
To try their courage, and their army lead.
Chance gave it for the White, that he should go
First with a brave defiance to the foe.
Awhile he ponder'd which of all his train
Should bear his first commission o'er the plain;
And then determined to begin the scene
With him that stood before to guard the Queen.

He took a double step: with instant care
Does the black Monarch in his turn prepare
The adverse champion, and with stern command
Bid him repel the charge with equal hand.
There front to front, the midst of all the field,
With furious threats their shining arms they wield;
Yet vain the conflict; neither can prevail
While in one path each other they assail.
On ev'ry side to their assistance fly
Their fellow soldiers, and with strong supply
Crowd to the battle, but no bloody stain
Tinctures their armour; sportive in the plain
Mars plays awhile, and in excursion slight
Harmless they sally forth, or wait the fight.
  But now the swarthy Foot, that first appear'd
To front the foe, his pond'rous jav'lin rear'd
Leftward aslant, and a pale warrior slays,
Spurns him aside, and boldly takes his place.
Unhappy youth, his danger not to spy!
Instant he fell, and triumph'd but to die.
At this the sable King with prudent care
Removed his station from the middle square,
And slow retiring to the farthest ground,
There safely lurk'd, with troops entrench'd around.
Then from each quarter to the war advance
The furious Knights, and poise the trembling lance:
By turns they rush, by turns the victors yield;
Heaps of dead Foot choke up the crimson field:
They fall unable to retreat; around
The clang of arms and iron hoofs resound.

But while young Phœbus pleased himself to view
His furious Knight destroy the vulgar crew,
Sly Hermes long'd t' attempt with secret aim
Some noble act of more exalted fame.
For this, he inoffensive pass'd along
Through ranks of Foot, and midst the trembling
 throng
Sent his left Horse (that free without confine
Roved o'er the plain) upon some great design
Against the King himself. At length he stood,
And having fix'd his station as he would,
Threaten'd at once with instant fate the King
And th' Indian beast that guarded the right wing.
Apollo sigh'd, and hast'ning to relieve
The straiten'd Monarch, grieved that he must leave
His martial Elephant exposed to fate,
And view'd with pitying eyes his dang'rous state.
First in his thoughts however was his care
To save his King, whom to the neighbouring square
On the right hand, he snatch'd with trembling
 flight;
At this with fury springs the sable Knight,
Drew his keen sword, and rising to the blow,
Sent the great Indian brute to shades below
O fatal loss! for none except the Queen
Spreads such a terror through the bloody scene.
"Yet shall you ne'er unpunish'd boast your prize,"
The Delian God with stern resentment cries;
And wedged him round with foot, and pour'd in
 fresh supplies.

Thus close besieged, trembling he cast his eye
Around the plain, but saw no shelter nigh,
No way for flight; for here the Queen opposed,
The Foot in phalanx there the passage closed:
At length he fell; yet not unpleased with fate,
Since victim to a Queen's vindictive hate.
With grief and fury burns the whiten'd host,
One of their Tow'rs thus immaturely lost.
As when a bull has in contention stern
Lost his right horn, with double vengeance burn
His thoughts for war, with blood he's cover'd o'er,
And the woods echo to his dismal roar,
So look'd the flaxen host, when angry fate
O'erturn'd the Indian bulwark of their state.
Fired at this great success, with double rage
Apollo hurries on his troops t' engage,
For blood and havoc wild; and, while he leads
His troops thus careless, loses both his steeds:
For if some adverse warriors were o'erthrown,
He little thought what dangers threat his own.
But slyer Hermes with observant eyes
March'd slowly cautious, and at distance spies
What moves must next succeed, what dangers next arise.
Often would he, the stately Queen to snare,
The slender Foot to front her arms prepare,
And to conceal his scheme he sighs and feigns
Such a wrong step would frustrate all his pains.
Just then an Archer, from the right-hand view,
At the pale Queen his arrow boldly drew,

Unseen by Phœbus, who, with studious thought,
From the left side a vulgar hero brought.
But tender Venus, with a pitying eye,
Viewing the sad destruction that was nigh,
Wink'd upon Phœbus (for the Goddess sat
By chance directly opposite); at that
Roused in an instant, young Apollo threw
His eyes around the field his troops to view;
Perceived the danger, and with sudden fright
Withdrew the Foot that he had sent to fight,
And saved his trembling Queen by seasonable flight.
But Maia's son with shouts fill'd all the coast:
"The Queen," he cried, "the important Queen is
lost."
Phœbus, howe'er, resolving to maintain
What he had done, bespoke the heavenly train.
"What mighty harm, in sportive mimic fight,
Is it to set a little blunder right,
When no preliminary rule debarr'd?
If you henceforward, Mercury, would guard
Against such practice, let us make the law:
And whosoe'er shall first to battle draw,
Or white, or black, remorseless let him go
At all events, and dare the angry foe."
He said, and this opinion pleased around:
Jove turn'd aside, and on his daughter frown'd,
Unmark'd by Hermes, who, with strange surprise,
Fretted and foam'd, and roll'd his ferret eyes,
And but with great reluctance could refrain
From dashing at a blow all off the plain.

Then he resolved to interweave deceits,—
To carry on the war by tricks and cheats.
Instant he call'd an Archer from the throng,
And bid him like the courser wheel along:
Bounding he springs, and threats the pallid Queen.
The fraud, however, was by Phœbus seen;
He smiled, and turning to the Gods, he said,
"Though, Hermes, you are perfect in your trade,
And you can trick and cheat to great surprise,
These little sleights no more shall blind my eyes;
Correct them if you please, the more you thus
disguise."
The circle laugh'd aloud; and Maia's son
(As if it had but by mistake been done)
Recall'd his Archer, and with motion due,
Bid him advance, the combat to renew.
But Phœbus watch'd him with a jealous eye,
Fearing some trick was ever lurking nigh,
For he would oft, with sudden sly design,
Send forth at once two combatants to join
His warring troops, against the law of arms,
Unless the wary foe was ever in alarms.

Now the white Archer with his utmost force
Bent the tough bow against the sable Horse,
And drove him from the Queen, where he had stood
Hoping to glut his vengeance with her blood.
Then the right Elephant with martial pride
Roved here and there, and spread his terrors wide:
Glittering in arms from far a courser came,
Threaten'd at once the King and Royal Dame;

Thought himself safe when he the post had seized,
And with the future spoils his fancy pleased.
Fired at the danger a young Archer came,
Rush'd on the foe, and levell'd sure his aim;
(And though a Pawn his sword in vengeance draws,
Gladly he'd lose his life in glory's cause.)
The whistling arrow to his bowels flew,
And the sharp steel his blood profusely drew;
He drops the reins, he totters to the ground,
And his life issued murm'ring through the wound.
Pierced by the Foot, this Archer bit the plain;
The Foot himself was by another slain;
And with inflamed revenge, the battle burns again.
Towers, Archers, Knights, meet on the crimson ground,
And the field echoes to the martial sound.
Their thoughts are heated, and their courage fired,
Thick they rush on with double zeal inspired;
Generals and Foot, with different colour'd mien,
Confusedly warring in the camps are seen,—
Valour and Fortune meet in one promiscuous scene.
Now these, victorious, lord it o'er the field;
Now the foe rallies, the triumphant yield:
Just as the tide of battle ebbs or flows.
As when the conflict more tempestuous grows
Between the winds, with strong and boisterous sweep
They plough th' Ionian or Atlantic deep,
By turns prevails the mutual blustering roar,
And the big waves alternate lash the shore.

But in the midst of all the battle raged
The snowy Queen, with troops at once engaged;
She fell'd an Archer as she sought the plain,—
As she retired an Elephant was slain.
To right and left her fatal spears she sent,
Burst through the ranks, and triumph'd as she
went;
Through arms and blood she seeks a glorious fate,
Pierces the farthest lines, and nobly great
Leads on her army with a gallant show,
Breaks the battalions, and cuts through the foe.
At length the sable King his fears betray'd,
And begg'd his military consort's aid:
With cheerful speed she flew to his relief,
And met in equal arms the female chief.
Who first, great Queen, and who at last did
bleed?
How many Whites lay gasping on the mead?
Half dead, and floating in a bloody tide,
Foot, Knights, and Archer lie on every side.
Who can recount the slaughter of the day,
How many leaders threw their lives away?
The chequer'd plain is fill'd with dying box,
Havoc ensues, and with tumultuous shocks
The different colour'd ranks in blood engage,
And Foot and Horse promiscuously rage.
With nobler courage and superior might
The dreadful Amazons sustain the fight,
Resolved alike to mix in glorious strife,
Till to imperious fate they yield their life.

Meanwhile each Monarch, in a neighbouring cell
Confined the warriors that in battle fell,
There watch'd the captives with a jealous eye,
Lest, slipping out again, to arms they fly.
But Thracian Mars, in stedfast friendship join'd
To Hermes, as near Phœbus he reclined,
Observed each chance, how all their motions bend,
Resolved if possible to serve his friend.
He a Foot-soldier and a Knight purloin'd
Out from the prison that the dead confined,
And slyly push'd 'em forward on the plain;
Th' enliven'd combatants their arms regain,
Mix in the bloody scene, and boldly war again.
So the foul hag, in screaming wild alarms
O'er a dead carcase muttering her charms,
(And with her frequent and tremendous yell
Forcing great Hecate from out of hell)
Shoots in the corpse a new fictitious soul;
With instant glare the supple eyeballs roll,
Again it moves and speaks, and life informs the whole.
Vulcan alone discern'd the subtle cheat;
And wisely scorning such a base deceit,
Call'd out to Phœbus. Grief and rage assail
Phœbus by turns; detected Mars turns pale.
Then awful Jove with sullen eye reproved
Mars, and the captives order'd to be moved
To their dark caves; bid each fictitious spear
Be straight recall'd, and all be as they were.

And now both Monarchs with redoubled rage
Led on their Queens, the mutual war to wage.
O'er all the field their thirsty spears they send,
Then front to front their Monarchs they defend.
But lo! the female White rush'd in unseen,
And slew with fatal haste the swarthy Queen;
Yet soon, alas! resign'd her royal spoils,
Snatch'd by a shaft from her successful toils.
Struck at the sight, both hosts in wild surprise
Pour'd forth their tears, and fill'd the air with cries;
They wept and sigh'd, as pass'd the fun'ral train,
As if both armies had at once been slain.
And now each troop surrounds its mourning chief,
To guard his person, or assuage his grief.
One is their common fear; one stormy blast
Has equally made havoc as it pass'd.
Not all, however, of their youth are slain;
Some champions yet the vig'rous war maintain.
Three Foot, an Archer, and a stately Tower,
For Phœbus still exert their utmost power.
Just the same number Mercury can boast,
Except the Tower, who lately in his post
Unarm'd, inglorious fell, in peace profound
Pierced by an Archer with a distant wound;
But his right Horse retain'd its mettled pride,—
The rest were swept away by war's strong tide.
But fretful Hermes, with despairing moan,
Grieved that so many champions were o'erthrown,
Yet reassumes the fight; and summons round
The little straggling army that he found,—

All that had 'scaped from fierce Apollo's rage,—
Resolved with greater caution to engage
In future strife, by subtle wiles (if fate
Should give him leave) to save his sinking state.
The sable troops advance with prudence slow,
Bent on all hazards to distress the foe:
More cheerful Phœbus, with unequal pace,
Rallies his arms to lessen his disgrace.
But what strange havoc everywhere has been!
A straggling champion here and there is seen;
And many are the tents, yet few are left within.
Th' afflicted Kings bewail their consorts dead,
And loathe the thoughts of a deserted bed;
And though each monarch studies to improve
The tender mem'ry of his former love,
Their state requires a second nuptial tie.
Hence the pale ruler with a love-sick eye
Surveys th' attendants of his former wife,
And offers one of them a royal life.
These, when their martial mistress had been slain,
Weak and despairing tried their arms in vain;
Willing, howe'er, amidst the Black to go,
They thirst for speedy vengeance on the foe.
Then he resolves to see who merits best,
By strength and courage, the imperial vest;
Points out the foe, bids each with bold design
Pierce through the ranks, and reach the deepest line:
For none must hope with monarchs to repose
But who can first, through thick surrounding foes,

Through arms and wiles, with hazardous essay,
Safe to the farthest quarters force their way.
Fired at the thought, with sudden, joyful pace
They hurry on; but first of all the race
Runs the third right-hand warrior for the prize,—
The glitt'ring crown already charms her eyes.
Her dear associates cheerfully give o'er
The nuptial chase; and swift she flies before,
And Glory lent her wings, and the reward in store.
Nor would the sable King her hopes prevent,
For he himself was on a Queen intent,
Alternate, therefore, through the field they go.
Hermes led on, but by a step too slow,
His fourth left Pawn: and now th' advent'rous White
Had march'd through all, and gain'd the wish'd for site.
Then the pleased King gives orders to prepare
The crown, the sceptre, and the royal chair,
And owns her for his Queen: around exult
The snowy troops, and o'er the Black insult.
Hermes burst into tears,—with fretful roar
Fill'd the wide air, and his gay vesture tore.
The swarthy Foot had only to advance
One single step; but oh! malignant chance!
A tower'd Elephant, with fatal aim,
Stood ready to destroy her when she came·
He keeps a watchful eye upon the whole,
Threatens her entrance, and protects the goal.

Meanwhile the royal new-created bride,
Pleased with her pomp, spread death and terror wide;
Like lightning through the sable troops she flies,
Clashes her arms, and seems to threat the skies.
The sable troops are sunk in wild affright,
And wish th' earth op'ning snatch'd 'em from her sight.
In burst the Queen, with vast impetuous swing:
The trembling foes come swarming round the King,
Where in the midst he stood, and form a valiant ring.
So the poor cows, straggling o'er pasture land,
When they perceive the prowling wolf at hand,
Crowd close together in a circle full,
And beg the succour of the lordly bull;
They clash their horns, they low with dreadful sound,
And the remotest groves reëcho round.
But the bold Queen, victorious, from behind
Pierces the foe; yet chiefly she design'd
Against the King himself some fatal aim,
And full of war to his pavilion came.
Now here she rush'd, now there; and had she been
But duly prudent, she had slipp'd between,
With course oblique, into the fourth white square,
And the long toil of war had ended there;
The King had fallen, and all his sable state,
And vanquish'd Hermes cursed his partial fate:

For thence with ease the championess might go,
Murder the King, and none could ward the blow.
With silence, Hermes, and with panting heart,
Perceived the danger, but with subtle art,
(Lest he should see the place) spurs on the foe,
Confounds his thoughts, and blames his being slow.
" For shame! move on! would you forever stay?
What sloth is this, what strange perverse delay?—
How could you e'er my little pausing blame?—
What! you would wait till night shall end the game?"
Phœbus, thus nettled, with imprudence slew
A vulgar Pawn, but lost his nobler view.
Young Hermes leap'd, with sudden joy elate;
And then, to save the monarch from his fate,
Led on his martial Knight, who stepp'd between,
Pleased that his charge was to oppose the Queen.
Then, pondering how the Indian beast to slay,
That stopp'd the Foot from making farther way,
From being made a Queen, with slanting aim
An Archer struck him; down the monster came,
And dying shook the earth: while Phœbus tries
Without success the monarch to surprise.
The Foot, then uncontroll'd, with instant pride,
Seized the last spot, and moved a royal bride.
And now with equal strength both war again,
And bring their second wives upon the plain.
Then, though with equal views each hoped and fear'd,
Yet, as if every doubt had disappear'd,

As if he had the palm, young Hermes flies
Into excess of joy; with deep disguise,
Extols his own Black troops, with frequent spite
And with invective taunts disdains the White.
Whom Phœbus thus reproved with quick return—
"As yet we cannot the decision learn
Of this dispute, and do you triumph now?
Then your big words and vauntings I'll allow,
When you the battle shall completely gain;
At present I shall make your boasting vain."
He said, and forward led the daring Queen;
Instant the fury of the bloody scene
Rises tumultuous, swift the warriors fly
From either side to conquer or to die.
They front the storm of war: around 'em Fear,
Terror, and Death, perpetually appear.
All meet in arms, and man to man oppose,
Each from their camp attempts to drive their foes;
Each tries by turns to force the hostile lines;
Chance and impatience blast their best designs.
The sable Queen spread terror as she went
Through the mid ranks: with more reserved intent
The adverse dame declined the open fray,
And to the King in private stole away:
Then took the royal guard, and bursting in,
With fatal menace close besieged the King.
Alarm'd at this, the swarthy Queen, in haste,
From all her havoc and destructive waste
Broke off, and her contempt of death to show,
Leap'd in between the monarch and the foe,

To save the King and state from this impending
blow.
But Phœbus met a worse misfortune here:
For Hermes now led forward, void of fear,
His furious Horse into the open plain,
That onward chafed, and pranced, and pawed
amain.
Nor ceased from his attempts until he stood
On the long-wished-for spot, from whence he could
Slay King or Queen. O'erwhelm'd with sudden
fears,
Apollo saw, and could not keep from tears.
Now all seem'd ready to be overthrown;
His strength was wither'd, ev'ry hope was flown.
Hermes, exulting at this great surprise,
Shouted for joy, and fill'd the air with cries;
Instant he sent the Queen to shades below,
And of her spoils made a triumphant show.
But in return, and in his mid career,
Fell his brave Knight, beneath the Monarch's spear.
Phœbus, however, did not yet despair,
But still fought on with courage and with care.
He had but two poor common men to show,
And Mars's favourite with his iv'ry bow.
The thoughts of ruin made 'em dare their best
To save their King, so fatally distress'd;
But the sad hour required not such an aid,
And Hermes breathed revenge where'er he stray'd.
Fierce comes the sable Queen with fatal threat,
Surrounds the monarch in his royal seat;

Rush'd here and there, nor rested till she slew
The last remainder of the whiten'd crew.
Sole stood the King, the midst of all the plain,
Weak and defenceless, his companions slain.
As when the ruddy morn ascending high
Has chased the twinkling stars from all the sky,
Your star, fair Venus, still retains its light,
And, loveliest, goes the latest out of sight.
No safety's left, no gleams of hope remain;
Yet did he not as vanquish'd quit the plain,
But tried to shut himself between the foe,—
Unhurt through swords and spears he hoped to go,
Until no room was left to shun the fatal blow.
For if none threaten'd his immediate fate,
And his next move must ruin all his state,
All their past toil and labour is in vain,
Vain all the bloody carnage of the plain,—
Neither would triumph then, the laurel neither gain.
Therefore through each void space and desert tent,
By different moves his various course he bent:
The Black King watch'd him with observant eye,
Follow'd him close, but left him room to fly.
Then when he saw him take the farthest line,
He sent the Queen his motions to confine,
And guard the second rank, that he could go
No farther now than to that distant row.
The sable monarch then with cheerful mien
Approach'd, but always with one space between.
But as the King stood o'er against him there,
Helpless, forlorn, and sunk in his despair,

The martial Queen her lucky moment knew,
Seized on the farthest seat with fatal view,
Nor left th' unhappy King a place to flee unto.
At length in vengeance her keen sword she draws,
Slew him, and ended thus the bloody cause:
And all the gods around approved it with applause.
The victor could not from his insults keep,
But laugh'd and sneer'd to see Apollo weep.
Jove call'd him near, and gave him in his hand
The powerful, happy, and mysterious wand
By which the Shades are call'd to purer day,
When penal fire has purged their sins away;
By which the guilty are condemn'd to dwell
In the dark mansions of the deepest hell;
By which he gives us sleep, or sleep denies,
And closes at the last the dying eyes.
Soon after this, the heavenly victor brought
The game on earth, and first th' Italians taught.
For (as they say) fair Scacchis he espied
Feeding her cygnets in the silver tide,
(Scacchis, the loveliest Seriad of the place)
And as she stray'd, took her to his embrace.
Then, to reward her for her virtue lost,
Gave her the men and chequer'd board, emboss'd
With gold and silver curiously inlay'd,
And taught her how the game was to be play'd.
Ev'n now 'tis honour'd with her happy name;
And Rome and all the world admire the game:
All which the Seriads told me heretofore,
When my boy-notes amused the Serian shore.

THE END.

www.ingramcontent.com/pod-product-compliance
Lightning Source LLC
LaVergne TN
LVHW020219110826
845151LV00003B/766